Sociological Reasoning

Sociological Reasoning

Towards a Past-modern Sociology

ROB STONES

St. Martin's Press
New York

St. Martin's Press, Scholarly and Reference Division, 175 Fifth Avenue, New York, N.Y. 10010

First published in the United States of America in 1996

Printed in Malaysia

ISBN 0-312-16076-3 (hardcover)
ISBN 0-312-16077-1 (paperback)

Library of Congress Cataloging-in-Publication Data
Stones, Rob, 1957–
Sociological reasoning: towards a past-modern sociology / Rob Stones.
p.   cm.
Includes bibliographical references and index.
ISBN 0-312-16076-3 (cloth). — ISBN 0-312-16077-1 (pbk.)
1. Sociology—Philosophy.   I. Title.
HM24.S765   1996
301—dc20   95-48379
                                                      CIP

For Mum, Dad, Dave, Liz and Mike

Contents

List of Figures		*ix*
Acknowledgements		*x*
List of Abbreviations		*xii*
Introduction		1
1	Contemporary Developments in Social Theory: The Right Time for a Past-modern Sociology	13
2	A Rich and Complex Ontology	40
3	Analysis and Textuality: Players, Dreamers and Despots in Sociological Research	64
4	The Pivotal Role of the Methodological Focus: A Positive Critique of Anthony Giddens	88
5	Contextualising, Floating and Dreaming: Variations from the Sociologies of Politics, Culture and Ethics	118
6	A Positive Scepticism Towards Claims about Empirical Evidence	151
7	Past-modern Sociology and Textual Critique	167
8	Exemplary Critiques of Sociological Modernism I: Comparative Citizenship and State Autonomy	192
9	Exemplary Critiques of Sociological Modernism II: The Flying Sorcery of Sylvia Walby's Patriarchal Systems	207
	Conclusion	232
	Bibliography	236
	Index	247

List of Figures

2.1 Giddens' stratification model of the agent 43

Footnote Figure 1 (Chapter 2): An amendment to the
model of the agent 63

3.1 Dimensions of research shared by player and dreamer
models 66

3.2 Key dimensions of the player model of sociological
research 72

3.3 Player grid of levels and types of contextualisation 75

3.4 Dreamer grid with defining characteristics and types
of analysis 78

3.5 Key elements in the dreamer model of sociological
research 79

4.1 Focus of institutional analysis and systems analysis as
defined by Giddens and Cohen 98

4.2 Relevant spheres of analysis for the contextualised
reconstruction of an individual's frame of meaning in
relation to a situated practice 100

4.3 Elaborated version of player grid, including a wider
range of methodological bracketing 106

4.4 Elaborated version of dreamer grid, including
methodological bracketings of focus 108

4.5 Focus on 'routines' or on 'routines & deviations from
routines': illustrated in relation to the TPA Floater box 109

7.1 Stages in a cross-questioning analysis of a sociological
text 170

9.1 Walby's 'private and public patriarchy' 216

Acknowledgements

I would like to thank the following people for those various mixtures of friendship, support and inspiration that sustained and heartened me through the highs and lows of writing a whole book: my wife Ja and my children Klong and Pimai; my mother, father, sister and brothers, to whom this book is dedicated; Zowie Atkins; Sally Hoskyns; Mike Mills; Oriel Sullivan; Bob Jessop, whose ghost lurks behind many a page; Phil Lyons, who taught me how to read properly; Ian Craib, for reading the entire manuscript and providing me, typically, with invaluable written comments that prompted me to rush home and change what I *had* written to what I had *thought* I had written but hadn't; Ted Benton, for forcing half-baked intuitions to be spelt out and defended; Lydia Morris and Richard Wilson for reading sections of the manuscript and providing me with helpful suggestions.

I would also like to thank heartily all those MA and undergraduate students who have taken my courses in the philosophy of the social sciences and in political sociology and contemporary social theory over the past few years. Their enthusiasm and engagement – week in, week out – with many of the ideas in this book helped more than I can say to improve upon the rough-hewn raw materials I started out with.

I would like to acknowledge the generous and invaluable study leave provided by the University of Essex; a grant from the Centre for Advanced Research at the University of Essex to undertake some preliminary work on the notion of 'citizenship' together with Bryan Turner and Joe Foweraker, which led, indirectly, to the work of Michael Mann being chosen as an exemplar in Chapter 8; and the opportunity given to me by Andrew Sayer and the other organisers of the Conference on Realism and the Human Sciences at the University of Sussex in the summer of 1991 to air some first thoughts on the implications of postmodernism for realism in the social sciences. Thanks in particular to Andrew Sayer, William Outhwaite and Christopher Norris for comments on that talk that helped me to bring the project more sharply into focus.

Finally, but by no means least, I would like to thank Frances Arnold and Catherine Gray at the publishers: Frances for getting me started and Catherine for keeping me going, and going, until I ended up with the book we both wanted.

The author and publishers wish to thank the following for permission to use copyright material:

Basic Books, a division of HarperCollins Publishers, Inc, for material from Judith Stacey, *Brave New Families*. Copyright © 1990 by Judith Stacey; Blackwell Publishers for table from Sylvia Walby, *Theorizing Patriarchy*, Blackwell Publishers, 1990, Table 1.1; Beacon Press for material from Jürgen Habermas, *The Theory of Communicative Action Vol II*, Polity Press and Beacon Press. Copyright © 1987 by Beacon Press; Faber & Faber Ltd, with Key Porter Books Ltd and Alfred A. Knopf Inc for material from Kazuo Ishiguro, *The Remains of the Day*, 1989, published by Faber and Faber Ltd, Lester Orpen & Dennys, Toronto and Alfred A. Knopf Inc. Copyright © 1989 by Kazuo Ishiguro; and material from Peter Carey, *Oscar and Lucinda*, 1989; Macmillan Publishers for material from G. Ingham, *Capitalism Divided?: The City and Industry in British Social Development*, 1984; and Figure 2.1 from A. Giddens, *Central Problems in Reasoning*, Macmillan Press Ltd, p. 56; Verso for material from Janice Radway, *Reading the Romance: Women, Patriarchy and Popular Literature*, Verso/New Left Books, 1987.

Every effort has been made to trace all the copyright holders but if any have been inadvertently overlooked the publishers will be pleased to make the necessary arrangement at the first opportunity.

List of Abbreviations

ACA   agent's conduct analysis
TPA   theorist's pattern analysis

Four phrases used regularly in the text that include the abbreviations ACA and TPA are as follows: **ACA Contextualiser; ACA Floater; TPA Contextualiser; TPA Floater.** The relationship of these categories to each other is shown in Figure 3.3 and they are defined and explained on p. 75. Each of the respective categories refers to one of the four boxes in Figure 3.3. Whenever the categories are used capital letters are used, thus differentiating them, for example, from subcategories within the four boxes, which are referred to without capital letters.

Used as an acronym ACA/agent's conduct analysis is an umbrella term which includes both agent's conduct analysis *and* agent's context analysis. See p. 99.

Introduction

The Enemies

This is a book about how sociology should respond to the time in which it finds itself. I call the response I would like to see 'past-modern realism' or 'realism beyond modernism'. I argue that contemporary social theory has consolidated a much richer and more sophisticated view of the social world than the one with which modernist sociology worked. This rich and complex social *ontology* (what sorts of things the social world is made up of) has not, however, been matched by a corresponding development in the sophistication of research guidelines. In this latter sphere of epistemology and methodology, the state of the art is trailing forlornly some way behind. This uneven development is extremely important because sophisticated research guidelines are a necessity if we are to find out about the particular shapes, colours and details that the basic social entities of ontology take on in specific times and places. My argument is that sociology needs to provide itself with guidelines on how to traverse the bridges and the junctions that connect the insights of ontology and high theory to the empirical evidence necessary to make claims about the real world of any one moment. I argue strongly that we need to maintain a clear sense of the real, but that we also need to acknowledge the complexity of that real and the enormous demands of subtlety that this imposes upon anyone wanting to come anywhere near an apprehension of it in a given time and place. In the process of arguing for a past-modern sociology, I will also mark out two alternative responses to the present moment as inadequate, misguided and, in important ways, intolerable. These 'enemy' positions are:

1 The complacency of sociological modernism. I use the notion of 'sociological modernism' as an ideal type to try to capture a set of features that have dominated, and continue to dominate, many areas of sociology, both theoretical and empirical.[1] These features include a severe underestimation of the rich complexity and diversity of the social world, and a corresponding overestimation of the ability of sociologists to obtain accurate and truthful knowledge about that world. Sociological modernism is associated with an overweening

1

confidence in the ability of social scientists (or, in modernism's less academic guise, the ability of 'experts'), now or later, to know all there is to know, without doubt and without blinkers.

2 The defeatism of that dominant trend of postmodernism, which wishes to deny any difference at all between fictional stories and the accounts of social sciences. While, on the one hand, it places what I think is a healthy, and celebratory, emphasis on the plurality of different perspectives on the world, the diversity of that world, and the obstacles to obtaining accurate, truthful, knowledge of that world, on the other, it moves far too quickly from these insights to an attitude of hopelessness about our ability to make comparative judgements about the quality of different knowledge claims. This loss of critical capability means that all stories – accounts – are believed to be as good as each other as far as accuracy or truth are concerned. Thus, when a postmodern sociologist prepares an account of the world, she accepts no constraints of coherency of perspective, accurate representation, empirical data or logical connections. Her motto can be said to be 'anything goes and in just any old way'.

A Rickety Old Makeshift Bridge

The first of these enemy positions radically understates the problems of bridge-building between high theory and empirical evidence of the real world. The second position believes that the problems are insurmountable and gives up the whole enterprise. As stated above, I believe that the problems involved are not as insurmountable as the defeatist postmodernists would have us believe, but that sociological modernists have severely underestimated them. Related to their respective positions on the insurmountable difficulties of, or the ease of, bridge-building, the defeatist postmodernists decry any notion of realism, while the sociological modernists work, implicitly or explicitly, with a crude form of realism in which the reality of the social world is all too unproblematically apparent to the favoured theoretical framework, whether this be Marxism, functionalism, modernisation theory, systems theory or whatever. In these latter cases, far too much of the burden of proof is placed upon the theoretical framework, to the detriment of an adequate stock of empirical knowledge. As a corollary of this, of course, the techniques and skills of bridge-building between theoretical framework and empirical evidence are also neglected and remain poorly developed. One often wonders whether sociological modernists have ever noticed the chasm that separates the two.

Where empirical evidence does rear its head, it is typically presented as if the 'facts' will speak for themselves, that they are transparently a validation of the theoretical framework, that no explicit rules or guidelines are needed in order to demonstrate the links between the theoretical and conceptual apparatus of the 'high theory' and the 'facts' that are said to correspond to it. Without such links, or controlling guidelines, it is very difficult to judge the status of the facts, and the theories become very difficult to falsify. Consequently, the authors of these sociological works are afforded the kind of omniscience and omnipotence that literary critics typically associate with the classical realist novelists of the nineteenth century (see Chapter 1): they simply know all that is going on everywhere and in every moment associated with their story, and it is with effortless ease that they move between abstract reflections and the most microscopic aspects of the real events of their characters' lives. The formidable accuracy of these renderings, the uncanniness with which barriers to access seem to melt away, and the virtuous quality of truthfulness that authors insist upon, are all manifestations of this omnipotence. In short, real events, objects, actions, processes and structures are too often too complacently transparent to sociological modernists for us to be comfortable with their claims for knowledge.

Laying Bare the Conventional Foundations for a Much Improved Bridge

How do we go beyond the enemy positions of *either* giving up on *or* underestimating the problems of bridge-building between high theory and empirical evidence? The first step is to develop some basic concepts about the world and how to find out about it (ontology and epistemology). However, to advocate such a realist position is to invite the derision of defeatist postmodernists, who will accuse one, not least, of succumbing to 'foundationalism'. Foundationalism is one of the greatest crimes in the postmodern law book, and the desire to avoid committing it is one of the reasons why defeatist postmodernists reject the possibility of bridge-building. They believe that all constructions of high theory necessarily involve foundationalism. What, then, is foundationalism? And can we build bridges without committing its sins?

Foundationalism involves claiming that your theoretical framework is true beyond all doubt and is not open to questioning, because the framework is not one of human linguistic construction according to potentially fallible hunches, concepts, perceptive insights and empirical observation, but is transparently and resolutely how things are. It is probably true that sometimes – perhaps quite often, and for reasons not unconnected to the points made above about sociological modernism – social scientists slip into a mode of writing and lecturing that invites such accusations, so it is important to keep reminding ourselves of the fragility of our theoretical frameworks. At the same time, however, I think that, when addressed explicitly, there is much more of a consensus against any sort of preconventional foundationalism in sociology as a whole than postmodernists allow. More heat than light tends to be generated in the attacking of foundationalism. Light, I suggest, would be much better generated by switching the focus to the exploration and explicit elaboration of the respective sets of conventions, hunches and so on that underpin different theoretical frameworks. These metatheoretical conventions (see Chapter 1) – these philosophical assumptions about the nature and reality of the social world and the obstacles in the way of getting knowledge about it – must be recognised as being very closely bound up with particular sociologists' claims about more local and contextual manifestations of real social processes and events.

On with the Building

As a positive alternative to these 'enemy' positions – in place of either a defeatist rejection of realism or a complacent belief in a transparent realism – I advocate a sophisticated form of realism, which rejects the defeatism of postmodernism and also moves beyond modernism's complacency. There are two main maxims for this past-modern sociology, which provide the framework within which the other guidelines should be considered:

1 It should be more aware of the limitations of its efforts successfully to forge the links betweeen philosophical and theoretical frameworks and relevant empirical evidence – it should be highly reflexive, modest and sceptical. It should learn to accept that it works with fragments of the real rather than with complete stories.

2 It should be more aware of, and more reflexively vigilant in relation to, its own conventions of both analysis and textuality.

These points are explicated in the chapters that follow. Each chapter plays its part in a long-sustained argument in relation to which the various subjects are broached in as logical and sequential an order as I could manage.[2] In **Chapter 1**, I give a brief overview of developments in literature, literary theory and contemporary social theory that have undermined any sense that facts speak for themselves, that reality can be represented directly and transparently by words and narrative forms that simply mirror the world. This is followed by a brief discussion of defeatist postmodernism's overeager move from the valid recognition that reality cannot be directly represented to the invalid claim that reality cannot therefore be represented at all, that the only alternative to a crude form of realism is a 'fictional' postmodernism. I take the position that there can be a positive alternative form of realism. I also signal a set of secondary themes, to be addressed in the course of the book, which revolve around a series of either/or alternatives that postmodernism sets up, which I believe to be unnecessary and overly restrictive. Developing this I, first, draw briefly on an influential post-structuralist work (Joan Scott's *Gender and the Politics of History*, 1988) to indicate how the authors of such works would actually find it very difficult to do without some sort of commitment to realism.

Second, I begin the positive task of constructing the alternative to a naïve realism by taking the first step of laying out my reasons for choosing a particular ontology, a particular set of metatheoretical conventions about the nature of the social world. I draw on the theoretical realism associated with the work of the philosopher Roy Bhaskar and on the sociological version of realism offered by Anthony Giddens' structuration theory. It is suggested that these positions are consistent with general developments in contemporary social theory away from the rather flat and insipid view of the world associated with empiricism – and, more broadly, with sociological modernism – and towards a richer, more complex, ontology. This new ontology provides a basis for the methodological bridge that can be built between the high theoretical conventions of analysis, on the one hand, and sociological research claims about more local, contextual and contingent forms of real social processes and events, on the other.

This forms the backdrop to **Chapter 2**, which is a more detailed elaboration of what is meant by a rich, complex ontology. Using graphic illustrative examples taken from literature, I try to show ontology in action, bound up in the intricacies of everyday life, demonstrating the way in which an explicit ontology directs us to think in certain ways, to notice certain things, to acknowledge complexity and richness where it exists, and not to prejudge reality as a flat, humdrum cycle of predictable monotony. Influenced by developments in contemporary social theory, one key aspect of this rich ontology lies in its emphasis on meaning, its stress on the webs of linguistic meaning within which we exist, think and act in the social world; another is the emphasis on the hermeneutics of potentially creative agents situated within such webs of meaning. There is also a stress upon the local, the contextual and the contiguous in time and space (that is, the proximity of events to each other in time and space, the extent to which they are 'next to each other'). Where others have only emphasised the elements of radical disjuncture between postmodernism and previous positions in the social sciences, I want to emphasise some of the continuities and resemblances between postmodernism and developments in other areas of contemporary social theory in the realm of ontology. It seems to me that there has been a convergence here on the attention given to meaning, the local, the contextual, and to the linguistic and symbolic mediation of reality. In this respect, it is essential to differentiate the emphasis of contemporary social theory on these dimensions from the flat and underdeveloped ontology of sociological modernism.

In accordance with these points, the rich complex ontology presented in Chapter 2 draws on exemplars of contemporary social theory and, more briefly, of postmodernism. Specifically, it draws heavily on the work of Giddens; brings out congruencies with central elements in the writings of Jürgen Habermas; is commensurable with many aspects of contemporary realist philosophy of the social sciences as found, for example, in the work of Bhaskar, Andrew Sayer, William Outhwaite and Ted Benton; and is shown to be consistent with central dimensions of the postmodern position of Zygmunt Bauman.

On the other hand, if contemporary social theory has appreciated and developed our understanding of the richness of social ontology, its advances in this sphere have not been matched by a corresponding degree of sophistication at the level of epistemology and methodology, that is, at the level of exploring the obstacles in the way of obtaining knowledge about a rich and complex world. In order for sociology fully to harness the positive legacy endowed by contemporary social theory, it needs to fill in this missing dimension in its stock of intellectual resources. **Chapter 3** begins to do this. It begins the job of developing new epistemological and methodological rules commensurable with the ontology of Chapter 2. Categories of types of sociologist or sociological research – the contextualiser, the floater, the dreamer and the despot (for example the sociological modernist) – are identified and developed, and their relation to two models of sociological research – the player model and the dreamer model – is set out.

These are introduced in order to illustrate the range of relationships that a sociologist can develop with the rich and complex social world she studies. It is argued that the contemporary developments in ontology logically entail that a much higher degree of reflexivity is required in order to sustain a consistent and disciplined relationship between high theoretical assumptions and empirical knowledge claims. 'Old' ideas of falsification are indispensable but must be developed in order to cope with a much more sophisticated ontology than the flat empiricist one they were designed for. The crucial benchmark here is the one of total contextualisation, the answering of a research question with utterly exhaustive detail; absolutely everything relevant to a question in terms of, for example, hermeneutics and contiguity (these are my focus here), or power or material resources, must be included in order for an account to be exhaustive and closed to any further extension. This benchmark is, of course, Utopian, but is useful as a point of reference by which we can judge how far our accounts fall short of the rich reality of events. Some accounts (contextualised accounts) will be nearer to it and others (floater accounts) will be further away. A high degree of reflexivity is needed in order to keep a grasp on the degree of contextualisation called for by a particular question and then attained in the attempted answer.

The player and dreamer models provide guidelines on what sorts of thing need to be taken into account in attempting to track the relative adequacy of a research answer to a particular question. Understanding the status of a particular account – its strengths and its limitations, identifying the gaps that are left and the precise nature of the fragments that have been acquired – allows one a basis on which to begin to compare different accounts in a research area, to look at their respective strengths and weaknesses, and to begin to see where they might be extended. One important salutary consequence of this approach is that it allows one to acknowledge the ontological significance of the local and the contextual, while still allowing the validity of a whole range of research projects, from the small scale to the grand scale. Sociologists convinced by postmodernism's critique of the presumptiousness of modernist grand narratives have begun to be critical of large-scale sociological sweeps, such as those typically found, for example, in histor-ical sociology.[3] However, they have also felt uneasy about retreating solely to the level of the micro and the contextual, relinquishing any sense of the wider picture. The past-modern guidelines I propose free up this stalemate, simply by accepting the virtues of the longer and the wider sweep, but demanding that their authors reflexively acknowledge just how far away their empirical evidential base is from the benchmark of ontological exhaustiveness (see Chapters 3 and 4).

Chapter 4 closely analyses the epistemological and methodological dimensions of the work of Giddens, as an important representative of ontological developments in contemporary social theory, in order to show the extent to which these former dimensions have been neglected. Epistemological and methodological rules remain poorly developed and unable to harness the power of ontological advances. The analysis of Giddens' work, particularly in relation to his advocacy of nothing more than a loose, sensitising link between ontology and empirical research, suggests that even contemporary social theorists are still modernist in their complacent attitude to the dimension of epistemology and methodology. The opportunity is also taken to show how the close critique of one contemporary social theorist, in this case Giddens, can provide a fruitful basis for the production of additional guidelines for the reflexive identification of appropriate types, levels and specific details of empirical evidence.

Chapter 5 draws on a whole series of examples of sociological research in the areas of political sociology, the sociology of culture and the sociology of ethics, in order to illustrate the usefulness of a past-modernist sociology to an analysis of a range of different examples with varying degrees of contextualisation, hermeneutic grounding, time–space contiguity and claims to generalisation. Each of the examples is measured against the rich complex ontology developed by contemporary social theory. The various accounts within and between subdisciplines are compared and contrasted in terms of their research questions, their methodological focus and the status of the fragments of evidence with which they work, and in terms of the type of evidence about which, just as significantly, they are silent.

Chapter 6 attempts to deepen the sceptical and provisional spirit of a past-modernist sociology by tackling head-on the most powerful arguments of poststructuralism and postmodernism for the radical undecidability of all knowledge claims – for the implied futility of attempts to provide intersubjective social scientific rules that can help one to adjudicate between competing accounts of the real in terms of accuracy and truthfulness. While wishing to retain the emphasis on the undecidability and provisionality of knowledge claims, I also uphold the possibility of adjudicating between competing (commensurable) accounts on the basis of degrees of relevant contextualisation and the corresponding quality of empirical evidence. Radical undecidability, it is argued, is a limit case, but, likewise, so is radical decidability. There will generally be many ways in which an account and its evidence can be challenged: as incomplete, misinformed or ambiguous in meaning or significance. In developing a number of categories of scepticism in this respect, I draw upon, and merely touch the surface of, work in a number of academic disciplines (see below), which have increasingly questioned various aspects of modernism's epistemological complacency. The Utopian, but ontologically real, benchmark of exhaustiveness means that indeterminacy and undecidability will be the norm, and that judgements of validity, accuracy and relative superiority will typically have to be made against this background. They will have to be made in the spirit of modest provisionality, with the spectre of Karl Popper's ethic of falsification needing to acquire much more sophistication and flexibility as it haunts a richer world than he would ever allow into his scientific outlook.

Reflexivity in relation to the high theory/empirical evidence relationship must go far beyond the loose relationship propagated by sociological modernism and must apply not only to the moments of sociological analysis but also to the moments of textuality, to the presentation of sociological research within a textual narrative. Modernist and postmodernist literature and literary theory are drawn upon in this respect as, more than any other disciplines, they have explored the autonomy of the text in the context of a continuing concern with the relationship of the text to the real world. They have also stressed the limitations and fallibilities of human perceptions and knowledgeability, restricted as they are by situation and by human idiosyncracies. In the latter respect, they share much with modernism and postmodernism in the arts, and with contemporary developments in anthropology, feminism and philosophy, among others, which have exercised a deep scepticism in relation to supposedly objective, neutral, accurate and truthful knowledge claims, which, on closer examination, turn out to be based on very dubious or partial foundations, and to have been formulated within very limited perspectives. It is an irony of *sociological* modernism that a resumé of its major failings should turn out to include both an absence of a sense of the limitations of perspective, and the neglect of the flux and specificity of the hermeneutic moment. Both these dimensions have been defining characteristics of modernism in the arts and in literature.

Immersed in the same complex 'ontological mood' that lies behind developments in contemporary social theory, modernist and postmodernist novels have gone further in the respect of dwelling long and hard upon our limitations in relation to knowledge of the real. While modernist sociologists, in general, have not done very much positively to bring to the fore the limitations of our knowledgeability, and defeatist postmodernists have celebrated scepticism to such an extent that they have relinquished any role at all for the regulatory notion of the real, modernist novelists stayed very close to the real, to the minute details of everyday life. However, they reacted against the omniscience of the nineteenth-century novelists by resolving to highlight the situated and limited perspective of the narrator of an account. Postmodernist novelists have continued this emphasis, while going even further in drawing attention to the rhetorical and formal techniques used in the construction of the text, and to the leeway that the autonomy of the text provides for the author to represent reality as she likes, unconstrained by the shackles of accuracy and truthfulness. Postmodernist novelists have typically exposed this leeway by breaking into their own stories in order to hold an explicit discussion of their authorial power, their textual strategies and the alternative options available to them. The second part of Chapter 3 introduces these themes in order to recommend that the positive guidelines of a modest and sophisticated realism should be spiced with a healthy dose of scepticism in the form of explicit textual reminders about the limitations of perspective and the potential for dissembling inherent in the autonomy of the text.

Following immediately on from the introduction of the player and dreamer models, the suggestion is thus that a past-modern sociology should combine its ontological boldness with caution, scepticism and reflexivity in relation to epistemology and methodology, and that it should be as explicit as possible about the textual construction of its narratives and knowledge claims. Past-modern sociologists should find ways of breaking into their own stories with tales of how much they really know and how much they do not, what they would have liked to know but could not find a way to, and how they are writing with particular textual strategies and eschewing others that might have had another effect.

While Chapters 4, 5 and 6 are devoted to an elaboration of reflexivity, precision and scepticism in relation to the epistemology and methodology of the sociological analysis, **Chapter 7** focuses on the relative autonomy of the sociological text from that analysis. As texts are not transparent windows onto the reality of the sociological analysis, as they have idiosyncrasies, conventions and rhetorics of their own, it is important that we learn to distinguish the knowledge claims *implied* by the rhetorical tropes and narrative structure of the text, from the knowledge claims as systematically assessed according to the linguistic conventions and models of sociological research. Accordingly, Chapter 7 begins to develop tools for the recognition and critical analysis of the various literary devices that can be used to imply epistemic authority for the author by way of allusion, connotation, insinuation, framing and diversion. Four categories of technique are singled out for attention, and are illustrated with examples taken from anthropology, literature and poststructuralist literary theory, and an extended sociological case study in the form of an episode from Judith Stacey's *Brave New Families* (1990). Stacey's account is particularly useful as she is unusually self-reflexive about her role in both the ethnographic and the textual processes. These various literary techniques, in turn, are systematically related back to: (1) the actual sociological analysis; (2) the critical assessment of this as more or less adequate to the claims made for it; and, finally, (3) to the benchmark of a rich complex ontology. These are presented as various stages in the cross-questioning of a sociological text.

Chapters 8 and 9 attempt to demonstrate the utility of the inter-related stages of a past-modern sociology for the detailed analysis and critique of three case studies, which are all clear examples of the most stubborn elements of sociological modernism. The case studies are of: comparative citizenship (Michael Mann); the autonomy of the state in relation to the financial institutions of the City of London (Geoffrey Ingham); and the particular systems of patriarchy that are said to have existed in Europe and North America in the last century or so (Sylvia Walby). Whereas the sociological case study discussed in Chapter 7 is a highly contextualised ethnographic and local study, these cases are all examples, more or less, of the large sweep. The three examples are particularly pertinent as each of these authors is distinguished by having gone some way to an appreciation of the rich, complex ontology of contemporary social theory, criticising the *ontological* reductionism of sociological modernism along the way. However, like Giddens, their epistemological, methodological and textual perspectives are all radically underdeveloped. A critical analysis of their accounts shows that, whereas they actually pitch their analyses primarily at the floater and the dreamer levels, they claim much more for them in their textual presentations. Their analyses are criticised for their lack of epistemological and methodological reflexivity, their consequent misunderstanding of the status of their own evidential base, and their textual complacency and highly premature closure of alternative possibilities. The concluding chapter briefly points to the dangers to sociology of tolerating the weaknesses manifest in the complacency of sociological modernism and in the defeatism of nihilistic postmodernism. Conversely, it commends the advantages of a past-modern sociology and calls for more work to be done in developing its various dimensions at the levels of ontology, epistemology and methodology, and textuality, and in their synthetic combination in the critical analysis of existing sociological texts and the creative production of new ones.

Notes

1 I am keenly aware of, and have sympathy with, the irritation of an older generation of sociologists who feel that the intellectual positions that they themselves have previously held, or still hold, are caricatured by postmodernists. I have no wish to follow postmodernists into this trap. While obviously believing that my ideal type of sociological modernism captures central features of the dominant positions in twentieth-century sociology, I also – again, of course – accept that there will be elements of sociological approaches (more in some than in others) within the general orbit of sociological modernism that will be less guilty than others. These elements will be more sensitive to the richness and complexity of ontology and to the limitations of their knowledge in relation to it. In this sense, the appropriateness of the ideal type to any particular individual piece of sociological research remains an open question, to be settled by a specific analysis of that work. The same, incidentally, goes for the ideal type of contemporary social theorists with respect to their alleged inattention to epistemology and methodology (see below and Chapter 4) and, similarly, to the works of any one postmodern theorist as regards the various charges that I lay at the door of the ideal type of defeatist postmodernism.

2 One consequence of the argument and its chains of reasoning being the focus of the book is that my primary objective is not to attempt to provide a series of potted summaries of everything and anything about all the various schools of thought that currently inhabit the sociological marketplace. Thus, some schools of thought, some theorists, will only be mentioned in passing rather than dealt with in detail. I make no apologies for this. The argument, once formulated, can always be extended to confront other paradigms, other theorists. On the other hand, I do attempt to focus specifically on appropriate authors wherever possible, in order to pre-empt the charge that my ideal types bear little relation to the work of real authors.

3 For the seminal critique of grand narratives or metanarratives, see Lyotard (1984). It should be noted, however, that the use of these terms in the postmodern literature is ambiguous and ill-defined. It covers a whole spectrum of presumed normative and descriptive ills. In my experience, however, the disreputable features of grand narratives are always said to include their vastness of scale and their presumptiousness with regard to the local and the contextual. In any case, I have tried to be very clear in the course of this book as to what I myself consider metanarratives to be in all the various forms relevant to my argument – forms benign and not so benign (see the floater, dreamer and despot categories in Chapter 3).

Chapter 1

Contemporary Developments in Social Theory: The Right Time for a Past-modern Sociology

I will begin the task of crafting an alternative between defeatist postmodernism and the complacency of sociological modernism by, first, looking at the ways in which transparent forms of realism have been undermined by contemporary developments in literature, literary criticism and philosophy. I will then go on to question what I believe to be a series of false dichotomies supposed by defeatist postmodernists, the most central among these being that between a crude transparent realism, on the one hand, and the impossibility of any sort of realism, on the other. I will briefly suggest that even those most deeply responsible for the undermining of a transparent and complacent realism are still necessarily committed to some notion of the real as long as they have an interest in political, ethical or practical issues. I finish the chapter by introducing some of the metatheoretical principles that inform my advocacy of a past-modernist sociology. I stress the linguistic and paradigmatic conventions of these principles, as well as their provisional and nonfoundational character. On the other hand, I also stress their regulative function in directing and focusing the sociologist to empirical data of theoretical significance.

The explicit recognition of the relationship between abstract categories of ontology and empirical research/evidence provides a coherent and systematic basis for intersubjective debate between sociologists on the adequacy of empirical evidence to the ontological categories, and vice versa. Without such an explicit framework we are well and truly lost – the crude dichotomy between fictional postmodernism and transparent realism would be the only one available. The more sophisticated realism I propose thus retains a commitment to the regulative function of the real in the context of metatheoretical principles that are acknowledged as conventional and corrigible. Equally, in the course of the book, I will also draw on a range of postmodern concerns that pose a formidable reminder, from within the practical framework of this more defensible realism, that it should not lose the constant humility that should accompany a sense of its own very real and inevitable limitations: its perspectival bias, and its fallibility, provisionality and consequent instability.

Realism under assault

Literature and literary criticism

In the humanities, it has been literary theory that has led the assault on the 'transparent real', with its translation of the ideas of structuralism and poststructuralism into the language of the literary criticism of novels, drama and poetry. 'Reality' has here acquired inverted commas, and its representation in literary texts is said to be less the product of some external reality 'out there' and more the result of particular traditions and conventions of language use. In other words, the apparent references to the real world that appear in the novels of Gustave Flaubert, George Elliott and Charles Dickens, for example, are primarily, or at the extreme no more than, literary imaginings. They could hardly be anything else because we are trapped, to quote the oft-quoted title of Frederic Jameson's (1972) book, in a 'prison house of language'. The words we use for things in the world are in an important sense arbitrary; that we call a particular type of flower a rose and not a chocolate mousse is purely a matter of convention. Words for things just have to be, on the whole, different from other words, other sounds, so that we do not get confused. All the rest – which words for which objects – has been up to the many linguistic cultures to work out for themselves.

In turn, the meanings we create with the words we do come to use soon become layered with allusions and connotations and cannot be pinned down naïvely and pristinely to a particular object out there in the world. Even when it is fairly clear which object is being referred to, our understanding and apprehension of that object does not stand discretely on its own untainted by other meanings. Rather, it will be interpreted within a web of pre-existing meanings and layered allusions accrued within our minds as interdependent stocks of cultural knowledge gleaned from past experience.

Each separate word in a realist novel, with its weight of connotation, is placed next to other such words to form a sentence, which is in turn placed among many other sentences, which are strung together into a narrative form by an author. The author is more or less aware, more or less in control, of what she is producing, but in any event she cannot float free from the linguistic world of which she is a product, from which she draws her material (her intertexts), and within which she wishes to find an audience with which to communicate. The author can only play at the edges of the particular conventions (novelistic, dramatic, poetic) and subconventions (for example realist, modernist or postmodernist) within which she is writing. Realist conventions of narrative construction, for example, call for a clear beginning, middle and end. Poststructuralist critics point to the artificiality of this injunction to forge out an arbitrary starting point, a middle and a neatly packaged ending from the amorphous flux and flow of events in a world that is, in actuality, in constant process. By pointing to the artificial nature of realist texts, these literary critics foreground the conventionality, the literary conventions, whereby what passes for reality is actively produced. Heightened awareness of these conventions has produced responses not only from literary critics but also from postmodernist novelists, so that in John Fowles' *The French Lieutenant's Woman* (1977) we have a choice of two endings, in Graham Swift's *Waterland* (1983) the chronological ending appears in the middle of the book, and in John Berger's novel *G* (1989), for example, we find the following enigmatic and suggestive passage:

> I cannot continue this account of the eleven-year-old boy in Milan on 6 May 1898... To stop here, despite all that I leave unsaid, is to admit more of the truth than will be possible if I bring the account to a conclusion. The writer's desire to finish is fatal to the truth. The End unifies. Unity must be established in another way (Berger, 1989, p. 77; cf Hutcheon, 1989, p. 69).

Philosophy, and Philosophy of the Social Sciences

In the social sciences, there is a long tradition of thought that has been suspicious of claims to have direct and objective access to the real world. This is a tradition of scepticism often associated with the Scottish philosopher David Hume, who was only too aware of the tricks we can play on reality with our wilful 'habits of the mind' (Hume, 1975; cf Ayer, 1980). However, and somewhat ironically given its pedigree, this scepticism was lost with the ascendancy of empiricism and its near-cousin logical positivism to their position of pre-eminence in the social sciences. Although there were always dissenters from this position, its pre-eminence only began to be significantly challenged in the late 1960s and 70s, as primarily, but not only, philosophical developments in the recognition of the importance of language and meaning, and their structuring influence on the communities (academic and social) in which they existed, began to filter through into the social sciences. Major influences here were the figures, in other ways diverse, of Wittgenstein (1973), Saussure (1974), Gadamer (1976), Austin (1975), Winch (1958), Kuhn (1970) and Derrida (1973, 1978). An important cumulative consequence of these influences was a deepening scepticism towards the often smug claims to objectivity voiced both by philosophically formalised empiricism and, in a more intuitive but no less confident manner, by a range of practically oriented forms of empirical social science. Their claims to objectivity were questioned in a number of areas, all of which revolved around the themes of meaning and understanding. Max Weber, following the lead of Schleiermacher, Dilthey and others in the hermeneutic tradition, had made important moves in the direction of acknowledging the importance of *verstehen* (or understanding) as a moment in the social scientist's method of grasping what is going on in any particular social circumstance. However, the general reception of Weber's work, rightly or wrongly, treated verstehen as an aspect of method to be combined with a more orthodox empiricist attachment to a quest for objective causal laws, which would parallel the laws of nature investigated and unearthed by natural scientists (cf Cuff et al, 1990, p. 142; Outhwaite, 1986, pp. 46–55).[1] Moreover, Weber's interest in verstehen was restricted to the realm of method; he did not explore the radical possibilities opened up by considering verstehen as an essential part of ontology, understanding meanings as an intrinsic and unavoidable part of everyday life itself (Giddens, 1993, p. 24). It was these neglected possibilities that were brought to light by the major figures listed above.

For the philosopher Hans-Georg Gadamer, hermeneutic understanding and dialogue were chronic features of everyday life; one could never quite escape from one's own view of the world, one's own background of understanding, so that one was always caught within a 'hermeneutic circle'. Understanding others and communicating with others thus involved what Gadamer called a 'fusion of horizons', whereby one necessarily had to attempt to grasp another's world view, or aspects of it, from within one's own world view or horizon of meaning (cf Warnke, 1987, pp. 107–8). For Wittgenstein, and in a wider sense for Winch, forms of everyday life are in a sense language games, in which one has to know the linguistic, cultural rules in order to be able to 'go on' in a reasonably successful manner. To know the meaning of a word, a sentence or a social practice is to know the social rules that govern its use. Thus, what counts as praying, or voting, or politeness, or vulgarity, or *risqué* behaviour, can only be settled within a form of life. A corollary of this is that social practices do not exist independently of the concepts in terms of which social agents think about those practices. Rationality for Winch was something that only made sense from within the network of norms and beliefs that made up a culture. Thus, for example, a belief that all people not following certain rituals were witches and should be killed might be a totally rational thing to believe within the network of meanings and norms that constitute a particular form of life. It would only become irrational if you refused to accept, for example, that your brother was a witch after he had failed to follow the prescribed rituals.

For J. L. Austin also, again drawing on Wittgenstein, it was important to note that language did more than just help to describe the social world: it also helped to constitute it, to produce it (cf Skinner, 1988a, pp. 83–6). One of the most important aspects of language games was their 'performative' (or illocutionary) function: language was used for promising, lying, expressing affection and loyalty, undertaking tasks, co-ordinating action, causing offence and smoothing ruffled feathers. For the philosopher of science Thomas Kuhn, academic communities researching in their own specialised areas took part in their own specialised language games, which he called 'paradigms', within which and through which they constructed and investigated a field of study, whether in the natural sciences or, in later incarnations, the social sciences (cf Barnes, 1985, pp. 83–100). Knowing the paradigm was knowing how to 'go on' in your community. Scientists did not approach reality directly or head-on; they did so using the concepts, the models, the metaphors and the general presuppositions of their host community of scholars. They approached the world out there from within the hermeneutic circle of their own paradigm; evidence was evidence when it made sense within the paradigm, falsification was falsification only when the linguistic community agreed it was. A central part of Kuhn's argument was that even the apparent empirical falsification of a claim made from within a linguistic paradigm and following the terms of the paradigm was usually not enough to endow it with significance. Scientists and social scientists had so much invested in their paradigms that it would take years of empirical evidence that did not fit, or years of no explanatory progress (or, more cynically, a change in the sources and ideology of research funding) in order for a community to decide to abandon a paradigm.

For Saussure, the emphasis was on the way in which languages are structured according to a system of differences, as mentioned above in relation to the rose and the chocolate mousse. For Saussure, one would expect to find that within a particular language culture, a given word with a particular sound and spelling (signifier), say 'chocolate mousse', would refer to a fixed concept, say a slightly wobbly brown milky substance, which would, in turn, have a fixed referent in the real world. Poststructuralists, however, want to show that the sounds and marks on a page that are used in communication have no fixed signified, no fixed concept or image that they signify. The meanings attached to a signifier are forever in flux and can expand, narrow or change completely, one set of meanings being effaced by others. Think of the signifiers 'Mrs Thatcher', 'Marxism', 'black', 'Sarajevo', 'Robert Maxwell', 'flared jeans', '*en suite*' and 'sliced white loaf'. And think of trying to alight on a rigorous definition of, say, 'Mrs Thatcher' and trying to adhere to it rigorously, constantly and without tensions, shifts and slippages throughout the course of a book. The result is to drastically problematise the ability of language to directly represent or mirror a world out there that somehow has its own meaning beyond language (cf Culler, 1983, p. 85ff; Hoy, 1986, pp. 43–64; Norris, 1991, pp. 18–55).

Essentially the same point has been made by the American philosopher Richard Rorty (Rorty, 1980; 1987, pp. 241–59), who expresses it by saying that we have to accept that the things out there in the real world do not have their *own* meaning; it makes no sense to look for 'nature's own language', as if the fields and the hills and uranium and bauxite would have 'fields' and 'hills' and 'uranium' and 'bauxite' written all over them. They are called these things because we call them these things; these are the signifiers that can take on a range of signifieds beyond which we cannot go to uncover the real, fixed meaning. Incidentally, in the case of the real world referent of 'chocolate mousse', it does appear in the supermarket with its name written all over it, but this is only because we, or someone like us, have put it there! The signifier 'chocolate mousse' can be changed because, like all signifiers, its use is conventional. The same, as we have seen, goes for what it signifies (the signified), probably even more so, as connotations accrue, layer and gather with the wind.

The upshot of all these influences, from literary theory, philosophy and the philosophy of the social sciences, is that it is harder than ever to claim to have direct access to an objective real world out there that is independent of our world in here, as it were. Instead of carrying on as if all this makes little difference to the real stuff of getting out there into the world, 'getting our hands dirty' (interviewing, correlating, observing!), and then unproblematically telling it like it was – the truth, the facts of the matter – we should be aware that the reality we describe is always highly mediated. First, one has to acknowledge the hermeneutic frame of meaning of one's own academic paradigm, which is then easily extendable into an acknowledgement of the formative influences of our own cultural, linguistic, political and general biographical experience on our particular hermeneutic frame of meaning. Second, there is the fact that the everyday world out there, for social science researchers, involves encountering linguistic communities with their own hermeneutic frames of meaning to which they have privileged access, and through which they co-ordinate action in the social world. So not only is there the combination of the individual social analyst and her paradigm's perspective on what reality is, but there is also the everyday social actor's perspective on what reality is.

Third, both social analyst and everyday social actor form their perspectives on what constitutes reality in a world in which the meanings that words (or images) – signifiers – have are purely conventional and are potentially open to constant flux, losing, gaining and changing connotations and denotations. In order to have a shot at what reality is at a particular place and time – including in relation to a particular strip of interaction in a very specific setting – one would be advised to get to know as much as possible about how to 'go on' in such a densely textured linguistic and cultural community, open to the likely flux of meaning and aware of the many meanings and allusions that will no doubt pass one by.

Fourth, how does one combine an attempt to get at reality with an awareness of the artificial textual conventions of aesthetic realism? Can a sociological realist analysis of the world out there be transferred into text on the basis of conventions that avoid the artificiality of which Berger tries to struggle free? Or, if, as it seems, all conventions are artificial, yet we are condemned in both analysis and writing to follow conventions, are there 'artificial' forms of textuality that are more appropriate to a sociological realism than the aesthetic realism associated with nineteenth-century novelists?

The Specious Dichotomy of Crude Realism and 'Fictional' Postmodernism

How does postmodernism respond to all these mediations – (1) social scientists' frames of meaning; (2) social agents' frames of meaning; (3) the slipperiness and the context-dependency of meanings; and (4) the 'artificiality' of forms of textual representation – which undermine any notion of having direct and unmediated access to the reality of social practices? At its most defeatist, the postmodern response to this complexity is simply to counterpose, on the one hand, the consequent impossibility of an objective, transparent and total representation of the real, and, on the other, a position, which it endorses, that has no truck whatsoever with any attempt to represent the real, with any attempt, that is, to critically analyse and textually present real social and material relations (cf Rosenau, 1992, p. 80 and *passim* for a review of the literature). Rejecting the possibility of any sort of realism in this way, defeatist postmodernism involves a complete repudiation of the distinction between fictional and nonfictional accounts of the world. If we have no notion of the real, we can have no notion of the nonreal, as the two logically entail one another. Just about anything would go, and in any old way, for a sociology constructed on the basis of such a position. The basic idea is that there are so many obstacles in the way of an objective, transparent account of the real that one should just give up the ghost; not to do so is to persist in a lie. There are said to be many reasons why the lie is perpetuated, including those to do with sectional power interests camouflaging their preferred view of reality as *the* objective account of reality, with the desire of professionalised 'experts' to dignify the knowledge they claim to have acquired about the real world with the hierarchical privilege of 'truth', and with the generalised modernist will to mastery and control over nature and society.

Defeatist postmodernists seek to expose the lie so as to rid it of all power. I want to do something different. I want us to persist with the notion of the real – because I believe that our social practices have their own specific realities – but to expose the devices, linguistic and otherwise, that we employ in our attempts to say something about whatever slice of reality we are currently aiming at. There is a middle way between a naïve notion of realism and a naïve rejection of it. One can accept the difficulties posed by the four types of mediation listed above but still believe that a social researcher should be guided by some regulative notion of the real. One can still make the effort to get at the real while understanding all the obstacles in the way. The difficulties and the mediations should be acknowledged to the full, but, equally, there are many things that have really happened, and are really happening, in the world, which we have many good reasons for finding out about in as accurate a way as possible, even if the accuracy will be imperfect and provisional, and representation mediated by linguistic, theoretical and textual forms.

Taking on board both a sense of scepticism and provisionality in relation to truth claims, on the one hand, and a commitment to a real, on the other, means for me developing some clear markers by which we can understand what our perspective on the real is at any one time. These markers will provide a basis from which we can then go on to identify the empirical evidence that would be appropriate to the substantive fleshing out of that perspective in relation to a particular social practice at a given time and place. We need to understand the relation between ideas and the specific real world conjuncture. This means, first, developing a useful and defensible account of what is in the world, a realist ontology, in a way that pays heed to the conventionality of, and thus the inevitable provisionality of, such an account. Such an ontology would respect the potential richness and complexity of the social world, taking on board, not least, the mediations stressed by the 'linguistic' and 'hermeneutic' turns, especially those encapsulated in (2) and (3) above. In itself, it would consist of fairly low-level generalisations about the nature of, for example, social agents, social meaning, resources, power, social norms, discourses, time and space. The ontology should be as broadly conceived as possible, so that – again, as far as possible – all individual, idiosyncratic, historically and culturally specific aspects of an element are left out of the picture. Thus, an ontology of agency, time or space would either be about all agents, all times and all spaces, or, in a more periodised form, about all agents, all times and all spaces *within* a given social, temporal and geographical location, for example, modern Western industrialised societies. The breadth of the generalised conception means that it can act as a structuring, orienting frame, while allowing as much latitude as possible for variations when brought to the investigation of specific instances.

Second, it means linking this realist ontology – combining it – with a means of gaining the best and most appropriate knowledge available about particular events at particular times and in particular places in the real world. In other words, it means translating the provisional realist ontology into an affirmative past-modern knowledge of events, which, in turn, is partial, fallible, provisional, unstable and limited by perspective, presuppositions and textual presentation, but which is, nevertheless, the nearest shot at the real that one can manage. Despite all my caveats concerning our chances of getting at the real, I reject the position taken up by the defeatist postmodernists, because to me a recognition of our inability to achieve absolute or perfect truth about the real does not mean that we cannot attain any useful information at all. As Craig Calhoun has put it, in an essay on the relationship between postmodernism and social theory, 'Choices are made with regard to epistemic gain, not absolute truth; political advantage, not political certainty; and so forth' (Calhoun, 1992, p. 261; see also Taylor, 1985).

The cogent answer Calhoun proposes to the problem of the imperfections of theories, to their fallibility and provisionality, is not to ignore them but to bring to the fore their assumptions, their procedures, their biases and their paradigms. He argues for a position in which theorists and researchers acknowledge as fully as possible the linguistic, cultural and historical conditions under which, and through which, they produce what passes for knowledge. In other words, they should 'thematise reflexivity'. He argues strongly against the defeatist postmodern view that just because theoretical discourse cannot live up to its own ideals, we must forfeit those ideals as regulative constructs. We must make choices among available theoretical options or abandon a great deal of contemporary scholarly, political and ethical discourse. The path of avoiding such choices, of letting the inadequacy of all available theories be a licence for dismissing them all, is far more radical and problematic than many of its seeming advocates suppose (Calhoun, 1992, pp. 261–2).

Three More Unnecessary Dichotomies Associated with Postmodernism

I also want to say where my argument in this book differs from defeatist postmodernists on three other points. Postmodernists argue, respectively, for: (1) respecting the existence of a plurality of perspectives, as against a notion that there is one single truth from a privileged perspective; (2) local, contextual studies in place of grand narratives; and (3) an emphasis on disorder, flux and openness, as opposed to order, continuity and constraint. Whereas these postmodern positions are often seen as being intimately and necessarily bound up with an antirealism, I want to show in the course of this book that there is no necessary relationship between them. The defence of what is of value in the positions that postmodernism advocates *does* necessarily entail a critique of sociological modernism's particular form of realism, with its aggrandising, complacent approach to knowledge, but it *does not* necessarily entail a rejection of all forms of realism. Moreover, with a more sophisticated realism, there is no need to choose between the supposedly irreconcilable alternatives of points (2) and (3); I will show that a past-modern sociology can provide the space for both local, contextual studies and certain forms of grand narrative, and for studies of both disorder and order, openness and constraint.

To take the three points in order. First, it seems to me that postmodernists (and poststructuralists, and others for that matter) have been right to insist that we understand and respect the multiplicity of perspectives that can be taken – which are often taken – on any particular social situation or practice; that we acknowledge that some perspectives are typically marginalised or ignored altogether and thus do not appear in any of the established accounts of the said reality. This point is obviously consonant and consistent with mediations 1–3 above, and in many ways grows from them. Thus, along with the postmodernists, I am all for emphasising multiple perspectives, but I want to specify my understanding of their significance in a way that is consistent with a sense of the reality of social processes. There is no need to choose between the two. Thus I hold that: (1) any one reality can be appreciated from many different angles, and that the vantage point provided by each of these angles will mean that the reality *that is seen and appreciated* will be more or less different from that seen from other vantage points; and (2) that there are many different real events and processes in the world that can be taken account of, including many that have been traditionally marginalised (those involving women, ordinary people, workers, colonised peoples and many other 'Others').

I also believe that two accounts of the same event seen from two different angles can be equally valid. However, I still believe that two competing accounts of the same reality viewed from the same angle, each claiming to be true, can be judged as more, less or just about equally adequate in terms, not least, of their empirical sufficiency as measured by their own respective theoretical frameworks. Some theoretical categories can emerge – if only temporarily and provisionally – as being more fruitful than others in allowing us to taste those multiple realities. Some categories will, therefore, be chosen as better than others for certain purposes.

Second, postmodernists have targeted grand narratives of a whole host of complexions as being worthy of the utmost disdain as the apotheosis of modernist social science's arrogant drive towards totalising accounts on the barest of evidential grounds. Grand narratives, or metanarratives, typically encompass large historical sweeps of actual time – notching up tens or hundreds of years in their causal accounts – or else pronounce on history and its mechanisms from a place somewhere outside actual social time, in a world of concepts and their mutual consistency. In either case, they typically feign to tell us about a lot without actually telling us about a lot. Details, meanings, contexts, the specificity of contingencies, the time of seconds and hours as opposed to years and decades (and much more besides), all either disappear from view or are never deigned to be important enough to appear from the very beginning (cf Seidman, 1991a, 1991b). The response of postmodernism to the arrogance of grand narrativism has been to retreat into the local, the contextual and the specifics of the situated perspective (relativistically in the case of defeatist postmodernism) and to reject the large sweep, the big picture as an arrogance to be shunned (cf Lyotard, 1984; Marcus and Fischer, 1986, pp. 7–16; Sarup, 1988, p. 131ff).[2] I share postmodernism's disdain for grand narratives that claim to know far more than they do (see 'Despots', below), and for those that totalise *their* account of the large sweep as *the* account, thus marginalising many other takes on the social processes that took place in that same slice of time–space, but I very much want to retain a place for the wide angle, bird's-eye view of history and geography, which could easily be lost as an overreaction to the impudence of modernism.

The crux of my argument is that a large sweep should recognise from the start that its strengths will also be its limitations. What it gains from being able to look at the big picture, it will tend to lose in terms of detail and nuance of colour. The claims that large sweeps make for themselves should be provisional and tentative, with a sense of proportion consonant with their lack of specificity. As we will see, there are many different forms of 'grand narrative' and I will indicate the reflexivity in relation to methodology and epistemology that is required if any one type of grand narrative is to be able to recognise itself – including its weak points and blemishes – in the mirror.

Third, postmodernists tend to strongly insist that we privilege disorder, flux and openness and, conversely, that we reject accounts focusing upon order, continuity and constraint (cf Marcus and Fischer, 1986, Chapter 1; Flax, 1990, pp. 41–3; Bauman, 1992, Chapter 9). I understand the reaction against modernism's overemphasis on the latter here (although we should not forget to put theories of conflict and class struggle onto the scales) but, notwithstanding this, I do not see why we should choose, *a priori*, one or the other. I will address some of the exigencies of my position as I return to this theme at various points in the book (see below, Chapter 2 and Chapter 4).

It is an essential point for me that none of the above three positions necessarily entails a rejection of the kind of sophisticated realism advocated by a past-modern sociology. Any sociologist with a view to saying something about the world – politically, ethically or practically – that she wishes to be believed, or which she hopes to rely upon as a guide to action, must surely stand to benefit from the development of a sophisticated sociology, which could develop the utility, discipline and flexibility of the regulative ideal of the real. Many writers influenced by critiques of transparent realism and the 'linguistic turn' in contemporary metatheory, and by the emphasis on multiple perspectives, the related critique of hegemonic grand narratives, and the arguments in favour of focusing on discontinuity and instability, still have a strong desire – despite their press and their sometime equivocations – to say something about the real. To take just one example, Joan Scott's extremely influential *Gender and the Politics of History* is strongly influenced by Derrida's radical insistence on the volatility and instability of the relation between signifier and signified, and would clearly have no truck with any claims to represent the real directly. Nevertheless, some sort of commitment to the real is an essential aspect of her work. On the one side – the sceptical, liguistically mediated, non-totalising side – Scott argues that the deconstructive exposure of the fluidity and instability within and between supposedly fixed and self-evident oppositions of categories (for example relevant and irrelevant human agents and events, men and women, colonised and colonisers, the significant and the insignificant, postmodernism and realism!) has meant an undermining of the historian's ability to:

> claim neutral mastery or to present any particular story as if it were complete, universal, and objectively determined. Instead, if one grants that meanings are constructed through exclusions, one must acknowledge and take responsibility for the exclusions involved in one's own project. Such a reflexive, self-critical approach makes apparent the particularistic status of any historical knowledge and the historian's active role as a producer of knowledge. It undermines claims for authority based on totalizing explanations, essentialized categories of analysis (be they human nature, race, class, sex, or 'the oppressed'), or synthetic narratives that assume an inherent unity for the past (Scott, 1988, pp. 7–8).

At the same time, Scott is clear about her commitment to trying to produce knowledge about the real world. She expresses this in terms of the contribution of academic studies to feminist politics, in terms of the role that works like hers can play in the collective attempt to confront and change existing distributions of power. Academic studies, says Scott, can interpret the world while trying to change it, insisting upon 'the need to examine gender concretely and in context and to consider it a historical phenomenon, produced, reproduced, and transformed in different situations and over time' (Scott, 1988, p. 6). Scott is particularly interested in how the subjective and collective meanings of 'women' and 'men' as categories of identity have been constructed, and in the ways in which these categories have entered into the working definitions of the whole gamut of institutional practices, including those within the workplace, the community, wars and the 'high politics' of governments and states, as well as within the family and the home, the traditional sites of gender within much of social history (Scott, 1988, p. 6). The emphasis throughout is on specific variations in meaning, context and the concrete in historical conditions, which are never produced once and for all but whose reality is in more or less constant flux. Definitions of reality are always open to contestation, struggle and exposure, but the definitions are clearly not thought to be arbitrary; while the historian has an active role in the production of knowledge, she does not have total autonomy from the specificities of the real. She must, to repeat, 'examine gender concretely and in context', and her accounts would therefore, logically, be open to provisional validation or falsification on the basis of relevant evidence about that context. It is difficult to see what would be gained by eschewing the resources of a more sophisticated and linguistically mediated realism developed beyond modernism.

A Sophisticated Realism

Ontological Similarities Between Contemporary Social Theory and Postmodernism

The reason, therefore, for insisting on developing a defensible and definite ontology of the sorts of thing that exist in the real social world is that this can act as a regulative construct, which helps to marshal and discipline accounts of more conjuncturally specific social events and processes. Although provisional and defeasible, it can help to allay the retreat into a defeatist postmodernism in which just anything goes in just any old way. My stress on the provisionality and the fallibility of the ontology that I will sketch out here, and with which I propose to work, carries with it the implication that this ontology is by no means thought to be the only one possible, or to be definitely superior to other possible ontologies. This last point does not contradict the fact that the reason I work with it is because it is the most powerful one I know about, at present, for the purposes I am engaged in. Unless one begins from a reflexively explicit ontology, it will be impossible to use it in order to discipline what passes for systematic knowledge. A reflexively explicit ontology is the first brake on the 'just any old how' mentality.

The ontology that I will be using as my regulative construct, and which I will present in Chapter 2, is a synthesis informed by the various complementary developments in the philosophy of the social sciences outlined above. One of my central contentions is that contemporary social theory of a sophisticated realist kind has been radically and widely influenced by those developments – stressing meaning, hermeneutics, specificity, the linguistic and symbolic mediation of reality – in relation to both traditional and new areas of study. We shall see that these emphases have been translated into sociological theory in a number of different ways, not least in a rethinking of the classical structure–action question, and have been supplemented by other moves, such as the resurgent interest in the time and space dimensions of social relations. The *leitmotif* that I shall use as a shorthand to express these emphases of contemporary social theory will be that of 'contextualisation'. I set out to emphasise both the continuities within the different strands of contemporary social theory, and also those between the general thrust of contemporary social theory in the sphere of *ontology* and that of postmodernism in the same sphere. Where others have only stressed the radical disjuncture between contemporary social theory and postmodernism, I emphasise some central continuities and resemblances. When the dust settles, I hope that these will be seen as more important.

A Postempiricist Ontology and Linguistic Self-consciousness

What is left for me to do in the present chapter is to provide more of the background and reasoning behind the choice of a particular ontology in a world, a culture, in which we are all too aware that the choice is embedded in all sorts of cultural, linguistic and academic webs of presupposition and predisposition. Above all, I want, on the one hand, to clarify the postempiricist nature of the realist ontology I propose, and, on the other, to stress its linguistically self-conscious nature, the fact that it has taken on board the famous 'linguistic turn' that was evident in both the literary and philosophical inputs into the contemporary questioning of naïve realism.

For empiricist philosophies of science, all that could be known about causation came from the experience of observing over and over again a particular type of event. The sort of event that ensued when two objects came together, collided, were placed side by side or otherwise interacted in some way or another. This type of event became interesting when the result, the consequence, of the two objects meeting seemed to be constant, to have a regularity about it. Thus a piece of coal placed on a fire would regularly burn. A piece of iron released at a height would invariably drop towards earth. Water heated to a temperature of 100°C at sea level would consistently boil. Empiricists were interested in these regularities, which they called regular conjunctions of events. They believed that scientific knowledge consisted of laws derived from, or tested by, such regular conjunctions. In more sophisticated forms of empiricism, such as that espoused by Popper, scientists were seen as having a duty not only to formulate bold hypotheses about the effects that would be produced by the conjunction of events, but also to try every way they knew how to falsify the hypotheses, to prove them wrong by finding an exception to the rule (Popper, 1968; cf Cottingham, 1984, pp. 141–3).

The problem with the empiricist view of the world for realists such as Bhaskar lies in their reduction of scientific knowledge to what can be attained by means of looking at regular conjunctions. Bhaskar argues that this constitutes what he calls an 'epistemic fallacy', whereby what can be said about the nature of the world (ontology) is reduced to what can be known by means of a particular (that is, empiricist) epistemology, which is a limited and restrictive one (cf Bhaskar, 1978, pp. 36–8). For Bhaskar, as for Giddens and Habermas, this flattens out the richness and depth of reality; there is more to be said about the world than that which can be gleaned in those moments of regular conjunction. Each of these theorists sketches out an array of objects, entities and dimensions over and above regular conjunction, which they believe does more justice to the true richness and depth of reality. They each outline certain broad ontological objects and conditions, which, they suggest, are transhistorical, even though their detailed particular forms and interactions with other objects are greatly conditioned by the specific historical and social context in which they come to be situated.

Bhaskar and Giddens are at opposite ends of the spectrum in terms of the formalism through which they derive their key ontological concepts. There is something to be said for either strategy and, ultimately, the key point in judging the adequacy of an ontology is not the method by which it is arrived at but, rather, its explanatory effectiveness, the range of questions it allows one to address with relative success, however measured.

The Philosophically Inspired Sociological Realism of Roy Bhaskar

Intrinsic Causal Powers.   Bhaskar logically deduces a large part of his account of the world from the practices of the laboratory based natural sciences (cf Bhaskar, 1978, p. 54ff; Isaac, 1987, pp. 48–9). Briefly, he argues that scientific experiments only make sense if we believe that the properties and capacities of objects that we find out about and test for in the laboratory continue to exist when these objects leave the laboratory. The regular conjunctions that we carefully and skilfully produce in the 'closed' system of the laboratory, by restricting any impediments to an ordered and limited meeting of objects, are the exception to the rule. When experiments produce particular results, they do so because of the intrinsic properties of the objects involved, objects that we assume will continue to have these properties outside the rarefied conditions of the laboratory. Indeed, regular conjunctions, when they take place, are secondary events, in the sense that they depend on the setting into motion of prior properties, which are inherent in a particular object at a particular time. Thus, coal's rendezvous with fire is of consequence only because of the intrinsic properties of coal and fire respectively. For realists, it is the inherent properties and intrinsic causal powers of objects that are of primary importance. Both inanimate natural objects, such as coal and water, and animate actors, such as human beings, have intrinsic causal powers that can be identified irrespective of whether or not they are involved in the production of regular conjunctions of events. For example, human agents may have the potential to lift an arm, throw a ball, remember things, change a baby's nappy and conjure all the dishes onto the table at the same time while they are all steaming hot, but this does not mean that these particular capacities will necessarily be exercised (feminist observation suggests that 50 per cent or so of human agents very rarely exercise some, at least, of these capacities).[3]

The Stratification of Reality.   Thus, in the nonlaboratory conditions of the outside world, natural and social objects may or may not have their intrinsic properties activated (copper may or may not come into contact with electricity, so may or may not conduct electricity; a couch potato may or may not do the washing up), but this does not (at least in the short term – many human capacities wither with long-term disuse) significantly alter those intrinsic potential powers. There would be no sense in having experiments if we thought that objects might change their properties at any moment, that their properties were not relatively enduring. On the basis of these points, Bhaskar draws a three-fold ontological distinction between: (1) the real mechanism or an object's inherent powers; (2) the actual event (for example copper conducting electricity, or lying dormant, or, for example, in social relations, a person using her inherent capacity to run across a room, or a policewoman using her socially inscribed power to apprehend a criminal); and (3) the empirical event (the aspect, if any, of the natural or social event that is empirically observed). Empiricists restrict their ontology to the last of these dimensions of reality and eschew any talk of the other two as stretching too far beyond what can be known about. They thus drastically flatten the terrain of ontology.

Open Systems: The Differentiation of Reality.   Bhaskar calls this three-fold division the 'stratification' of reality, and he couples it with an appreciation of what he calls the relational 'differentiation' of reality, by which he means that neither natural or social objects exist in a vacuum without contact with other objects or other causal power mechanisms (Bhaskar, 1978, pp. 163–85; Sayer, 1984, pp. 108–11; Outhwaite, 1987, pp. 45–6). Even in a laboratory experiment (leaving aside experiments involving vacuums!) objects are deliberately placed in conjunction with other objects, and it is the interaction of their *differentiated* powers that produces the result (cf Outhwaite, 1987, pp. 45–6).

The capacities that objects and agents possess as potentials, which may or may not be drawn upon or activated, exist in a field of many different objects and agents, each with diverse characteristics and capacities. In Bhaskar's terms, they exist in 'open systems', so that even when a capacity, for example throwing a ball, is exercised, the intended consequence of, for example, the ball being caught by a member of the same sports team may not come about. This may be due to the interception of the ball by an opponent, or by its inadvertently hitting the referee, or by one's team-mate fumbling the catch. The final consequence of an action in an open system depends on many contingently intervening factors.

If this is true for something as localised as the throwing of a ball during a team game, it is even more so for an action such as a national government's economic policy decision to control inflation by increasing interest rates. Such a decision has consequences that stretch over a much greater spatial distance and involves all sorts of imponderables that are often beyond the playing vision of the Minister or Secretary of State responsible for the final decision. All sorts of intervening factors, from a sudden increase in the price of imported goods and components necessary for the production of goods in the manufacturing sector, through a rise in wages in some sectors of the economy, to a simple loosening of non-interest rate terms and conditions on loans demanded by banks and building societies, may intervene between the initial decision and the subsequent figures for inflation in the following quarter. All decisions by all governments to raise interest rates in conditions of inflation are not invariably followed by a reduction in inflation rates. One would look in vain for a regular conjunction here. Open systems are much too complicated and contextualised to be captured by a simple empiricist logic.

Causal chains can be infinitely complex, and both their complexity and their potential for contingency will usually be expected to grow as their spatial and temporal breadth grows. Thus, the narrator of Ian McEwan's novel *Black Dogs* (1972) reflects, towards the end of the book, upon the many strands, the disparate and contingently related set of conditions, that had conjoined to produce his present circumstance. While a proper sense of the meaning and significance of each strand would only become apparent upon reading the novel itself, these reflections help to illustrate the mixture of grand and lowly, personal and impersonal, public and private, highly structured and barely structured events and processes, which, in combination, can have a significant determining effect on the production of an outcome. They also neatly bring out some of the accidental, contingent and open dimensions of social relations:

> Since June's death, when we inherited the bergerie, Jenny and I and our children have spent all our holidays here. There have been times in the summer when I have found myself alone in the last purple light of the evening, in the hammock under the tamarisk tree where June used to lie, wondering at all the world historical and personal forces, the huge and tiny currents, that had to align and combine to bring this place into our possession: a world war, a young couple at the end of it impatient to test their freedom, a government official in his car, the Resistance movement, the Abwehr, a penknife, Mme Auriac's walk – 'doux et beau', a young man's death on a motorcycle, the debts his shepherd brother had to clear, and June finding security and transformation on this sunny shelf of land (McEwan, 1992, p. 173).

Outside experimental conditions, in 'open' systems, the number of different objects pertinent to a given outcome is potentially very great indeed. Sociologists, in this context, need only think of commentators from Emile Durkheim to Norbert Elias who have stressed the increasing complexity of the division of labour and the corresponding intensification of interdependency in social systems.

The Existential Reality of Social Practices.   The final major ontological building block of Bhaskar's realism is that of the *existential reality* of actions, processes and events in the world, and the *existential*

independence of these from the concepts, theories and methodologies
by which researchers attempt to tell us what this reality consists of, or
consisted of (Bhaskar, 1979, p. 60).[4] In Bhaskar's words, intransitivity
means that 'things exist and act independently of our descriptions'
(Bhaskar, 1978, p. 250). In some cases, this is obvious. Marx's concepts
and theories, for example, did not affect the course of the French
Revolution; and sociological observers of impeccable discretion may
manage not to have any effect on the current social relations they are
studying; most lay actors in the world are probably witness most days
to many social interactions upon which they have no effect at all – the
interactions have their own existential independence, their own
existential reality. And even if they do have an effect upon the action
they witness, if they get involved in the production of that interaction,
the interaction still happens, it still takes place, it still has a reality of its
own, which is irreducible. It has happened, no matter how it was
produced. Having a reality, they can thus be objects of social analysis
for researchers wanting to describe that reality, or aspects of that reality:
What really happened? How much money changed hands? Did she
really kick him? What were the real motivations? Who really took the
final decision? What was the reality of the chain of command?

The independent existential reality of what is produced from its
causes is important, in that there is always a real process, real powers,
real actions and consequences, and a reality to modes of understanding, discourses, ways of feeling and so on, which can be the objects of a
realist analysis. Among other things, this should indicate that there is
no contradiction between accepting that events, actions and institutions are social constructions, and accepting that they have an existential reality of their own; they are constructed in particular ways at
particular times and places, and the goal of the realist sociologist is to
get as close as possible to being able to recreate those particular ways, to
come as close as possible to being able to 'tell it like it was'.

The Sociologically Inspired Sociological Realism of Anthony Giddens

Giddens, at the other extreme from Bhaskar, relies on a much less
formal, much more common-sensical method of constructing an
ontology on the basis of a selective critique (of the sorting the chaff
from the grain variety) of a range of social theories and philosophies,
on the basis of his own perspective on a wide range of theoretical and
substantive literatures – and, presumably, everyday life! Influenced by
the general trends of contemporary social theory, his ontological
impulse is towards a combination of increased complexity and internal

consistency, which has led him to attempt to weave the many dimensions of social relations into a richer, potentially more variegated ontological tapestry than had previously been accommodated. His negative critique, on the other hand, is focused on those aspects of theories that he believes reduce or flatten out the many dimensions of social relations.

Despite the marked difference from Bhaskar in the strategy through which Giddens produces his ontology, he ends up with some remarkably similar conceptualisations. In my view, all of the points made above in relation to Bhaskar, covering causal powers, stratification, differentiation and contingently interacting mechanisms in open systems, all apply equally to Giddens' view of ontology. Indeed, Giddens has indicated in a number of places his own belief that his ontology is consistent with a realist epistemology of the type produced by Bhaskar (cf Giddens, 1982, p. 14). The difference, I believe, in addition to the one of strategy already noted, is that Giddens produces a much broader, more socially and sociologically informed picture of ontology than the one outlined by Bhaskar. As we will see in greater detail in the next chapter, Giddens elaborates on a whole series of ontological concepts clustered around, and developed in careful consistency with, his core concepts of: structures and agency (both of which are internally differentiated); what he calls 'the *duality* of structure and agency'; the open-ended structuration of social relations; and sensitivity to time–space context and to the distancing of social relations in time and space.

A Hermeneutically Informed Social Theory.   An essential aspect of Giddens' outlook is captured in his insistence that structuration theory is a 'hermeneutically informed social theory'. In this, he follows the lead of Gadamer, Winch and others, who have emphasised the role that understanding plays in everyday interaction. It is as important to grasp the implications of this emphasis as it is to be clear that for Giddens, just as for Habermas and Bhaskar, there is very definitely more to social life than just understanding. First, there is the material substratum of objects, be these human embodiment or weapons, money, food, clothes, CDs, electric lighting, washing machines, wells, coffee, roads of tarmac, buildings of steel, concrete, glass and much more, computers and computer network systems, and so on and so on. Second, there is also the time–space location of these objects and their distance from other objects. Both of these additional aspects, of course, have an intimate, albeit contingent, relationship with the realm of understanding, with how we perceive their significance from within a particular culture or discourse: a washing machine might as well not have the intrinsic capacities of a washing machine if we do not perceive it as a washing machine and wash our clothes in it; a CD is of no use as a CD if we eat our dinner off it. However, it is equally of no use training our understanding to believe that we have a washing machine in our home when the nearest one is about half a mile away in somebody else's home; what we would have here is a gap (a half-mile gap) between understanding and material substratum.[5]

However, to reverse the emphasis back towards hermeneutics, the radical emphasis on the role that understanding plays at the heart of social relations poses questions for the notion of real causal mechanisms – the intrinsic powers of objects – proposed by Bhaskar and other realists. This is so even though both camps would clearly come together in opposition to the empiricist stress on regular conjunctions and invariable universal laws; hermeneuticists stress the causal importance of contextualised, nonuniversal, cultural ideas and the ability of thinking agents to 'say no' to supposed laws of behaviour. The tension between realism and hermeneutics remains despite their mutual emphasis on a rich and complex world beyond regular conjunctions. For although both ontologies suggest a world of contextualised potentials and possibilities, which may or may not be acted upon, the potentials and possibilities that realists tend to feel most comfortable with are those of material objects. Examples of causal mechanisms given by realists are usually examples taken from the natural or physical sciences. Thus we have examples of the potential power of an aeroplane to fly, whether or not it actually does so, or the potential of gunpowder to explode, which exists as a potential even if it is never ignited, or the potential of iron to rust. It seems to me that this penchant for physical rather than social mechanisms is no accident.

The whole picture becomes far more complex when human agents and the hermeneutic dimension are introduced. In accordance with the points made above, a causal mechanism would now be composed of both a material substratum and a realm of motivating ideas and understandings. Now, in one sense, it is reasonably clear how this latter dimension could fit into the model of a causal mechanism that has an identifiable set of potential powers. Jeffrey Isaac, for example, in his realist analysis of *Power and Marxist Theory* (1987), uses the example of a teacher who has a certain range of potential powers available to her by virtue of her social position as a teacher. The conditions for the exercise of these powers are partly constituted by material infrastructures, such as classrooms, desks and white boards, gathered together in a specific locale. They also rest, however, on a range of understandings – the teacher's own, her pupils', her employers', and so on – which are regularly translated into fairly predictable social practices. We can begin to see the usefulness of such an approach; powers constituted by both material and ideational factors are clearly exercised in the creation of everyday life. Our feelings of reassurance are probably heightened by the sense of routine, of predictable social practices.

Hermeneutics and Open Systems.   However, the picture is messier once we begin to introduce the element of contingency in human interpretations and choices, together with the question of causality within these. Why, for example, is a particular potential power drawn upon at a particular time and place. (Why not draw instead on one of the other potential powers? Why draw on any at all?) We know that the potential of coal to burn, inherent in its physical composition, has been activated by its proximity to fire, but in the case of human agents, we need to know about more than a material substratum. In the case of a teacher's decision to spend two and a half hours each week teaching her class of 13-year-olds about the history of the Vietnam War, a whole array of institutionally transmitted codes of practice, mutually understood norms and career designs is involved.

The difference in emphasis arises when, in contrast to the natural transformation of coal by fire, one asks why social possibilities become translated into actual events by thinking, knowledgeable agents. Knowledgeable agents usually have a wide range of understandings and emotions, which are advertently or inadvertently drawn upon in responding to a situation or in deciding whether or not to do something. These understandings and emotions are knitted together in all sorts of weird and wonderful patterns, which may quite often include shades, shapes and combinations that are unique. A reader of *Black Dogs*, for example, will know that there is an idiosyncratic story behind 'June finding security and transformation on this sunny shelf of land'. To know how it was that June found security, one needs to know much more than the fact that June was placed next to the bergerie, as a piece of coal is placed next to fire. To understand the causes of June's security, one needs also to enter the web of June's understandings and experiences, the present ones overlaid and co-mingling with those of the past. One needs to know these things even to be able to suppose that June had the *potential* power to find security and transformation, given the right conditions. The range of potential powers intrinsic to human agents at a given point in time is constituted in significant part by their own hermeneutic frame of meaning.

In the case of the teacher, her reasons for doing what she does depend not only, likewise, on her own frame of meaning, but also – and this is usually more significant when we are discussing someone in her institutionalised social role, situated in some sort of hierarchy – on the frames of meanings and power resources of other actors in the educational system of which she is a part. The range of potential powers available to the teacher, together with the likely consequences of drawing on a particular one of those powers (that is, the rewards or punishments) are, again, constituted in significant part by the hermeneutic frames of meaning of a range of social actors. The powers of a teacher can be added to or diminished at any moment by other agents' decisions to act differently: pupils may not turn up for class or may challenge the authority of the teacher, the head of school may decide that the teacher is not fit to teach, a relevant local authority may decide that the teaching of the history of the Vietnam War is a double-edged sword that had best not be afforded, or the state or national government may decide to increase the burden of fixed curriculum testing, thus altering the autonomy of the teacher to arrange the teaching year in the way she favours. Thus, both the potential powers available to an agent at a given time and how those powers are drawn on are highly contingent upon the hermeneutic frames of meaning of themselves and of relevant others in an open system.

Implications for Research

I will close this section by quoting at length from Ira J. Cohen's study of structuration theory, in order to bring out clearly both the relative autonomy of realist ontologies and their dependence on empirical research for the production and defence of substantive claims. Cohen notes that structuration theory's realism is thoroughly consistent with a postpositivist view of the nature and objectives of ontological insights, but he also insists, on the other side of the coin, that unlike unfalsifiable metaphysical systems of thinking, it discourages those types of self-contained grand narrative (my words) that are immune to empirical refutation:

> The principal means to this end is the distinction drawn between ontological conceptualisations of fundamental entities or mechanisms on the one hand, and substantive theory and empirical research on the other. The ontological element of scientific theory can be understood as a series of internally consistent insights into the trans-historical *potentials* of the phenomena that constitute a domain of inquiry: i.e. fundamental processes

and properties that may be activated or realised in various ways in diverse circumstances and on different occasions. These potentials are irrefutable on empirical grounds because they are formulated without regard to their manifestations in the empirical flux of events. But for the same reason, the development of substantive theories is required to determine how these processes and properties operate and appear in any given context, and these theories are subject to empirical refutation. A primary consideration in the formulation of ontological concepts of this kind obviously must be to allow the widest possible latitude for the diversity and contingencies that may occur in different settings (Cohen, 1989, p. 17).

Thus, the realist approaches I have been outlining, on the one hand, have an explicit transhistorical ontology and, on the other hand, are concerned to see how this ontology of potentials manifests itself in a diversity of complex empirical cases. As Cohen indicates, these ontological approaches can be seen as tools with which to develop both substantive theories and individual case studies. The argument for a past-modern sociology rests upon the belief that the journey from ontology to substantive theory and empirical case study must be systematic and reflexive if the 'realist' dimension of sociological research is to stand for anything more than a vague or rhetorical gesture. It is imperative that we establish that realist ontologies have clear *methodological consequences* (cf Outhwaite, 1987, p. 36). This is all the more so in the face of a powerful postmodern scepticism towards claims to have knowledge about the real world. A central aim of this book is to establish an array of methodological guidelines, through which we can maximise our self-consciousness about the sort of knowledge we are producing and about the status (inflated? defensible?) of the claims we make for it. I will build into these guidelines what I consider to be the most challenging arguments of postmodern sceptics.

Bhaskar's realism, for example, involves the epistemological notion of 'retroduction' as a guide to methodology in the research process. Retroduction, for sociology, involves the postulation of social objects or mechanisms, with definable powers, whose existence or activation is thought to be making, or to have made, a significant causal contribution to a social phenomenon that a sociologist wants to explain. After postulating such a mechanism, the sociologist then has to demonstrate its existence and that it has been drawn upon in a particular manner, with specific consequences, in order to provide a convincing explanatory account. Thus, to combine a real definition of an object and retroduction in an explanatory account means, in common-sense terms, that one makes an informed guess as to what is doing the causing (retroduction), gives a clear and detailed definition of what this causal element is (real definition), and then shows clearly that it is indeed doing a significant amount of the causing. As we shall see in future chapters, postmodern scepticism would be directed at, among other things, the belief that one could recover a historical or social process in so accurate and self-contained a manner as to be able to envisage tracing a causal influence through a complex series of successive interactions. Precision and contextualised detail are called for in terms of delineating the potential powers, both material and hermeneutic, of a social object, and in terms of distinguishing the powers and influence of the specified social object from other causal influences. It seems to me that a serious engagement with the hermeneutic dimension, allied as it is to the realm of language, with all its slipperiness between and among signifiers and signifieds, poses the biggest challenge and promises the greatest potential rewards to a realist approach. It is certainly the dimension in which one feels that precision and contextuality will be hardest to come by.

It is clear (I hope) that a sociological realism beyond modernism must set itself very exacting terms of reference. If it is true that most sociology comes nowhere near meeting these necessary standards of precision and contextualisation, perhaps postmodernists are right to be sceptical about the claims to authority of sociologists and other social scientists. If it is true that sociology could never hope to get anywhere near such exacting standards, perhaps the defeatist postmodernists are right to insist that there is never any difference between fiction and putative sociological and historical fact. My aim is to show that: yes, the world is that complex; yes, it is often very hard to get at; yes, sociologists and other social scientists often claim an authority they have no right to; and, no, the defeatist postmodernists are not right to imply that the only alternative to a complete and total knowledge of a very complex world is a retreat into fiction. A past-modern sociology can, at one and the same time, aspire to the most exacting standards and levels of discipline, while also reflexively emphasising the ways in which it falls short of this ideal. The knowledge produced can thus be systematic, but equally it will typically be provisional, fallible, incomplete and extendable. The goal is epistemic gain rather than absolute truth, epistemic gain rather than a debilitating celebration of relativism without constraints.

Notes

1 But see Kalberg (1994) for an alternative interpretation of Weber's work, and for an interesting and intriguing review of the literature.

2 Seidman begs the question when he acknowledges that, while we may sometimes need pictures that cover large chunks of time–space, these should be 'deeply contextual' (Seidman, 1991a, p. 139).

3 It is also true that one may never quite be sure that one has a particular capacity until an exercise of it is attempted. The steaming hot dishes could stand as an emblem of this uncertainty.

4 Bhaskar uses the term 'existential intransitivity' to denote this insight, and differentiates it from the transitive realm of theory, concepts, and so on (cf Bhaskar, 1979; Benton, 1985; Collier, 1994, pp. 50–1). I prefer the terms 'existential reality' or 'existential independence' to 'existential intransitivity', because, quite simply, their meanings are more apparent to me. The book by Collier referenced here is an extremely clear overall introduction to Bhaskar's work.

5 Similar points are included in Habermas' critique of Gadamer and in Bhaskar's critique of hermeneutics. See Habermas, 1990, pp. 143–70; Bleicher, 1980, pp. 153–8; Holub, 1991, pp. 49–77; Bhaskar, 1979.

Chapter 2

A Rich and Complex Ontology

It is important to establish, with some degree of precision and clarity, the nature of the ontology with which I will work in constructing guidelines for a past-modern sociology. My strategy will be to centre my comments around the ontological building blocks developed in Giddens' structuration theory. One reason for this choice is the striking breadth of Giddens' ontological agenda, that sympathetically and critically encompasses major developments towards increased sophistication, complexity and a general antireductionism in so many areas of contemporary social theory. Ian Craib lists the striking number of source materials in Giddens' ontology as: linguistic philosophy, phenomenological sociology and ethnomethodology, Goffman, psychoanalysis, hermeneutics, structuralism and poststructuralism, Marxism, Heidegger and time-geography (Craib, 1992a, p. 19) – these being just the main sources.

In the course of expounding upon the finished products of Giddens' ontology, and of bringing added life and colour to them with illustrations drawn from literature, I will also indicate and suggest, all too briefly, the resonances, compatibilities and shared emphases that Giddens' work has with aspects of the work of another of the great synthesisers of contemporary social theory, the German social theorist and philosopher, Jürgen Habermas. The central significance that they both attach to hermeneutics and contextuality is striking. I regard all of the elements of both Giddens' and Habermas' ontology, which I will present here, as compatible with those aspects of contemporary realism associated with Bhaskar that were discussed in Chapter 1. Although I will not explicitly return to this work in the present chapter, the notions of differentiation, stratification and open systems are clearly consistent with what I write and, at times, directly inform my commentary.

Finally, I will close the chapter by signposting some of the many congruencies and shared emphases that exist between contemporary social theorists such as Giddens, Habermas and Bhaskar, on the one hand, and postmodernists, on the other. I will focus here on the work of Zygmunt Bauman, a postmodernist influenced, not least, by the interpretivist tradition and by the work of Norbert Elias on relations of interdependency. My aim is to stress the common emphasis of all these writers on the themes of ontological complexity and contextualisation. For all of them, there is a hell of a lot going on 'out there' in the world, and 'in here' in our worlds: both sets of sites are varied, multiple, local, contextual and saturated with meanings. As a corollary to these themes the writers share, too, a concern with the situated and limited knowledgeability and perspective of the knower/agent. However, first, let us turn to the localised, contextualised, contingent, actively created, structurally constrained and hermeneutically mediated world according to Giddens and Habermas – as I see it. If a sophisticated realist ontology is to have methodological consequences, and if these consequences are to be marshalled and tested according to an equally sophisticated and reflexive set of guidelines for sociological research – inspired not least by the spirit and resources of postmodern scepticism – we first have to be as clear as possible about the ontology.

Context and Hermeneutics in Giddens' Structuration Theory

A useful place to start to explore the meaning and importance of contextuality within the work of Giddens is a review article, written by Nigel Thrift, of Giddens' weighty summation of structuration theory so far, *The Constitution of Society* (1984). Thrift settles on the idea of context as being central to the objectives of structuration theory, and he relates a personal anecdote in order to try to convey the spirit in which Giddens treats the significance of context.

The young daughter of a friend of Thrift's returned home from infants' school one day with an important question for her father: 'Isn't it true, Daddy, that bears live in trees?' Her father, being a good geographer, answered that it certainly was true. The little girl's face brightened, but she was still puzzled about her teacher's behaviour that day. The teacher had handed out to each child a piece of paper with three pictures on it: a bear, a tree and a mouse. The children were told to circle the two pictures that went together. The friend's daughter had circled the bear and the tree, but on handing in her piece of paper she was told that she had got it wrong, and that it was the bear and the mouse that went together because they were both animals. The point of the story, of course, is that the category similarity between the bear and the mouse was a taxonomic abstraction lifted out of any real life context. The relationship between the bear and the tree, on the other hand, was from a real life situation. The emphasis in this example is on the fact that the two objects share the same physical space – bears live in trees – but this is just one aspect of any context or real life situation.

In addition to space, Giddens also emphasises time, and the relations between the two. People often live in houses or apartments, but they do not usually spend all day every day in them. They will typically have routine journeys that they make to other locations, such as to their place of work, shopping centres, the nursery or school, friends' houses, the video store, the sports centre, the bank or the railway or bus station. They will travel through space by bus, rickshaw, rail, bicycle, car, skateboard, foot or some other means of transport to get to these places. Much of social life is about the co-ordination of time and space – being in the right place at the right time – and modern life increasingly demands that on a single day we have many appointments to keep in many different places.

We experience the pressures of these demands as individuals, but demands are also placed on institutional collectivities, such as the post office, for example. Letters have to arrive at their place of destination within an acceptable period of time. The organisation that goes into getting a single missive from Sukhumvit Road, Bangkok, Thailand, to Eastbourne Grove, Bolton, Greater Manchester, UK, is immense. Time–space co-ordination here means success in the task of transporting a letter over 6000 miles of space within about 120 hours of time. The co-ordination is much more complex than, for example, the sending of a message within a feudal village. One of Giddens' key distinctions in this respect between modern and traditional societies is in the degree to which they co-ordinate interactions over long distances and, also, the way in which the institutions set up to do this in modern societies, such as post offices, tend to dig themselves in so that they perform this function over long periods of time. Giddens calls this process 'time–space distanciation'.

Much of the sort of organisation needed to keep modern societies going is distanciated over time and space. One need only think of the international and domestic banking systems, the multinational automobile industry making parts of the same car in several different countries, supermarket chains, airlines, the tourist industry or the supply of electricity to millions of homes. The list could obviously go on almost indefinitely. However, to keep our eye on the ball, it is important to remember, as we recognise the complex division of labour expanding over time and space, that each single component in the chain of co-ordination involves individual human beings located in their own little piece of time–space. This may be the post office worker at 3a.m. on a Thursday morning in a Cairo sorting office, or an air traffic controller bringing down a Boeing 747 onto runway 16 of John F. Kennedy airport, New York, or a supermarket chief in Basingstoke negotiating with a supplier over the price of a particular brand of liquid clothes wash. All these people are in a specific context – specific places at specific times. They have particular institutional positions and tasks to perform, with more or less discretion as to how they perform or alter the content of those tasks.

Enough about context for the time being, what about hermeneutics? Giddens talks about structuration theory being a 'hermeneutically informed social theory'. By this he means that the context in which a social action takes place is definable not only in terms of time and space and the division of labour, but also in terms of people's understandings of what they are doing. This theme is closely related to Giddens' model of agency, which is outlined in Figure 2.1, the categories written in italic constituting the three major analytical components of agency.[1] First, agents are self-aware and typically monitor their own actions and are able to adjust these actions if, for example, they are not producing the desired effect. In other words, they are self-reflexive.

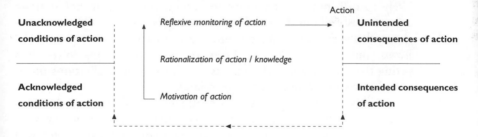

Figure 2.1 Giddens' stratification model of the agent

Second, agents are relatively knowledgeable about themselves and their social context: they are not 'cultural dopes', as some over-structuralist or functionalist theories would have us believe. The more knowledgeable agents are about their conditions of action (left-hand side of Figure 2.1) then, all things being equal, the less likely they are to engage in practices that then lead to unintended consequences (right-hand side). Conversely, the more that the conditions of action are unacknowledged – simply not known about – the more likelihood there will be of unintended consequences.

Third, actions are motivated by wants and desires, whether conscious or unconscious. Some actions are directly motivated, those, for example, that involve major decisions that stand out from the humdrum, everyday routines. Other actions, those which fit more readily into the rounds of everyday routines, are motivated only indirectly by a broader project such as 'getting a degree', 'making a comfortable living', 'being a law-abiding citizen' or 'climbing Everest', or, as we shall see in a later chapter, more sinister objectives such as 'the extermination of non-Aryans'. The intermingling of all three aspects of agency can be usefully thought of as meeting in the rationalisation of action (paired with knowledgeability in Figure 2.1), in which desires (motives) and knowledge of context combine in order to patch together a way of 'going on'. As motivation (desires or wants) comes up against reality in the form of knowledgeability, it may need to be attenuated. Thus, we may desire something very badly – use your imagination – but our knowledge of the real world context tells us that we had better not go for it. We should trim our sails. From the sublime to the not so sublime: we may not *want* to get out of bed in the morning, but we *know* that the exam starts at 9.30a.m. and we also *want* to pass it. Our knowledge of context and the probable consequences of acting within it – the punishments and rewards it is likely to dish out as a response to certain actions – means that we cannot satisfy all our desires. Our knowledge of hard realities makes us choose between wants. We become aware that we have a *hierarchy of wants*, and staying in bed an hour longer tends to rank lower than sitting that final exam (although, as for all social generalisations this is a tendency and certainly not an iron law).

It will be useful right away to consolidate the link between the stress on hermeneutics and agency, on the one hand, and the emphasis on contextualisation, on the other, by referring to one of the examples used above in looking at the co-ordination of actions over time and space. This is an extremely important link to make, because although the context of actions is partly constituted by aspects such as the time–space location of an action in a web of other interactions, it is also constituted by the meanings and understandings that agents bring to these interactions. Thus, when an air traffic controller gives her directions to airline pilots, she draws on the stocks of understandings that she takes to be shared by herself and by the relevant pilot. In providing the pilot with certain information, and using particular words or codes, she is relying on her belief that the pilot will understand what she is saying and doing. In other words, she is drawing on her knowledge of the mutual understandings shared by herself and the pilot, and, more widely, by the whole community of air traffic controllers and airline pilots. The work of air traffic controllers and pilots respectively is highly skilled, and the actors who undertake these jobs must have a great deal of knowledge about the technical aspects of their work. However, it would be of no use if they were to have their own private pet names for all the equipment and manoeuvres – a crucial part of their jobs lies in the sphere of communication. They must consequently also have a great deal of knowledge of shared language and mutual understandings about how to communicate practically about the technical aspects of, for example, bringing a plane down safely. Both these aspects – technical knowledge and knowledge of shared understandings about how to communicate – are involved in Giddens' notion of knowledgeability (Figure 2.1).

Analytical Aspects of Social Reality and Communicative Action in the Work of Jürgen Habermas

Having established through Giddens' notion of agency that a high degree of technical and social knowledge and successful communication is necessary in order to carry out what is nowadays a pretty routine exercise, we can turn to Habermas in order to look in more detail at some of the contingent and highly contextualised aspects of the process of communication. First, the pilot must trust the air traffic controller not only to be sincere in wanting to get the plane down safely, and therefore *truthful* in the information she gives about clear flight and landing paths, weather conditions and so on, but also to be completely 'in the know' about what she is saying. It is not much use having a controller oozing sincerity and goodwill but lacking adequate knowledge about the real conditions of the relevant flight paths, runways and weather. The controller also has to know how the pilot will 'really' understand certain instructions, codes and messages sent to her from the control tower. Successful practical communication relies on the controller being socialised to second-guess the way in which pilots will respond to certain linguistic or signalled prompts. In both these cases, there is a critical onus not only on sincerity or truthfulness, but also on getting it right, on getting at the *truth* about the real world at that particular place and time. What Habermas here calls 'the truth' is equivalent to what Bhaskar calls intransitive reality (see Chapter 1).

In other words, from a realist perspective, implicit in the mutual working out of the task that air traffic controllers and pilots of aircraft routinely perform is not only a shared understanding about what the real world is like, insofar as it affects airlines and their safe landing, but also a shared understanding about what the real communicative world of pilots and air traffic controllers is really like. For such people to deny that they had a shared conception of the real world, in either of these respects, which they rely upon to accomplish their crucial task, would be to be guilty of what Habermas calls a 'performative contradiction'. In other words, the assumptions they make when acting would plainly contradict their statements. They would be arguing one thing while doing another.

Habermas argues that claims to both truthfulness and truth are implicit in all acts of communication when such acts are measured against our deepest intuitions about what we feel we should rightfully expect in dialogue between human beings. He calls these implicit claims 'validity claims', and distinguishes between truth claims, claims to truthfulness (or authenticity) and claims to normative legitimacy. The latter we shall come to in more detail later, but suffice it to say for the time being that, in all normal circumstances, one would expect the claims of truth and truthfulness implicit in the interchange between pilot and air traffic controller to revolve around the shared normative assumption that it would be morally unacceptable not to pull out all the stops in order to get all 300 or more passengers and crew down onto the ground in safety. In terms of a spy thriller, along the lines perhaps of a James Bond plot, it is possible to imagine a situation in which both pilot and controller are in cahoots in a daring attempt to crash the plane while making it look like an accident – perhaps the President of the USA is on board and this is the first step in yet another plan to take over the world. In such a case, it is instructive to note that pilot and controller would still have to trust each other in the areas of truth and truthfulness, while they would also need to have a mutual understanding about their aberrant normative framework.

Habermas is drawing attention to three different aspects of everyday communicative practices. He links these aspects of truth, truthfulness and normative legitimacy to his notion of the three worlds: the objective, the subjective and the social worlds. Each of these has their own reality. A subjective desire, interpretation or intention to deceive is as real as (although, of course, different from) an objective aeroplane or the objective fact that a shop has closed for a half day on a Monday afternoon. Likewise, a social norm that two-year-olds should not be taken to dinner parties (this example has the advantage that one could quite expeditiously test it) is just as real as one's subjective belief that adults should loosen up a little. There are subtle differences between the objectivity of a shop being closed on a Monday afternoon, the social normativity of all shopkeepers in Bremen agreeing to close on a Monday afternoon and, finally, an individual shopkeeper's subjective adherence to that social norm. All of these have an intransitive reality, which can, in principle, be tested, but they are clearly different aspects of reality, hence Habermas' recourse to the three worlds metaphor in order to explore each of them and their interaction.

Context and Hermeneutics in the Causal Production of Social Reality

The emphasis of structuration theory in looking at the above example would tend to be on the conditions and processes that have brought about the reality of Monday afternoon closing through the agency of the individual shopkeeper's decision (and, by extension, that of other shopkeepers) to abide by the social norm of, precisely, closing on a Monday afternoon. In other words, it would be interested in how the process of agency in a given structural context leads to this particular consequence. For Giddens, it is axiomatic that social consequences are the outcome of human actions, of agency, in contexts (structures) that both enable and limit the range of possible outcomes. In turn, the consequences of actions help to alter or maintain the enabling and limiting context for the next round of actions. There is an eternal round of structure, agency, structure, agency.

Using Figure 2.1 (above) as a guide, one might ask about the motivation of an individual shopkeeper in closing his shop along with all the other shopkeepers. We assume that he is a knowledgeable agent, so knows about the social norm in the town, existing for the past five years, that shops should close on Monday afternoons. We assume that he reflexively monitors his situation, so is reasonably confident that there have been no recent changes to this norm. Indeed, we might come across a few ignorant and dozy shopkeepers who open on Monday afternoons because they have no idea about the social norm. On the other hand, we might find some shopkeepers who are just as knowledgeable and aware as our hero, but who decide anyway that they will defy the social norm and open on Mondays. It is at this stage that the motivation of the respective agents can be seen to make all the difference. Our hero may conform with the social norm due to a number of reasons. It may be because he would like a day off on Mondays to look after his children or to clean the toilet and bathroom, or it might be simply because he is frightened of the consequences of breaking the social norm. It could quite easily be a happy combination of these two reasons. However, he may be struggling to make ends meet during present opening hours and consequently badly resent the Monday norm. Nevertheless, he remains closed, owing to the fear of breaking the norm. Indeed, the rebels, those who do open, probably also fear the consequences, but open all the same. Their motives may be to do with the extra revenue gained from Monday afternoon trading or, alternatively, be based on *laissez faire* principles of unrestricted trading, or on a more specific judgement that the social norm is illegitimately grounded. For example, it may have been initiated by a rich cartel of retail chains in the town for their own selfish purposes.

The general point is that structuration theory would look for the way in which individual agents made decisions by drawing on their knowledge of context (what Giddens calls structures), filtering this through the prism of their own motives, and then acting accordingly. Structuration theory can help one to understand the processes that go into producing the routine or not-so-routine actions of individuals. All three elements of reflexivity, knowledgeability and motivation are seen to effect the final action. We can also see that if not complying with the social norm would have negative consequences, of whatever kind, dozy and ignorant shopkeepers who failed to comply out of ignorance and doziness would suffer unintended consequences of their actions (opening their shops), owing to acting in a context whose prevailing norms and power structures they had no awareness of (unacknowledged conditions of action). Equally, those more alert and knowledgeable shopkeepers who, in spite of their understanding of the probable negative consequences, still open their shops because they believe the norm to be illegitimate, are likely to suffer unwanted and unintended (the intention being to make a principled stand), but acknowledged, consequences of their actions.[2]

The Power of Context To Linger Beyond the Moment

One of the most important emphases of structuration theory is this radical dissolution of the idea that agents come to each new situation with their minds as empty spaces. They come, rather, with a battered portmanteau of personal and culturally nuanced ideas and memories. They cannot leave their luggage in the hallway while they encounter a new and pressing situation; they cannot help but see the new situation with cultural baggage in hand. They are who they have become through the years, and they see each new situation on this basis. They are more or less inhabited by past memories, attentive to the present moment, emotionally anxious or relaxed, and have a particular level and angle of spatial and intellectual awareness. The objects they see and respond to in a room are given a personal inflexion as they become objects for them.

For a number of issues in sociology, it is important to remember, in this respect, that life is 'processual': it is not divided into discrete parcels, with workplace, home, nightclub, media, political activity, crèche, bar, school, beach, supermarket, department store and so on each being the site of a self-contained activity. This is true not only for activities that have different spatial sites, but also for activities that are divided temporally, in the sense that they belong to a different stage in one's life. Thus, the experience of one workplace is carried over into a subsequent job – not just the skills that have been learnt, but also experiences of frustrated ambition, the taste of success, approval, discrimination, harassment, hierarchy and friendship. Influences over time and space overlap. Media images from romantic novels or *Mad Max* movies will also travel with you to your place of work, perhaps even role models from magazines last read when you were 15, or Cordelia from *Lear* for the highbrow; these jostle alongside plans for the weekend, a shopping list in the pocket for the lunch hour, or the telephone number of a babysitter, a lover or an acupuncturist. One cannot discretely separate agency from the world-out-there, from this time and that place, these impressions, those memories. An implication of this is that, in order fully to contextualise what is happening in a single event, it is necessary to spread the net further than the event itself; the geographical local does not exhaust the contextual. This is close in spirit to what poststructuralists such as Derrida are saying when they criticise the 'metaphysics of presence': the make-up of the present event is never contained within the present but stretches beyond to absent memories and meanings, without which the present moment would be very different, or not at all.

Repair Work and the Hermeneutic Focus of Participant Actors

While social life and interaction are processual and involve an intimate relationship between past experience and present agency, each episode, at least in nonextreme circumstances, is also based on a substratum of mutually understood norms and meanings, knowledge of which is required in order to be an aware and competent member of a community (and to escape the sanctions associated with 'failing' in this regard). Habermas provides a detailed example of participants expressing themselves in situations that they have to define in common, to acquire a mutual understanding of, if they are to accomplish their goals. The situation, which I will describe, replicates the example of the pilot and air traffic controller but goes into more detail about the way in which the group's attention becomes focused by a social framework that pre-exists a particular interchange. Giddens would typically relate to this social framework saying that agents act by drawing on structures that provide the specific conditions for those actions, which means that, at the same time, not just anything goes, but actions are focused within limits (for example, the limits of mutual understanding) and constrained by structures. In addition to drawing out participants' focus of attention and the enablements and constraints of context, Habermas' example is also designed to highlight the regular *repair* work that gets done by individuals in conversation trying to understand each other. The goal of mutual understanding is not always as smoothly rehearsed and choreographed as it has to be between pilot and air traffic controller. There are usually many more failed attempts and second tries.

Habermas writes of an:

> older construction worker who sends a younger and newly arrived co-worker to fetch some beer, telling him to hurry it up and be back in a few minutes, supposes that the situation is clear to every one involved – here, the younger worker and any other workers within hearing distance. The *theme* is the upcoming midmorning snack; taking care of the drinks is a *goal* related to this theme; one of the older workers comes up with a *plan* to send the 'new guy', who, given his status, cannot easily get around this request. The informal group hierarchy of the workers on the construction site is the *normative framework* in which the one is allowed to tell the other to do something. The action situation is defined temporally by the upcoming break and spatially by the distance from the site to the nearest store. If the situation were such that the nearest store could not be reached by foot in a few minutes, that is, that the plan of action of the older worker could – at least under the conditions specified – only be carried out with an automobile (or other means of transportation), the person addressed might answer with: 'But I don't have a car.'…. the older worker, upon hearing the other's response, might realise that he has to revise his implicit assumption that a nearby shop is open on Mondays. It would be different if the younger worker had answered: 'I'm not thirsty'. He would then learn from the astonished reaction that beer for the midmorning snack is a norm held to independently of the subjective state of mind of one of the parties involved. Perhaps the newcomer does not understand the normative

context in which the older man is giving him an order, and asks whose turn to get the beer it will be tomorrow. Or perhaps he is missing the point because he is from another region where the local work rhythm, that is, the custom of midmorning snack, is not familiar, and thus responds with the question: 'Why should I interrupt my work *now?*' We can imagine continuations of this conversation indicating that one or the other of the parties changes his initial definition of the situation and brings it into accord with the situation definitions of the others. In the first two cases described above, there would be a regrouping of the individual elements of the situation, a Gestalt-switch; the presumed fact that a nearby shop is open becomes a subjective belief that turned out to be false; what is presumed to be a desire to have beer with the midmorning snack turns out to be a collectively recognised norm. In the other two cases the interpretation of the situation gets supplemented with respect to elements of the social world: the low man on the pole gets the beer; in this part of the world one has a midmorning snack at 9:00 A.M. (Habermas, 1989, pp. 121–2).

In this way, the participants in a situation establish beliefs about reality, which they all share. This example, again, brings into focus the intricacy and specificity of everyday hermeneutic interaction. It is important to remember that the 'situation' to which the participants are oriented here is not some objectivistic situation that somehow exists independently of the agents involved. It is obviously centred around the fact that they are working on a construction site, but then there are a thousand and one things going on at a construction site at any one point in time. The very specific focus of the interaction described by Habermas is thrown into relief by the theme (the mid-morning snack), and it is then sliced up even more specifically by the goal (taking care of the drinks) and the plan (to send the poor 'new guy'). Habermas calls these elements that define a situation the 'contexts of relevance' (Habermas, 1989, pp. 122–3).

These aspects that provide a focus for a practical situation – the theme, the goal, the plan of action, the temporal and spatial locations – are useful orienting tools for the sociologist who takes hermeneutics seriously precisely because they direct one to the hermeneutic focus of the participant actors. These aspects can be articulated simply with Giddens' model of agency, in that the goal decided upon within a certain theme, and the plan of action created to achieve it, are a product of the combination of agents' knowledgeability and desires or motivation. We clearly see both at work in the above example: knowledgeability of hierarchical norms, of the distance to the local shop, of the traditional time for a mid-morning snack within the regional subculture; the desire to drink some beer, to impose authority, to 'fit in'. We see also that through the possible 'repair' work that can go on in conversation, the new guy can extend the boundaries of his own acknowledged conditions of action – his knowledgeability of context is increased. The 'repair' work is also an extremely important factor in the co-ordination of action, in the co-ordination of plans. It has a close relationship to 'socialisation' or 'training' in the way it brings approbation to bear on ignorance or the transgression of norms.

The Hermeneutics of Varying Scenarios of Action
The Skilful Accomplishment of One's Own Subordination

An example taken from literature will perhaps help to illustrate the utility of these categories in exploring the hermeneutics of practical action. The example is an extract taken from Kazuo Ishiguro's novel *The Remains of the Day* (1989), narrated by Stevens the butler at the English stately home of Lord Darlington, and concerns an incident (a situation) that occurred during the inter-war years:

> As I recall, I was rung for late one night – it was past midnight – to the drawing room where his lordship had been entertaining three gentlemen since dinner. I had, naturally, been called to the drawing room several times already that night to replenish refreshments, and had observed on these occasions the gentlemen deep in conversation over weighty issues. When I entered the drawing room on this last occasion, however, all the gentlemen stopped talking and looked at me. Then his lordship said:
>
> 'Step this way a moment, will you, Stevens? Mr Spencer here wishes a word with you.'
>
> The gentleman in question went on gazing at me for a moment without changing the somewhat languid posture he had adopted in his armchair. Then he said:
>
> 'My good man, I have a question for you. We need your help on a certain matter we've been debating. Tell me, do you suppose the debt situation regarding America is a significant factor in the low levels of trade? Or do you suppose this is a red herring and that the abandonment of the gold standard is at the root of the matter?'
>
> I was naturally a little surprised by this, but then quickly saw the situation for what it was; that is to say, it was clearly expected that I be baffled by the question. Indeed, in the moment or so that it took for me to perceive this and compose a suitable response, I may even have given the outward impression of struggling with the question, for I saw all the gentlemen in the room exchange mirthful smiles.
>
> 'I'm very sorry, sir,' I said, 'but I am unable to be of assistance on this matter.'

I was by this point well on top of the situation, but the gentlemen went on laughing covertly. Then Mr Spencer said:

'Then perhaps you will help us on another matter. Would you say that the currency problem in Europe would be made better or worse if there were to be an arms agreement between the French and the Bolsheviks?'

'I'm very sorry, sir, but I am unable to be of assistance on this matter.'

'Oh dear,' said Mr Spencer, 'so you can't help us here either.'

There was more suppressed laughter before his lordship said: 'Very well, Stevens. That will be all.'

'Please, Darlington, I have one more question to put to our good man here,' Mr Spencer said. 'I very much wanted his help on the question presently vexing many of us, and which we all realize is crucial to how we should shape our foreign policy. My good fellow, please come to our assistance. What was M. Laval really intending, by his recent speech on the situation in North Africa? Are you also of the view that it was simply a ruse to scupper the nationalist fringe of his own domestic party?'

'I'm sorry, sir, but I am unable to assist in this matter.'

'You see, gentlemen,' Mr Spencer said, turning to the others, 'our man here is unable to assist us in these matters.'

This brought fresh laughter, now barely suppressed.

'And yet,' Mr Spencer went on, 'we still persist with the notion that this nation's decisions be left in the hands of our good man here and to the few million others like him. Is it any wonder, saddled as we are with our present parliamentary system, that we are unable to find any solution to our many difficulties? Why, you may as well ask a committee of the mothers' union to organize a war campaign.'

There was open, hearty laughter at this remark, during which his lordship muttered: 'Thank you Stevens,' thus enabling me to take my leave.

While of course this was a slightly uncomfortable situation, it was hardly the most difficult, or even an especially unusual one to encounter in the course of one's duties, and you will no doubt agree that any decent professional should expect to take such events in his stride... (Ishiguro, 1990, pp. 194–6).

This extract is a treasure trove of illustrations of sociological themes, from the implicit sexism of the good old mothers' union joke, the peculiarly British manifestation of class hierarchy, the emphasis on functional differentiation and the professionalisation of tasks that accompanies it (butlers are not financiers or diplomats; they are unable to assist in these matters). However, if our aim is to understand the focus and dynamics of the participants in the conversation, to find out what they think they are doing and how they achieve it, Habermas' categories of contextual relevance help us to home in on this.

The *theme* here for the three gentlemen is the fitness of parliamentary democracy for the handling of complex matters of state. The demonstration of the absurdity of such a system is the *goal* that is related to this theme. Mr Spencer has obviously hit upon the *plan* of bringing in Stevens to help achieve this goal. The social obligations associated with his status mean that, like the 'new guy' on the building site, he cannot easily get around this request, although in Stevens' case his personal *normative commitment* to his trade is so strong that he would not even think of trying to get around the social norms of the situation – 'any decent professional should expect to take such events in his stride'. The normative framework is clear, and it is complied with suavely by all present, without any cracks appearing in the edifice, despite the potentially humiliating position in which Stevens is placed. There is very little repair work that needs to be done, as the professional Stevens takes his cues and very quickly sees the 'situation for what it was' and responds accordingly. The action situation is, of course, defined *temporally* and *spatially* by the after-dinner conversation in the drawing room and by Stevens' availability. Theme, goal, plan, normative framework, temporal and spatial settings are useful tools to use because they orient one directly to the task of finding the focus of attention around which individual and potentially isolated subjectivities – in this case three gentlemen and one butler – attempt to translate themselves into a mutual understanding. The concepts help the theorist to understand what is really going on in a real world situation.

One hermeneutic aspect that is very decidedly absent from such an extract, because of its abstracted nature, is a more detailed knowledge of the personality, the world view, of the actors involved. For example, one would need to read much more of the novel to really get to know Stevens and, hence, to be able to make a more informed judgement of the ideals, principles, beliefs, desires and repressed needs that lie behind the overt and normative compliance with social norms. However, his understanding of what the social norms required and of how to play out his part successfully, and his normative commitment to doing just that, are very clear indeed.

Stevens' efforts to comply with the relevant normative framework are never in doubt. The only aspect of contingency is whether or not he will possess the skills and be quick enough on the uptake to succeed in playing his part in the maintenance of that framework. His training and the pride he takes in his work also combine together to limit contingency. One should not, however, get the impression that normative frameworks are *a priori* binding and constraining on the actions of individuals. There are many instances in which the normative framework is contingent because it is openly and defiantly contested. Skills matter here too, but their goal is disruption rather than conformity.

The Skilful Defiance of a Normative Framework and the Swift Return of the Constraining Context

A scene from Peter Carey's *Oscar and Lucinda* (1989) demonstrates the mechanics of such contingency and contestation admirably. Oscar is, among other things, a newly installed vicar at St John's, Randwick, in the heart of Sydney. He has been giving sermons against the sins of gambling and has also been betting surreptitiously at the local racecourse. From the racecourse, his clandestine messengers, runners, touts and spivs had soon acquainted him with the floating two-up games at the notorious 'five hotels', fan-tan down in George Street, swy and poker and every card game to be imagined among the taverns down in Paddington. Mrs Judd was Oscar's housekeeper at the Randwick vicarage, where she liked to keep an eye on things. The Judds were wealthy members of the congregation. Mr Judd had donated handsomely to the building and decoration of the vicarage, and also saw personally to its upkeep. At 6 o'clock one morning, he came to sweep up the clippings from the hedge cutting of the night before:

> He was surprised to see the lights on and the window unshuttered. He bade his wife stay on the path while he climbed – very quietly – on to the veranda, and peered in.
>
> Well, you know what he saw.
>
> There was also money on the table. He saw this, too. He saw a woman, cards moving, money. It was then that he started hammering on the pane (Carey, 1988, p. 311).

A stunned Oscar invited the intruders to come inside the house. Unwittingly, he stepped back from the window as if making way for the Judds to enter by this route, which they did, full of moral outrage, ready to attack:

> 'I'd not be the sort of fellow comes climbing through a window', he said. 'And you should know that of me by now. But I'll tell you this, sir – we will not have it! We will not'… But '"Be not drunk with wine,"' he had not meant to quote, but the words came to him. He could see no wine. It was not wine he was quoting. '"Be not drunk with wine,"' 'he looked at the

cards. They were in full view, and money too. '"Wherein is excess; *but be filled with the Spirit*; speaking to yourselves in psalms and hymns and spiritual songs, singing and making melody in your heart to the Lord.'"

This produced a silence. They all stood with red faces and tried to understand their situation...

'... you should not be gambling, sir. It is a folly and a sin.'(Mr Judd)

'... I have never heard of such a hypocrite. Yes, a hypocrite. We made him lovely vestments. You will not wear them, isn't that true? You think God would rather see you looking like a crow.' (Mrs Judd)

'I wear–' said Oscar, but was stopped from saying more.

'You dress like a scarecrow,' said Mr Judd.

'I will *not* be stopped. He dresses like a scarecrow,' she agreed, 'and throws out our *Messiah*, and here he is with cards and women in the temple, and –' she looked backwards to the open window, and stopped a moment. 'And here we are,' she said at last.

The normative framework of this encounter is set by the Judds, drawing on wider social norms that loathe gambling, detest what they see as hypocrisy, and would be scandalised by the thought of either, particularly the former, being practised by a clergyman. Their goal is to humble Oscar by confronting him with the enormity of his sins. This is what they are doing there when Mrs Judd proclaims, 'and here we are':

Lucinda had been quiet up until now, although she had thought Oscar's conciliatory tone quite inappropriate. She had been incredulous when he had said, 'come in':

'You are a rude woman,' she said, 'and you are a rude man.'

Mrs Judd opened her mouth. Mr Judd stood on his wife's foot. Mrs Judd's mouth stayed open and her head jerked sharply sideways as she tried to read her husband's face.

'You imagine', Lucinda pulled her skirt tight against her legs until she felt them burning, 'that you are civilized, but you are like savages with toppers and tails. You are not civilized at all, and if gambling is a sin it is less of a sin than the one you have just committed. You should pray to God to forgive you for your rudeness.'

Oscar was aghast to hear such patrician arrogance from a woman he had seen, half an hour before, light a cigarette and draw the blue smoke up into her flaring nostrils (an action he found sensual in the extreme). He would have apologized to the Judds but he did not have the opportunity.

'You may leave,' said Lucinda.

And the Judds, indeed, made uncertainly towards the door.

'Through the window,' said Lucinda.
And the Judds left through the window. Lucinda had them shut it after them...

Lucinda challenges the normative framework of the Judds, their righteous outrage is trumped and sent right back from whence it came – through the window. Contingency and agency are two sides of the same coin here; Lucinda's agency exposes the contingency of the Judd's normative framework and rejects its claim to have a binding power on her attitudes to their accusations. She refuses to be humbled and penitent.

On the other hand, taking this one scene out of the context of the wider society would be to misunderstand the extent of Lucinda's victory and the Judd's defeat. Oscar knows, at the very moment that Lucinda speaks, that he is done for. He knew all along, as Giddens would put it, that the normative framework being invoked by the Judds was tied to – was drawing upon and faithfully representing – the normative structures of the wider local community. On slowly coming to realise Oscar's distress, Lucinda 'was like an athlete who, with her body warm, has ripped a muscle and not felt it. As she cooled, she stiffened, and felt – it hurt more than you would think possible – the damage' (Carey, 1988, p. 319).

Oscar's intuitive invitation to the Judds to 'come in', his conciliatory tone that Lucinda had found so inappropriate, and the apology that Lucinda's *coup de grace* denied him the opportunity of giving, were all prompted by his knowledge of structural factors that stretched beyond the immediate scene of action. Lucinda's virtuoso performance was motivated by indignation; she had no thought of the wider conditions of action or the consequences that would be likely to follow. Oscar's performance was motivated by the desire to maintain his status, his calling, his house and his livelihood, and his agency was thus linked inextricably to his knowledge of how those with power over his station in the local community would interpret the meaning of this morning's episode, and how they would measure this against their own rather rigid normative standards. If for Lucinda the consequences of her actions were unintended, for Oscar the consequences were painfully plain to see, 'sitting back on an ugly green chair with his hands plunged into his unruly rusty hair'. Indeed, while the fact and the manner of Lucinda's exposure of the contingency of the Judds' normative framework is what gives the action sequence its cathartic aesthetic power, it is the dawning reality of the social price that will have to be paid for this expression of autonomy that provides a counterpoint aesthetic of poignant resignation. If Lucinda represents the transformative power of individual agency, Oscar's reaction symbolises the punishing constraints of structural context.

The Profound Effect of Context on Motivations and Desire

Oscar's knowledgeability of his context, its power relations and its sanctions is what led him to attempt the 'repair' work with the Judds, which Lucinda could not bear. His actions show yet again the way in which the world-out-there inhabits and influences the world-in-here; they show the duality of context and agency. They also show that the world-out-there does not just affect knowledgeability, but also has a profound effect upon motivation and desire. Just how profound this power can be is brought out vividly in Gary Nelson's (1993) discussion of Toni Morrison's novel *Beloved* (1987), a discussion that is informed by the ontological concerns of this chapter. He writes that the novel presses us to situate ourselves in terms of the co-mingling of social context and personal agency within the character of Sethe, in order that we should try to understand the motives that led her to kill her second daughter:

> Throughout the novel, it is made clear to the reader that the situation of slavery is truly horrific. All freedom is lost in this situation; not just the obvious freedoms of not being able to decide what to do, when to do it, and how, but more fundamental issues. The reader is made aware of the fact that Sethe was not given the freedom to provide milk for her child, that this milk was stolen from her breasts by two adolescent white boys, and that in return for her complaint to her owner about this situation her heavily pregnant body was beaten so badly that the scars on her back resembled a tree and its branches… Sethe makes her decision because she has a high degree of knowledgeability. Her awareness of slavery is first hand. She is able to look at the options that are open to her when the Schoolteacher – her new owner – arrives, accompanied by the sheriff and two other men to reclaim his escaped property – Sethe and her children. She is well aware of what it is to be a slave, and it is this which constrains what she can do. She has very few real options: she can give in and be retaken into slavery along with her children. However, she is aware that by doing this there will be certain probable outcomes: she will probably be separated from her children, whom she has taken the unusual liberty – for a slave – of loving, she will also probably be forced to 'breed' with men other than her husband, in order to create more producers for her owner. On the other hand, she can, as she tried to do, take a more drastic course of action by trying to kill herself and her children. The only real consequence of this is that she will die along with her children without having to go through the pain and agony of slave life (Nelson, 1993).

Nelson's account goes on to probe the ways in which changing boundaries of knowledgeability in relation to acknowledged or unacknowledged conditions of action could have altered Sethe's motivation to commit the worst injury to herself that a parent could imagine. He asks a series of counterfactual, or 'what-if', questions:

> One can look at the fact that Sethe was not aware that she would not be able to complete the task of killing herself and her children. She was also not aware that she would be haunted by her dead child as a result of her murderous action. Nor was she aware that the murder and the haunting would cause her two sons to run off and leave her. She was unaware that if she had given in when she saw Schoolteacher, her children would not have spent all of their lives in slavery, since once the Civil War was won by the Yankees slavery was abolished (Nelson, 1993).

The Salutary Heaviness of the Unfolding Process of Social Being

The importance of hermeneutics and contextuality for a morally sensitive sociology should be apparent. Both these dimensions will always be major constituent parts of the reality within which moral choices, implicit as well as explicit, are made. They are part of the *unfolding process* of social life, within which moral choices co-mingle with the acceptance or contestation of normative sanctions, with attempts at instrumental and communicative understanding, with 'repair' work in strips of social interaction, with acknowledged and unacknowledged conditions of action, and with wanted and unwanted, intended and unintended consequences of action in the context of systems of more or less openness. The unfolding process of social life is full of contingency. It has not yet unfolded, not yet become the past, a past that will have happened in a particular way, taken a particular route and not another. The *unfolded past* loses its contingency in the very moment that it becomes the unfolded past; it passes over all the other contingent possibilities that were potentially open. It is the illicit slippage involved in reading back the unfolded process into the unfolding process that marks out social determinism. It is the reinvigorating movement of putting back the sense of an unfolding process into the unfolded past that, for me, marks out the spirit of contemporary social theory's complex ontology. In *The Unbearable Lightness of Being* (1985), Milan Kundera talks about Nietzsche's idea of eternal return:

> to think that everything recurs as we once experienced it, and that the recurrence itself recurs ad infinitum!... If the French Revolution were to recur eternally, French historians would be less proud of Robespierre. But

because they deal with something that will not return, the bloody years of the Revolution have turned into mere words, theories and discussions, have become lighter than feathers, frightening no one. There is an infinite difference between a Robespierre who occurs only once in history and a Robespierre who eternally returns, chopping off French heads.

Let us therefore agree that the idea of eternal return implies a perspective from which things appear without the mitigating circumstance of their transitory nature... In the world of eternal return the weight of unbearable responsibility lies heavy on every move we make. That is why Nietzsche called the idea of eternal return the heaviest of burdens (das schwerste Gewicht).

If eternal return is the heaviest of burdens, then our lives can stand out against it in all their splendid lightness.

But is heaviness truly deplorable and lightness splendid?

The heaviest of burdens crushes us, we sink beneath it, it pins us to the ground. But in the love poetry of every age, the woman longs to be weighed down by the man's body. The heaviest of burdens is therefore simultaneously an image of life's most intense fulfilment. The heavier the burden, the closer our lives come to the earth, the more real and truthful they become.

Conversely, the absolute absence of a burden causes man to be lighter than air, to soar into the heights, take leave of the earth and his earthly being, and become only half real, his movements as free as they are insignificant.

What then shall we choose? Weight or lightness? (Kundera, 1985, pp. 3–5).

For me, the hermeneutics, contextuality and contingency of agency and open systems are all about weight, about making social thinking heavier, bringing it closer to the social earth, to the reality of unfolding social relations. If I were to stress the discontinuities between contemporary social theory and defeatist postmodernism, I would say that the latter was light, reducing all to fictions without weight, lighter than feathers. I want, however, to stress here the continuities between contemporary social theory and the more affirmative aspects of postmodernism, so I want to indicate ways in which some of postmodernism's preoccupations cajole and entice us to think in ways that compound the sense of being there – a sense of the social conditions surrounding and inhabiting the 'being there' – within an unfolding process that matters and whose nature we cannot properly grasp from the soaring heights.

Context and Complexity in Postmodernism: Zygmunt Bauman

Postmodernism, like contemporary social theory, and with a renewed vigour, directs us to the many, many ways and conditions of being there. It directs us to multiplicity, pluralism, variety, difference, contingency, ambiguity, indeterminacy and ambivalence (cf Flax, 1990, p. 183; Bauman, 1992, p. 187). It directs us to a complexity that is specific to context.

In *Intimations of Postmodernity* (1992), Bauman contrasts these postmodern predilections with a view of the institutions of modernity, which sees them as struggling for universality, homogeneity, monotony and clarity; struggling for control and mastery in a manner that requires the elimination or concealment of all the differences, multiplicities and potentially disruptive contingencies that contemporary social theory and postmodernism positively affirm (Bauman, 1992, p. 188). Bauman characterises the cognitive perspective of sociological theories in the age of modernity as totalising theories of systems, obsessed with monotony, homogeneity and equilibrium, at the expense of his own preferred vision of social relations as 'essentially and perpetually unequilibrated; composed of elements with a degree of autonomy large enough to justify the view of totality as a kaleidoscopic – momentary and contingent – outcome of interaction… All order that can be found is a local, emergent and transitory phenomenon' (Bauman, 1992, p. 189). He places an emphasis on all found – they cannot be assumed to exist – structures as 'emergent accomplishments', and believes that equal attention should be given to 'the unpatterned and unregulated spontaneity of the autonomous agent' (Bauman, 1992, p. 190). The focus of sociology for Bauman should be on agents operating in a specific habitat (or context), inside which both the freedom and the dependency of this and other agents are constituted. All he says is highly reminiscent of the duality of structure and agency:

> Unlike the system-like totalities of modern social theory, habitat neither determines the conduct of the agents nor defines its meaning; it is no more (but no less either) than the setting in which both action and meaning-assignment are *possible*. Its own identity is as under-determined and motile, as emergent and transitory, as those of the actions and their meanings that form it.
>
> There is one crucial area, though, in which the habitat performs a determining (systematizing, patterning) role: it sets the agenda for the 'business of life' through supplying the inventory of ends and the pool of means… All states the habitat may assume appear equally contingent (that is, they have no overwhelming reasons for being what they are, and they

could be different if any of the participating agencies behaved differently). The heuristics of pragmatically useful 'next moves' displaces, therefore, the search for algorithmic, certain knowledge of deterministic chains (Bauman, 1992, pp. 191, 193, original emphasis).

Epistemological Agnosticism in the Face of Ontological Complexity

In order not to get too carried away with Bauman's emphasis on leaving room for openness and possibility, we should remember that when we engage in any one particular piece of research, we may well, of course, find that the totalising tendencies of *modernity* **are** still at work (Habermas, for example, certainly thinks they are, in the form of capitalistic and bureaucratic relations), trying to control and suppress difference and deviance. We need to hold open precisely this possibility that a more contextualised sociology may find a reality that is more stable and orderly than Bauman would like. However, in any event, the move away from sociological *modernism*'s all-knowingness from up on high, towards a less arrogant, more inquisitive and contextually sensitive sociology, is more likely to engender an ability to discover, and be richly surprised by, the multiple, the contingent and the ambivalent. Contingency may or may not lead to monotonously reproduced practices; the surprise may lie as much in discovering the reasons for continuity and the absence of perceived choices as in changes and discontinuities in practices. For me – and I am not clear, for example, whether this is true for Bauman – the acceptance of a rich, complex ontology entails no more than an agnosticism about the degrees of openness and closure in the situations facing agents in particular locations. It also entails an agnosticism about the degree of reflexivity and choice actually engaged in by such agents. To commit oneself to anything more than agnosticism about particular social situations – purely on the basis of ontology – would be to engage in a presumptuous reductionism *either* of necessary contingency and openness (a reductionism common among postmodernists) *or* of a necessary determinism and closure (common among those sociological modernists who invoke 'structure' or 'system' as a supposedly equivalent substitute for analysis of particular conjunctures). Neither is acceptable.

Notes

1 When presenting his diagram, Giddens does not include acknowledged conditions of action or intended consequences of action. I have included these because I think it clarifies Giddens' position.

2 It can be seen that, strictly speaking, the right-hand side of Giddens' diagram, represented in Figure 2.1, should have two sets of categories – intended and unintended consequences of action – and also acknowledged probable consequences and unacknowledged probable consequences of action. Thus, the present example would look like this in diagrammatic form:

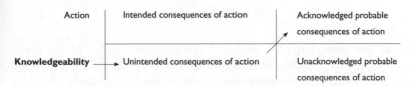

Footnote Figure for Footnote 2 An amendment to the model of the agent

Chapter 3

Analysis and Textuality: Players, Dreamers and Despots in Sociological Research

In the previous chapter, I outlined and illustrated some of the main ontological assumptions shared by a number of influential contemporary social theories. In other words, the chapter dealt with what the social world is like, what it is made up of and what is in it. I outlined many of the bold ontological assumptions of these realist metatheories. If ontology tells us what *is* in the social world, epistemology asks how we *know* that such and such is in the world. In the present chapter, and in the remainder of the book, I want to shift the focus of attention to the latter sort of question, to epistemology and methodology. I will argue that the increased appreciation given by contemporary social theory to the richness and complexity of the social world needs to be accompanied by a parallel appreciation of the difficulties and obstacles confronting attempts to gain knowledge about that complexity. Increased sophistication in the former needs to be matched by a corresponding increase in the latter. Elements of such sophistication have been surfacing in different parts of the epistemological pool – those relevant to my argument here emerging in the main from anthropology, literary theory, feminist theory and philosophy – but they have not been systematised in relation to models of the research process as a whole, nor to the sociological research process in particular.

The position I want to develop is quite consistent with the description of contemporary realism as *ontologically bold* and *epistemologically cautious* (Outhwaite, 1987, p. 34). Among those influenced by the work of Bhaskar, this motto invokes a widely shared belief in the combination of a strong commitment to a realist ontology and a keen awareness of the difficulties of finding out what is going on in the world at any one particular point in time and space. On the basis of the previous chapter, it should not be too difficult to accept a rather easy affinity between an ontology that stresses the importance of hermeneutics and contextuality, for example, and an epistemology that is obsessed by the difficulties that stand in the way of finding out about motives, world views, cultural meanings, knowledgeabilities and all the specific details of context that constitute a particular event or process. It is difficult to see how the sort of ontological boldness that refuses to leave out hermeneutics and contextuality could be anything else than epistemologically cautious. Indeed, it is no accident that the examples in the previous chapter were taken from literature. The novel, by its very nature, gives the story-teller a privileged access to 'what really happened' – at least, and we will come on to this, from their own perspective. Kazuo Ishiguro's narrator, the butler Stevens, could know what went on in the drawing room conversation because he was there; Ishiguro, in turn, could remember all the words of the characters just as they were because he was, in fact, inventing them. Ishiguro had the privilege of writing down *verbatim* every word that was uttered without making the characters observed become self-conscious and unnatural under his scrutiny.

This emphasis on the significance of the viewpoint and authority accorded to the narrator of a text provides part of the basis for a third heuristic category, which I would like to add to the two that adorn the realist motto cited above. Thus, in addition to being ontologically bold and epistemologically cautious, a sophisticated realism should also be *textually bold.* Before I can go on to clarify what I mean by this, it is necessary to outline some general ground rules for theory construction. Suffice it to say, for the moment, that a main plank of my argument will be that there are inestimable gains to be had from the combination of a sustained cultivation of a healthy epistemological scepticism in relation to social analysis, on the one hand, and a cultivation of insights about the construction of texts (books, articles, papers) derived from literary modernism and postmodernism, on the other.

Analysis: Player and Dreamer Models of Research and Theory Construction

Dimensions of Research Shared by both Player and Dreamer Models

I will begin the task of providing reflexive guidelines for a past-modern sociology by presenting two interrelated models for sociological research, which are designed to respond to the richness and complexity of the ontology presented in the last chapter. I will call these the player and the dreamer models respectively. The reality of our knowledge will always be less than this. The models have a number of different dimensions, and the pretensions of an account to represent the real in some way, however limited these claims are, can be challenged at the site of any one of these. I will begin by presenting the dimensions of research that are shared by both models, before going on to specify their differences.

Ontology and its Methodological Consequences

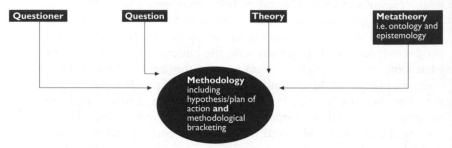

Figure 3.1 Dimensions of research shared by player and dreamer models

Consonant with the emphasis of Chapter 2, I will begin with *ontology* (top right-hand corner in Figure 3.1) and try to draw out the consequences of a bold ontology for the nitty-gritty empirical work of social analysis. From the perspective of realism, the major question to be answered is whether or not realist ontologies can be said to carry consequences for methodology and hence for research findings. In other words, does the commitment to a realist ontology make any difference to the sort of research findings one comes up with. Why not be an idealist or not bother with an ontology at all: why not just settle for 'anything goes in just any old way'.

If one prefers to work with a realist ontology, presumably the reason is that one feels it will make a difference to the sort of knowledge about the world which it leads one towards. This is the question of realism's *methodological consequences*. In order that the claims of, for example, structuration theory and the theory of communicative action to a realist dimension can maintain any credibility, they must develop clear methodological guidelines for the translation of ontology into empirical research. In the absence of such guidelines, the relationship between empirical research and the supposedly guiding ontology will be *ad hoc*, intuitive and unsystematic. At best, the ontology will act in a vague and unstructured manner to 'sensitise' the researcher to the relevant field of empirical material. To be content with such a tentative link between ontology and empirical findings is a way of generously providing grist for the mill of the defeatist postmodernists. We will come back to this point later. Suffice it to say here that if the link is not important enough to sweat over, it is perhaps not important at all. If empirical details are not to be guided and marshalled according to systematic ontological guidelines, perhaps the ontological guidelines do not have any significant effect. If this is the case, any claims to realism are more to do with wishful thinking or textual rhetoric than with logical and systematic argumentation and evidential support. My view, needless to say, is that the link between ontology and empirical findings is important and needs to be sweated over.

Ontology and Theories

There are a number of different ways to construct theory, which can be equally valid in their own ways; the adequacy of any particular ontology, like all other aspects of theory construction, is open to argumentation and dispute. However, if we are to take our preferred ontology seriously, we must assume that this will have implications for, and put constraints on, the *theories* (top centre in Figure 3.1) that we develop about particular aspects of the social world in particular times and places. The distinction between theories and metatheories is one that often confuses people. Perhaps the best way of making the difference clear is to say that, leaving aside certain qualifications, a metatheory is something that is more or less universal, applying in all times and in all places, whereas a theory, while ideally parasitic upon a metatheory – that is, faithful to the parameters and contours of its metatheory – is focused on a more circumscribed area of social relations. Thus, in our ontology, agents and structures are thought to exist wherever social relations exist. However, a theory of industrialism, for example, is designed to address a particular set of social relations, which is much more limited in time and space. Agents and structures will appear in, and inform, a theory of industrialism but theories of industrialism will not be relevant to all concrete manifestations of structure and agency.

An illustrative list of theories, more or less general, more or less specific, but all less general and more specific than ontological principles could include: theories of suicide; theories of suicide among adolescents in Hong Kong; theories of the State in capitalist societies; theories of the Italian State in the 1980s and 90s; theories of industrialism; theories of viewers' reception of soap operas; theories about the causation of the holocaust; theories about religion and its place in social life; theories about the place of Buddhism in the societies of Indo-China; theories about the role of the media; theories of patriarchy or gender construction; theories of modernity or postmodernity; theories of self-identity in modernity; theories of a new division of labour; theories of ethnic cultures; theories about new social movements; theories about the cultural influence of gay groups in the USA; theories of the pleasures of reading romantic fiction for particular social groups; and so on.

The Question and the Questioner: Keeping an Eye on the Angle of View

The range of any one of the theories mentioned above can be enormous, and which particular portion of a theory is relevant to an individual piece of research will depend upon *the question* (top left-hand side in Figure 3.1) that is asked. In turn, the significance and the contours of the question that is asked may be perceived differently according to the training, biography and experience of *the questioner* (top left-hand corner in Figure 3.1). Such a difference will obviously be the case where two researchers asking the same question are steeped in different theoretical paradigms, but it can also be so even when two questioners share the same theoretical presumptions. Their gendered experience, for example, may mean that one of them is keenly sensitive to aspects of the world towards which the other is blinkered. This issue of the 'focalisation' of the problem at hand was explored in some depth by modernist novelists who strove to highlight the situated and limited perspective of the narrator, who was often one of the characters taking part in the action of the novel. The narrative was thus said to be 'focalised' through the eyes of a particular character. As a consequence, the narrative was often written in the first person, but this was not always the case; a narrative could still be written in the third person (she did this, he did that) while being focalised through the character's perspective. Look at this example from Henry James' *What Maisie Knew* (1985):

> Maisie didn't know what people meant, but she knew very soon all the names of all the sisters; she could say them off better than she could say the multiplication tables. She privately wondered, moreover, though she never asked, about the awful poverty, of which her companion also never spoke (James, 1985, p. 44).

Whether in first or third person, this strategy casts a distinctive light upon the angle of vision from which the action and the other characters are perceived. Attention is still drawn to the 'world out there', but this is not presented as a supposedly transparent representation of reality revealing itself as it really is, irrespective of who is looking. The world 'out there' is apprehended 'in here' by the focaliser, who is more or less alert, knowledgeable, sophisticated, prejudiced or blinkered. Thus the little girl, Maisie, growing up in a corrupt world of adult intrigue and betrayal, would 'see much more than she at first understood'. In Malcolm Lowry's novel *Under the Volcano*, we are introduced to a herd of buffalo, which quickly turns out to be the phantoms of a character's mind – the character, Geoffrey Firmin, having distinct modes of perception that rest primarily upon the pillars of alcohol and paranoia (Lowry, 1962; Alexander, 1990). Saul Bellow's novel *Herzog* is dominated by the perspective of the subject of its title, Moses Herzog, but:

> while Herzog's vision and judgement dominate the novel's structure, they are [also] to a degree destabilised from within by the suspicion, communicated to the reader by other characters, that neurosis weakens the reliability of his judgements (Alexander, 1990, p. 96).

The significance of perspective, of bringing into the foreground the variety of limited, partial points of view on a set of events in the real world cannot be stressed too highly. One highly effective textual form in which the same set of real events and processes is shown to reveal itself in different ways to different perceivers is that contained in those novels, such as William Faulkner's *The Sound and the Fury* (1989) or Lawrence Durrell's *The Alexandria Quartet* (1961, 1963), in which a given set of events in the real world is narrated by a series of different characters, each with their own perspective, memories, emotions and style of telling.

Modernist literature was quick to make the inference – contained in the references to Firmin and Herzog – from the aesthetic promotion of a narrator with limited perspective to the possibility that this narrator might not be very reliable, might be prone to a whimsical memory, might embroider her past exploits, confuse fantasy with reality, might simply lie. Of course, sociologists never lie, but they may feel, consciously or unconsciously, that there is a virtue in the suppression or sidelining of some pieces of evidence in favour of bringing to the fore other pieces that are more convenient for their argument; they may embroider their own knowledgeability, and confuse what they would like to know with what they do know. Accordingly, it is even more important for sociological writing to develop methodologically and textually reflexive strategies that will highlight the perspective of the sociologist in knowledge construction and the way in which this perspective interacts with each of the research elements, and negotiates a personal settlement.

Drawing Things Together in a Methodological Focus

The questioner's particular inflexion, or limited point of view, is one element among others in the top line in the research model (Figure 3.1) that combine together to inform *the methodology,* which can be seen as the bridge between a sociologist's conceptual baggage and her immediate substantive analysis of the world. It is the place where the approach engendered by theoretical and personal perspective grapples with the problems posed by the exigencies of conceptualising, and gathering evidence, about an autonomous slice of the real world. The specific role played by methodology will differ according to the general principles of the player and dreamer models respectively.

In both cases, however, an aspect of methodology that I believe to be of enormous significance is captured in Giddens' notion of 'methodological bracketing'. We will explore this notion in some depth later, but the basic point of it, to my mind, is to draw together the elements of questioner, question, theory and metatheory, and to sort out their combined implications for identifying the field of vision of a research project. The delineation of an appropriate methodological bracket can allow it to act as a nodal point – a point of convergence and of sorting out what needs to be in focus and what is irrelevant to the quest – which helps one to keep a grip on the task at hand. For my present purposes, and without going into detail at this stage, I will treat the most basic forms of bracketing as:

1 A research project that includes an interest in the hermeneutics of how social actors draw reflexively on their knowledgeability and motivation in choosing how to act (Agent's Conduct Analysis – ACA). This bracket draws directly on Giddens, and all I have done is to change the term from 'strategic conduct analysis' to 'agent's conduct analysis' so as not to inadvertently suggest too narrow a focus.[1]

2 A research project that is not concerned with lay actors' conduct analysis but, rather, is interested in the researcher's analysis of social practices, from outside as it were (Theorist's Pattern Analysis – TPA).[2]

Where there is a broad hermeneutic dimension to this latter type of project, it is a hermeneutic appreciation of the general culture and not of the deliberations and conduct decisions of specific individuals or collective actors. Methodology and methodological bracketing are to be distinguished, in turn, from *methods,* which refers to the range of formal techniques available for conducting *empirical research*, from participant observation to semi-structured interviews, from documentary research to surveys, and so on, whose actual use is always informed by a methodology – more or less self-consciously, more or less systematically (cf Stanley and Wise, 1990, p. 26).

The Distinctiveness of the Player Model of Research

It is apparent from the sample list above that theories can aspire to be more or less general or specific to one case (for example the role of the state in capitalist societies versus the causation of the holocaust), and to be more or less contextualised or abstracted from the specific context (for example the pleasures of reading popular romantic fiction for particular social groups versus the nature of self-identity in modernity). In addition to noting whether a theory purports to be about single or multiple cases, and whether it is contextualised or abstracted, one can also ask if it involves an ACA, that is, whether it takes into account the hermeneutic understandings of the social actors involved. Thus we have three ideal type distinctions in relation to the type of knowledge that particular theories contain:

1 Single case: multiple case (generalising)

2 Contextualising: abstracted

3 Agent's Conduct Analysis: Theorist's Pattern Analysis

The realist ontology that I have so far identified with contemporary social (meta)theory, and to which I have referred approvingly as a suitable basis for a past-modern realism, gives an *ontological* primacy to the first of each of these binary oppositions. That is, the ontology of contemporary social theory emphasises the contextualisation and the hermeneutics of single cases. It does this because, for contemporary social theory, this is how things actually happen. Whatever similarities one social event or process has with other events and processes, it will have its own existential uniqueness. Its existential coming and going has a precise contextual location and is infused with, and surrounded by, meaning. Accordingly, the *player model* of theory construction (Figure 3.2) is designed to address contextualised single cases, sometimes, but not always (depending upon the question asked), including an analysis of the hermeneutic frames of meaning of social actors. Where the ideal type of player theory turns itself towards generalisations, it does so by being parasitic on its single, contextualised cases. Thus we have comparisons between studies of particular processes or events in specific places in specific times. Ideal player theory would be constructed in such a way that the findings of a case study would feed back into a precise body of theory about that type of case study. This body of theory would act as a storehouse of more or less contextualised, more or less hermeneutically sensitive, case studies of conjunctural events and processes that have addressed specifically phrased questions.

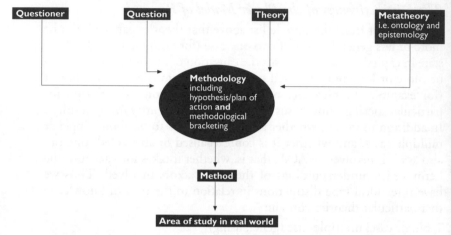

Figure 3.2 Key dimensions of the player model of sociological research

An Example of the Player Model of Theory Construction: Douglas' The Social Meanings of Suicide

An example of this 'player' type of theory building is contained in Jack Douglas' *The Social Meanings of Suicide* (1967). As Douglas is arguing against the traditional objectivistic approach of sociology to the study of suicide, he is close, in effect, to the position of building a completely new theory. Consequently, he begins primarily with his metatheory, within which an ontological concern with the hermeneutic framework of suicidal individuals figures large, and with a specific question. Douglas argues that in addressing this question of why a particular individual has committed suicide, sociologists should undertake a detailed analysis of the contextualised meanings of that particular suicidal act. They should do this through, among other things, interviews with 'survivors', medical and legal case reports, diaries and other documentary sources. Douglas combines an interest in the motivation of suicidal individuals with a focus on the context of social meanings upon which they draw (in Giddens' sense of drawing upon social structures). He argues that a culture's social meanings in relation to suicide can have an important influence on the meaning that an individual constructs for a suicidal act. In illustrating Douglas' point, Steve Taylor, in *The Sociology of Suicide* (1988), here gives as an example the idea that, in the modern Western world, suicide means that there is something drastically wrong with the individual and that people can be 'driven' to this desperate situation. This means that a person may feel that suicide can be used to indicate that others are to blame for this state of affairs. In other words, suicide can be used to inflict 'revenge' on others (Taylor, 1988, p. 42). Taylor quotes a particular case used by Douglas to illustrate this social meaning of suicide:

> A young clerk 22 years old killed himself because his bride of four months was not in love with him but with his elder brother and wanted a divorce so she could marry the brother. The letters he left showed plainly the suicide's desire to bring unpleasant notoriety upon his brother and his wife, and to attract attention to himself. In them he described his shattered romance and advised reporters to see a friend to whom he had forwarded diaries for further details. The first sentence in a special message to his wife read: 'I used to love you; but I die hating you and my brother too.'... Still another note read, 'To whom it may interest: The cause of it all: I loved and trusted my wife and trusted my brother. Now I hate my wife and despise my brother and sentence myself to die for having been fool enough to ever have loved anyone as contemptible as my wife has proven to be.'... The day before his death, there was a scene and when assured that the two were really deeply in love with each other, the clerk retorted: 'All right, I can do you more harm dead than alive' (Douglas, 1967, pp. 311–12, quoted in Taylor, 1988, p. 42).

The empirical findings that result from this type of investigation and that help one to construct a picture of what really happened in a given case can then be fed back into the construction of a body of theoretical knowledge about a whole series of cases, all derived from this 'player' source. In line with this, Douglas argues that one should look for recurring patterns of motivation and dimensions of meaning – the social meanings of suicide. Douglas begins to develop a body of theory based on the contextualised motivations of individual suicidal 'players' (Douglas, 1967, pp. 284–319); he argues that there are common patterns of motivation and meaning, of which some of the most common are 'revenge', 'the search for help', 'escape', 'repentance' and 'seriousness' (Taylor, 1988, pp. 41–2). These motivations draw on and are related to social meanings in different ways – for example, escape and revenge express very different relationships with one's social world – but in all cases one's attempt to get at the reality of what happened should be informed from the top right-hand corner of Figure 3.2 to the bottom by a model of reflexive and knowledgeable agents drawing on their context of social meanings.

As the researcher picks and chooses empirical evidence according to these guidelines, she must remember that, if the realist ontology is to have methodological consequences, the picking and choosing must be consistent with a continued respect for the ontology. It must not flatten out the rich and diverse textures of social life suggested by the ontology. Rather, the pragmatic partiality of focus and empirical selection, necessary in order to answer particular questions, must remain aware of itself as pragmatic, partial and selective. It must possess a continual self-reflexivity. One's grasp of the importance of this self-reflexivity grows in proportion to one's grasp of the complexity not only of ontology, but also of the process of acquiring knowledge about a complex world. By its very form, the player model emphasises the point that empirical evidence only makes sense within a process of research with many other elements, including ontology, none of which can be privileged *a priori*. Each of these elements has its own autonomy and is therefore underdetermined by each or all of the others. The process is an intricate and complicated one.

Mapping Contextualisation

Presented so formally, with such intricacy and complication, it is easy to see that the ideal type model is precisely what it says – an ideal. Correspondingly, it also becomes much easier to understand postmodernism's distrust of knowledge claims, especially (but not only) when one changes scale from a case study of a single event to claims that purport to embrace multiple cases, or from a study of two or three social interactions in close proximity to each other to a plethora of interactions stretching across large sweeps of time–space. The postmodernist distrust of, for example, the confident generalising metanarratives often associated with Marxism, Science, the Nation or Feminism – where these are seen to ignore or swallow up local differences and contingencies – is, among other things, a distrust of knowledge claims. The swallowing-up, or subsumption, of the diversity of contexts and people entails a general disregard for both the specificity and the potential plurality of the real world, and for the difficulties involved in producing knowledge about it.

The diagram reproduced below (Figure 3.3) is designed as a map, or a series of benchmarks, against which the types of knowledge produced by *player analyses* can be plotted. It is intended to facilitate the reflexive monitoring of knowledge by providing co-ordinates, which can be used to define the *degree to which* a case study is contextualised, and the *ways in which* it is (more or less) contextualised.

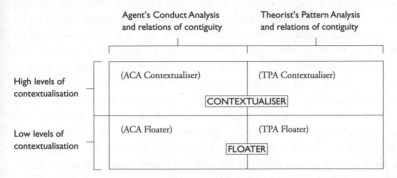

Figure 3.3 Player grid of levels and types of contextualisation

Agent's Conduct Analysis and Theorist's Pattern Analysis.   Some of the terms used here I have already introduced in the course of discussing the various aspects of the player model. By the term 'agent's conduct analysis' (ACA), I mean to refer to the analysis of the hermeneutic frames of meaning of lay actors (how they more or less reflexively draw on their knowledgeability of the context of action and their motivational orientations in the production of their own actions). This form of analysis is to be contrasted with 'theorist's pattern analysis' (TPA), which I have coined in order to refer to analyses that tell the story from 'outside,' as it were, without any recourse to a hermeneutic analysis of the agents involved in the social phenomena being studied.

Relations of Contiguity.   By *contiguity* I refer to immediate relations between things, agents and events in time and space; to the contiguous joins in time and space: (1) within the lifetime time–space paths associated with the personal biography of an actor(s); (2) within the present daily routines of an actor(s); and (3) within a system whose interconnections spread way beyond the time–space locations of its many constitutive actors. Contiguity can be studied from 'outside', on the basis of TPA, in which case it will track one or all of the three dimensions of contiguity – with more or less exhaustiveness, like either a zealous or a lazy private eye – depending upon the relevance of each dimension to the question at hand. Contiguity can also be studied from a perspective that includes an ACA perspective on the three dimensions (see Chapter 4 for an extended discussion of this) as well as the TPA perspective. The emphasis on contiguity is intended to bring to the fore the virtual impossibility of reporting every moment, of producing a thoroughly exhaustive account of social relations, even in their more basic TPA form. Reflexivity towards contiguity allows us to begin to see the gaps in our accounts of the real, gaps that we tend to play down, to efface through a use of 'joining' language that is second nature to us. The narratives we construct about the world are replete with formal and rhetorical leaps over missing days, months, marriages, deaths, political regimes and so on. Attention to contiguity is a logical corollary of an ontological emphasis on complexity, on the time and space contextualisation of social processes, and on the specificity of cultural meanings and agents' hermeneutic frames. If we take the ontology seriously, we need to be able to judge how much we know and how much we do not know. We need to be as aware of the possibly relevant gaps as we are of the probably limited knowledge.

The Benchmark of Exhaustive Contextualisation.   The general idea is that there is so much going on out there in the world in terms of hermeneutics, meaning and contiguity (and, for the sake of parsimony, I have not explicitly included power, although it is easy to see how attention to power could be developed along the same lines) that even in relation to a specific question, from a specific perspective (including our personal outlook, theoretical categories, metatheory and type of analysis), we still cannot hope to be thoroughly exhaustive of our object of study. The benchmark of exhaustiveness (the top line of the contextualiser boxes in Figure 3.3) must remain as an ontologically real but epistemologically Utopian benchmark. What we can do is attempt to be as reflexive as possible about all the constituent elements of our attempts to get at the world, including the degree and type of contextuality we are offering in the tentative and provisional answer to our specific question. Some studies will be more contextualised than others in terms of contiguity and also in terms of an agent's hermeneutics. Taking seriously the methodological consequences of a rich and complex ontology means paying serious attention to the degree of contextualisation produced in response to a given question. How much contextualisation – and of what type – is provided, for example, by those sociologists who provide the grand sweeps of history and of social systems? And if the contextualisation is limited by the scope of their enterprises – meaning the inevitability of massive gaps in contiguity – do they cut and trim their claims accordingly?

The Floater Metaphor.   The *floater* metaphor is directed towards this sort of question. It seeks to capture the way in which a certain type of study – and much comparative historical sociology is of this type – acquires a broader and longer perspective by means of floating over the surface of events, as if in a hot-air balloon, from which one's view is extensive but lacking in detail. Floater analyses, like hot-air balloons, can come down to land every now and again and, depending upon where they land – and for as long as they remain there – details, patterns and the nuances of social interaction can take on an unfamiliar richness and vibrancy. Even the words of lay actors can sometimes be heard before the balloonist floats upwards again and onwards over the next horizon. What distinguishes floater accounts from contextualised accounts is quite simply the dominance of the perspective from altitude, the surveying of vast expanses of time–space from up on high. Despite the ontological emphasis on complexity and contextualisation, there is no inherent hierarchy involved in the designations of contextualiser and floater. For some projects, with their own broad-scale questions and problems-to-be-investigated, a floater approach will be much more sensible and appropriate.

Triangulation.   Whether a particular case study is to be designated as contextualised or floating is partly a matter of judgement, according to the task at hand. This judgement, however, can be aided by a notion of *triangulation,* whereby one plots the level of contextualisation against two reference points. The first of these is the reference point of the complex realist ontology (the Utopian benchmark of exhaustive contextualisation). As this tells us that there is so much going on out there in terms of contiguity, meaning and all the other elements we have discussed, we can measure the level of our case study's contextual-isation against this benchmark. This will help us to be aware of the excessive claims made, for example, when a study from up on high presents itself as a streetwise view from street level. Against this somewhat fixed benchmark we can also have a second, more relativistic, benchmark or benchmarks. These would be other studies of cases similar to ours – the stuff of PhD literature reviews – which we might want to contrast with our own study. Our study may, thus, be less contextualised than the ontological apotheosis of exhaustiveness (the very top of the player grid) but much more contextualised than previous studies of the subject (which might appear in the floater boxes or just creep into the bottom of the contextualiser boxes). A future study by a young upstart, which provides much more contextualisation than yours ever did, may require you to review your judgement of designations and relative positions within the boxes. Ultimately, the grid is heuristic, of course, and may be more or less useful depending on the task at hand.

The Distinctiveness of the Dreamer Model of Research

At this point, I want to come on to my second ideal type of theory building, which I will label the *dreamer* model (Figures 3.4 and 3.5). My purpose in formally developing this model is in order to suggest a way in which we can still talk about another set of big questions, the multiple cases exhibiting general trends so beloved of the much-derided grand metanarrativists. I will first present and illustrate the dreamer model and then outline what I believe to be some of the crucial differences between dreamer theories and sociological modernism's grand metanarratives.

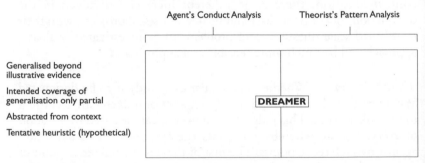

Figure 3.4 Dreamer grid with defining characteristics and types of analysis

It is best to start by distinguishing the dreamer model from the player model. In this model, instead of using the resources of theory and metatheory to ask a question in relation to a single contextualised case, one asks a question in relation to multiple cases abstracted from their specific contexts. One begins, as with the player model, with the diagram's top row of questioner, question, existing theory and metatheory. One then proceeds to a hypothesis about general trends or characterising features of an epoch or period in social life. I label this model of theory-building the 'dreamer' model, because although the hypotheses often draw on empirical research into specific cases, they do so in a limited way, using cases as illustrative examples of a more generalised trend. The more generalised trend is, in fact, the imagined (dreamer) hypothesis. It is creatively imagined rather than empirically grounded in knowledge of many specific cases, as with the player

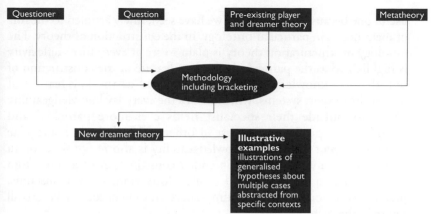

Figure 3.5 Key elements in the dreamer model of sociological research

model. Indeed, dreamer theory should be seen as, in a very strong sense, hypothetical; it is not grounded in the way that player theory is. The degree of imaginative freedom that it gains from being released from the rigours of playing at ground level is gained at the expense of the fine-grained perspective and contextuality that are the player's prerogative. I think that the creation of dreamer theory should be seen as positive, as long as it remains reflexively vigilant as to its own hypothetical status. In principle, dreamer theory should be capable of being fleshed out and tested by players; its worth as social theory can never be validated by fiat. It is when dreamers lose sight of the provisional, hypothetical nature of their conceptual innovations that they cease to be dreamers and become *despots* (see below).

An Example of the Dreamer Model of Theory Construction?: *Giddens'* Modernity and Self-identity

Giddens' *Modernity and Self-Identity: Self and Society in the Late Modern Age* (1991) is a good illustration of the formal possibilities of dreamer theory. In the introduction to the book, Giddens is explicit about the generalising and decontextualised nature of the study. As regards its generalising thrust, he writes that his aim is to try 'to identify some structuring features at the core of modernity which interact with the reflexivity of the self' (Giddens, 1991, p. 2). He is also very clear with regard to the abstraction of his theoretical claims from particular instances: 'I do not discuss in any detail how far some of the processes mentioned have proceeded in specific contexts, or what exceptions or countertrends to them exist' (Giddens, 1991, p. 2). The example is a useful one because Giddens is, as we have seen, finely attuned to the role of metatheory, in particular ontology, in the construction of theory. The ontology of structuration theory is plain to see at every turn: reflexivity is highlighted as the particularly modern feature of the construction of self-identity; knowledgeability is highlighted as the key feature of modernity's expert systems, which makes the everyday knowledgeability of agents outside their specialist fields ever more parochial and dependent on putting their trust in others. The glaringly inadequate bounds of agent's all-round knowledgeability is also responsible for an unwelcome rejuvenation of unintended consequences of action, from heart disease to environmental crisis. Motivation, the unconscious, practical consciousness and the time–space binding of social relations all figure in the picture.

As in the ideal type of dreamer theory, sketched out in Figure 3.5, Giddens creates his thesis by combining the basic ontology of structuration (meta)theory with existing theories of modernity and with occasional illustrative case studies, in order to address a nexus of questions about the relationship between structuring features at the core of modernity and the reflexive constitution of the self. Both Chapters 1 and 3, for example, begin with specific illustrative examples, which, when laid out on the tarmac alongside Giddens' ontology, are used as launching pads from which to make generalisations abstracted from the specific contexts in which it is suggested they exist.

The first of these is a:

> specific sociological study, plucked rather arbitrarily from a particular area of research. *Second Chances* (1989), by Judith Wallerstein and Sandra Blakeslee, is an investigation of divorce and remarriage. The book describes the impact of marriage break-up, over a period of some 10 years, on 60 sets of parents and children. Divorce, the authors point out, is a crisis in individuals' personal lives that presents dangers to their security and sense of well-being, yet also offers fresh opportunities for their self-development and future happiness. Separation and divorce, and their aftermath, can cause long-lasting anxieties and psychological disturbances but, at the same time, the changes brought about by the dissolution of a marriage provide possibilities, as the authors put it, to 'grow emotionally', to 'establish new competence and pride' and to 'strengthen intimate relationships far beyond earlier capacities' (Giddens, 1991, p. 10).

Giddens goes on to focus on the fact that although *Second Chances* is a work of sociology, it will not be read only by sociologists:

> Therapists, family counsellors, social workers and other concerned professionals are likely to turn its pages. It is perfectly possible that members of

the lay public, particularly if they have been recently divorced, will read the book and relate its ideas and conclusions to the circumstances of their own lives. The authors are clearly aware of this likelihood. Although the book is written mainly as a research study presenting a definite set of results, numerous passages scattered through the text suggest practical responses and courses of action which the newly separated or divorced might follow. No doubt few individual books influence overall social behaviour very much. *Second Chances* is one small contribution to a vast and more or less continuous outpouring of writings, technical and more popular, on the subject of marriage and intimate relationships. Such writings are part of the reflexivity of modernity: they serve routinely to organise, and alter, the aspects of social life they report on or analyse. Anyone who contemplates marriage today, or who faces the situation of the break-up of a marriage or a long-term intimate relationship, knows a great deal (not always on the level of discursive awareness) about 'what is going on' in the social arena of marriage and divorce. Such knowledge is not incidental to what is actually going on, but constitutive of it – as is true of all contexts of social life in conditions of modernity (Giddens, 1991, pp. 13–14).

The illustrative example that begins Chapter 3 is a book by Janette Rainwater entitled *Self Therapy: A Guide to Becoming Your Own Therapist* (1989), and is presented by Giddens along the same lines – the book is not only about something (self-therapy), but also helps to create the late-modern reality of the thing it is about – self-therapy. In this example, the link could not be more explicit: the book is a guide, a guide to systematic reflection on the course of one's life development. The central message of Giddens' book is that the self is a 'reflexive project', which is sustained through a perception of one's self-identity that is constantly revisable.[3] This is metatheory transposed onto modernity, metatheory negotiating with theories of modernity and with illustrative examples to produce a range of generalisations. The generalisations stretch way beyond the illustrative examples cited, to embrace distant other cases whose existence is suggested rather than demonstrated. It is these other, uncited, inferred cases that form the basis of dreamer theory; it is the supposition that these cases exist (or may exist) that provides the basis for dreamer theory's claims to be able to say something about general trends, about the widespread characterising features of whole societies or epochs. If these other cases did not actually exist, the narrow dividing line between dreamer theories and fictional imagining would then be breached. The more that player studies were able to show the existence of these inferred, hypothetical cases, then, *ceteris paribus,* the stronger those lines would be.

Summary Characteristics of Dreamer Analysis

The dreamer model of theory construction is much looser than the player model. It allows the theorist a great deal more licence to 'imagine' rather than 'find out about'. Indeed, for Giddens, this is its attraction. He sees 'conceptual innovation' in relation to large-scale, long-term processes of society as the main intellectual challenge provided by sociology (Giddens, 1987, p. 43). Such innovation should address questions such as: 'how should we best characterize modernity? What were its origins? What are the major transformations currently influencing the trajectories of development of world history?' (Giddens, 1987, p. 43). The major difference between dreamer theories and metanarratives is that the former's claims to knowledge are:

1 appropriately humble and tentative, owing to the fact that dreamers self-consciously surmise about instances that stretch beyond the cases they know something about;

2 aware of the limitations of their knowledge imposed by the fact that each individual instance (known about or imagined) of the generalisation has been uprooted and abstracted from its context in a complex open system;

3 aware of the partial nature of any generalisation – the extremely high probability of many exceptions to the generalisation (see Figures 3.4 and 3.5).

Sociological Despots (for example Modernists) Distinguished from Players and Dreamers

To the designations of players and dreamers, I want, finally, to add the category of sociological despot (for example sociological modernists). Despots are players or dreamers who squeeze the life out of reality by writing as if there is much less to knowing than there really is. They tend to write in an all-knowing, somewhat omnipotent manner about events, but this implied knowledge is not matched by the levels and types of empirical evidence that one would expect in the light of such confidence. They do not provide the evidence that would be required for us to believe that they know as much as they imply they know. They may do this intentionally or unintentionally, consciously or unconsciously, but they do it. The effect of doing this is to flatten the richness and the finely grained texture of reality. The world appears as less interesting, more one-dimensional, than it should do. Or, to put it another way, there is more in the construction of this world of the theorist, the researcher, than there should be. Claims are made that should not be made. They write as if they know more than they do. The specifics of this will, of course, vary from case to case, but the player and dreamer grids can provide us with some orienting benchmarks. On the basis of these benchmarks we can say that despots include:

1 Dreamers who write as if they are players. For example, they generalise beyond the instances they know about to other instances they do not know about – as a dreamer would do, partially, tentatively, hypothetically – but they do so without the tentative or hypothetical qualities of the dreamer. Rather, they present their imaginings, their extrapolations, as player knowledge of (many, many, many) particular cases in particular times and places. They write as if the whole world can be logically deduced from some concepts and an illustration or two. Their reductionism impoverishes the world which one would expect to find on the basis of a rich, complex ontology of potentials.

2 Floaters who write as if they are Contextualisers.

3 Theorist Pattern Analysts who write as if they have employed Agent's Conduct Analysis.

All three types of despot reduce the autonomy of the social world as against that of the sociologist; the sociologist dominates the text, refuses to allow all the possible surprises, differences and local variations contained in reality to disturb her neat algorithmic procedures.

Textual Boldness

The emphasis on the process of drawing out methodological consequences of a realist ontology has led me to lay out, somewhat didactically, the various elements – and combinations of elements – that cohere together to produce a varied range of sociological accounts. I have tried to stress the complexity and the intricacy of the research process, and the corresponding sophistication of the guidelines we need to develop for tracking this variety. With the acknowledgement of variety – a plurality of research possibilities and combinations – a premium is necessarily placed on the refinement of procedures of assessment.

Thus far in this chapter we have focused on epistemological and methodological guidelines. However, we can analytically distinguish this dimension of critical reflexivity from another dimension, namely that which is involved in the translation of an analysis into text, into the form in which it is to be presented to a readership or audience of some kind. For me, these two dimensions should be, respectively, those of epistemological caution and textual boldness, modesty and exhibitionism.

Moreover, the moments of epistemological caution and textual boldness should be intimately related, the text boldly drawing most attention to itself at those points at which it is making epistemological claims – claims about the process of acquiring knowledge. If this latter process is complicated and precise, and is engineered by a situated, partially sighted researcher of finite knowledgeability, its mechanisms must be laid bare for the cross-questioning reader to cross-question. The experiments of the postmodern novel can help us to think about how to bring to the fore these processes of textuality and their relation to the sociological analysis.

Postmodernist novelists have maintained the modernist emphasis on the situated perspective of the narrator – with all the epistemological caution and scepticism that this implies – but they have questioned the aesthetic of impersonality that accompanied it. For postmodernists, it is not possible completely to efface the author from the work; to assume that one can do this is nothing more than a misleading illusion. The author remains: selecting, choosing, highlighting, suppressing, designing. One must mistrust the author as well as the narrator; we should not only be aware of the author's credentials, but also demand justifications for the views, opinions and putative facts that she attempts to foist upon us. In sociological terms, we must not only be able to mistrust the lay actors – the interviewees, the informants, the observed – but also.be prepared to mistrust the sociologists who write about them.

For postmodern novelists, a central focus of this scepticism is the textual form in which knowledge claims are proffered. In a sense, these novelists work with the distinction between analysis and textuality, because, on the one hand, they continue the modernist awareness of the perspectival mediation of reality – and the caution that goes with this – while, on the other, they pay a great deal of attention to the formal construction of texts. With regard to the latter, they stress the obstacles, the problems involved in the process of narration, and also the opportunities presented by narration for dissembling, for the glossing over of ignorance, for evasions and ellipsis, for creating diversions and for all the tricks of rhetorical persuasion. One does not have to think too hard to make the link between these obsessions of the postmodern novel and the textual problems and opportunities available to sociologists. If contemporary social theory suggests that the world is a complex, contextualised and richly variegated place, and we also accept the many difficulties of getting to know about any one part of this world, we will then be presented with a range of problems and obstacles in our attempts to construct convincing and fluent narratives.

If the academic culture is one that disdains equivocation, gaps, ambiguity, hesitancy and provisionality in its authoritative narratives, the impulse towards exploiting the indelicate opportunities of textuality will then be great indeed.

One way in which postmodern novelists draw attention to the various strategies of the author of fiction – and, by analogy, to the temptations available to the sociological author – is to foreground *diegesis* – the direct speech of the author – by 'the explicit appearance in the text of the author as the maker of his own fiction, the fiction we are reading' (Lodge, 1990, p. 41). David Lodge notes that the Russian formalists called this 'exposing the device', and that the equivalent term used most consistently amongst postmodernists is 'metafiction' (cf Hutcheon, 1989). He compares the effect of this strategy with Erving Goffman's notion of social agents 'breaking frame' (Lodge, 1990, p. 43). Thus, John Fowles, in the famous Chapter 13 of *The French Lieutenant's Woman* suddenly intervenes in the flow of his imitation nineteenth-century novel: 'This story I am telling is all imagination. These characters I create never existed outside my own mind. If I have pretended until now to know my characters' minds and innermost thoughts, it is because I am writing in (just as I have assumed some of the vocabulary and 'voice' of) a convention universally accepted at the time of my story: that the novelist stands next to God. He may not know all, yet he tries to pretend that he does' (Fowles, 1969, p. 85, cf Alexander, 1990, p. 131). And Joseph Heller in *Good as Gold* suddenly begins to discuss the power that he has as author to negate the autonomy of Gold, the novel's chief protagonist (or so we thought), to do what he will with him: 'he would soon meet a schoolteacher with four children with whom he would fall madly in love, and I would shortly hold out to him the tantalising promise of becoming the country's first Jewish Secretary of State, a promise I did not intend to keep (Heller, 1980, p. 321; cited in Lodge, 1990, p. 42).

Kurt Vonnegut explores this same theme in *Breakfast of Champions*, when he, as author, decides to confront one of his characters, Kilgore Trout, late at night in Midland City, driving up alongside Trout who was walking on the sidewalk just outside the supply yard of the Maritimo Brothers Construction Company:

'Mr Trout,' I said, 'I am a novelist, and I created you for use in my books.'
'Pardon me?' he said.
'I'm your Creator,' I said. 'You're in the middle of a book right now – close to the end of it, actually.'

'Um,' he said.

'Are there any questions you'd like to ask?'

'Pardon me?' he said.

'Feel free to ask anything you want – about the past, about the future,' I said. 'There's a Nobel Prize in your future.'

'A what?' he said.

'A Nobel Prize in medicine.'

'Huh,' he said. It was a noncommittal sound.

'I've also arranged for you to have a reputable publisher from now on. No more Beaver books for you.'

'Um,' he said.

'If I were in your spot, I would certainly have lots of questions,' I said.

'Do you have a gun?' he said.

I laughed there in the dark, tried to turn on the light again, activated the windshield washer again. 'I don't need a gun to control you, Mr Trout. All I have to do is write down something about you, and that's it' (Vonnegut, 1992, pp. 291–2).

'All I have to do is to write down something about you and that's it.' How much autonomy do social actors have from the writers of sociology? How much licence do sociological writers have to disregard the autonomy of social actors, practices, causes, power relations, the realities of social relations? If their analysis is thinner than they would like, or is telling them something of which they do not approve, can they just write down something else, and that's it? How far does the power of the sociological writer go?

The implications for the social sciences of a will to 'expose the device' has a double edge to it through the tension between the commitment to a representation of the actual real world and the power to use textuality to play fast and loose with what one actually feels one knows about that world. There is a tension between commitment to the real and the power of fabrication, between a desire to be faithful to the real and a wish to be seen to know more (or less) about that real than one in fact does. The strategy of exposing the device can be useful to draw attention to very particular aspects of textual construction. In this respect, it is important to develop ways in which to expose the devices by which the analysis of particular elements in the player and dreamer models are translated into text, and to expose the techniques by which inadequacies of analysis are smoothed over and made invisible by the naturalising strategies and rhetoric of textuality. To break frame, to draw attention to the metadevices that textuality can employ in representing its relationship to sociological analysis, is, again, to promote the ability of the cross-questioning reader to cross-question. It is a form of self-conscious critique that helps to denaturalise what otherwise might seem natural, given and beyond questioning. It is to engage in what Linda Hutcheon in *The Politics of Postmodernism* has called the 'de-doxification' of cultural and social representations (Hutcheon, 1989, p. 4). To de-doxify a text is to reveal its mode of construction, to reveal its form and content as things as much sculpted as found, to reveal the text as much more – and also as much less – than just a transparent representation of 'the way things are'. Note: Move onto the next chapter. Make the neat transition you've been planning.

Notes

1 On reflection, and from the experience of presenting papers on 'strategic context analysis', I am now convinced that the use of the word 'strategic' suggests too narrow, too instrumental a focus to too many people (cf *inter alia*, Habermas' use of the term 'strategic' in *The Theory of Communicative Action*, 1989, 1991) for it to be adequate as a means of signifying what is meant to be a much broader focus on all types of agency hermeneutics that may have a bearing upon social practices. For a list of abbreviations used, see p. x of this book.

2 In a previous article (Stones, 1991), I labelled this 'visible pattern analysis', but was persuaded in personal correspondence with Ira Cohen that such a term could misleadingly suggest an objectivism that is not intended. The advantage of 'theorist's pattern analysis' is that it draws explicit attention to the theoretical and personal perspective of the person who is viewing, interpreting and selecting the pattern to be analysed.

3 For a powerful critique of certain aspects of Giddens' thesis, see Craib, 1994, pp. 112–32.

Chapter 4

The Pivotal Role of the Methodological Focus: A Positive Critique of Anthony Giddens

In the last chapter, I stressed the complexity, intricacy and variety of the research process, and the premium this places on the refinement of procedures of assessment, on the developing of guidelines that can help us to track this variety. I went on to discuss the relationship between research and writing and how the guidelines must help us to track the research within – and often in spite of – the writing (or whatever textual form it appears in). Reflexivity should be part of, directed towards, both research and writing, analysis and textuality. The display of reflexivity in the text should be a display of reflexivity about the analysis, and about the moves made in the construction of the text – it should reflect upon and expose its textual devices.

From one extreme to another. The stance that Anthony Giddens – the hero of Chapter 2 – has taken towards methodology and episte-mology would, if it were to find in us a receptive audience, lead us away from the development of a past-modernist sociology. It would see such an endeavour as fiddling while Rome burns, as the sociological equivalent of medieval theological debates about the number of angels on the head of a pin. Giddens' primary metatheoretical concern is with ontology, with the definition, redefinition and elaboration of broadly consistent ontological concepts, of the kind we met in Chapter 2. He feels that these should loosely sensitise research but that an attempt to develop any further methodological rules for them is misguided. I suspect that the reason he takes this stance is that his targeted notion of epistemology and methodology is taken from the past, from a period dominated by empiricism, when methodological rules were mean-spirited and narrow, desiring to squash all the variety of the world into the same small bottle. Giddens was not thinking of rules that can maintain diversity while also guiding reflexivity, that can tell us where we are, what we are doing and how it is different from what others are doing. That is, I think this is what he was not thinking of. Perhaps I am right. In any case, the rules that I am proposing do not attempt to simplify reality. Each step in the player or dreamer models has its own relative autonomy; the integrity of the individuality, contingency and contextuality of each empirical case is not compromised by the development of methodological guidelines. Indeed, the determinedly sceptical, reflexive and pedantic nature of the guidelines is necessary precisely to safeguard the integrity of each empirical case and the potential for uniqueness implied by the ontological stress on hermeneutics and contextuality. What *are* compromised are the potentially haphazard and capricious implications of a vaguely defined sensitising approach.

Critiques of Giddens' Lack of Interest in Epistemology and Methodology

Giddens has been taken to task for his lack of concern with method-ological and epistemological issues by a number of commentators. I will concentrate here on the comments of Thrift and Cohen, and on the replies by Giddens to this sort of criticism. In the course of this discussion, and in the elaboration of the methodological concept of bracketing that follows, I hope to highlight the way in which the adoption of Giddens' position would severely weaken the ability of sociologists to draw methodological consequences from a realist ontology. Both Thrift and Cohen are sympathetic to the ontological concerns of structuration theory, and their criticisms are directed, in effect, against Giddens' lacklustre claims for the methodological and empirical implications of the structurationist ontology. In a review of *The Constitution of Society*, Thrift declared himself to be 'deeply disappointed' by the final chapter, in which Giddens discusses this subject at some length. Thrift quotes a passage from the chapter in order to highlight what he finds so unsatisfactory:

> There is, of course, no obligation for anyone doing detailed empirical research, in a given localised setting, to take on board an array of abstract notions that would merely clutter up what could otherwise be described with economy and in ordinary language. The concepts of structuration theory, as with any compelling theoretical perspective, should for many research purposes be regarded as sensitising devices, nothing more. That is to say, they may be useful for thinking about research problems and the interpretation of research results (Giddens, 1984, pp. 326–7; quoted in Thrift, 1985, p. 620).

Thrift believes that this notion of social theory as, in a rather vague and unspecified way, an 'approach,' comes very close to a rather conventional 'take it or leave it' attitude, which inevitably leads to a radical curbing of ambitions; the ontology of structuration theory suddenly seems far less consequential than should be the case. Thrift finds it difficult to square Giddens' remarks in this respect with his insistence elsewhere that structuration theory should lead to more social researchers taking on hermeneutic concerns, to social researchers taking the complexities of the constitution of human agents more seriously and to more social researchers taking time and space into account. In short, Thrift believes that 'structuration theory, with its contextualising tendency, should have a considerable amount to say about epistemology and about the conduct and methods of research' (Thrift, 1985, p. 621). For him, the major import of structuration theory lies in its empirical pay-off. His image of the next book he would like Giddens to write is one that would see the development of structuration theory in the arena of a particular place in a particular historical period of time, showing structuration in process, contextual-ising in context. The book would have to show how structuration theory can act as a basis for challenging existing interpretations of historical events (Thrift, 1985, p. 621).

Cohen endorses Thrift's call for a book devoted exclusively to the implications of structuration theory for empirical research, and for much the same reasons. However, referring directly to that side of Giddens' persona that had previously shown more enthusiasm for methodological issues – the Giddens of methodological bracketing – he suggests that such a project should consist not just of one empirical study but of several:

> Ideally all studies would focus on different elements of the same historical theme. But the reason why a series of studies is required is that the guidelines for research in structuration theory can be expected to vary depending upon which level of analysis is involved and the methodological brackets appropriate to that level (Cohen, 1989, pp. 283–4).

The Negative Response: Giddens as a Defeatist Postmodernist?

Giddens has responded to this type of criticism in his 'A Reply to my Critics', which appears as the concluding chapter of the collection edited by Held and Thompson entitled *Social Theory and Modern Societies: Anthony Giddens and his Critics* (Held and Thompson, 1989, pp. 249–301). The comments I refer to are addressed most immedi-ately to criticisms made in the collection itself by Nicky Gregson[1], but

Giddens also takes the opportunity to voice a rejoinder to Thrift. He defends his view that structuration theory 'should be utilised only in a selective way in empirical work and should be seen more as a sensitising device than as providing detailed guidelines for research procedure' (Giddens, 1989, p. 294). Accordingly, he expresses his own disappointment with the way in which researchers have employed his concepts in their work. In particular, he regrets the fact that they have tried to import his concepts *en bloc* into their research, 'seemingly imagining that this will somehow lead to major methodological innovations' (Giddens, 1989, p. 294).

Giddens' reply to Thrift and Gregson does clarify some things about his position on empirical research. Certainly, one cannot argue with his belief that ontological and theoretical notions, while indispensable to empirical work, must be drawn on selectively in the sense that not all notions will be relevant to a specific empirical problem. As Giddens says, 'the category "empirical work" is very large... and covers numerous different sorts of inquiries' (Giddens, 1989, p. 295). The heart of Giddens' objection to providing more detailed guidelines for empirical research is his belief that this would not be compatible with the acknowledgement of empirical research as a hydra-headed endeavour directed at a multiplicity of specific problems concerning specific contexts. While ontology is also contextual, in the sense that it is also geared to given objects in a given time and space, these givens, as we have seen, are much less specific:

> The main tenets of structuration theory... are intended to apply over the whole range of human social activity, in any, and every context of action (Giddens, 1989, p. 295).

Thus Giddens can quite happily combine a belief that structuration theory should sensitise researchers to a range of ontological features of social practices, such as those mentioned by Thrift, with an unmoving conviction that 'Structuration theory is not intended as a method of research, or even as a methodological approach' (Giddens, 1989, p. 296).

I think that Giddens is right to stress the multiplicity of empirical research problems and contexts but wrong to suggest that recognising this puts the kibosh on any sort of attempt to develop more generalised methodological guidelines. Of course, these guidelines would not consist of an attempt to impose a single uniform method that would somehow link the structurationist ontology to any and every project of empirical research in a mechanical fashion. As he says, this was one of the main errors of those who formulated canons of research under the aegis of logical empiricism (Giddens, 1989, p. 295; cf Rorty, 1982). Rather, the guidelines would strive to be flexible enough to respect a wide range of research contexts, indeterminate enough to allow for wide variations of subject matter and empirical evidence, and clear enough as benchmarks for researchers to be able to gauge reflexively what they are actually doing. The real issue is about the relevance of methodologies and methods in the plural, and their adaptation to a myriad of different research questions in relation to a plurality of different areas of empirical research. The question is whether or not, on acknowledging this diversity, one just gives up the ghost on any attempt at producing guidelines that will help to ensure that given ontological presuppositions will have confining consequences for methodology. In my view, the vagueness of the sensitising attitude is giving up the ghost. I think it is also the key to understanding why there is a certain amount of plausibility in the suggestions of some commentators that Giddens' work is in some sense postmodernist (cf Hawthorne, 1990; Craib, 1992a). This claim is initially somewhat counterintuitive because Giddens clearly sees himself as a realist. Of course, I share Giddens' view here that his ontology is indeed consistent with a (suitably modified) realist epistemology and methodology. However, there is a world of difference between potential compatibility and actual practice. And here Giddens' disinterest in epistemological matters and his loose and unsystematic attitude to methodology mean that, in practice, he has few rules of sociological research. In this sense, there are indeed similarities with postmodernism.

Some Positive Methodological Guidelines: Giddens as Realist Beyond Modernism

From my perspective, Giddens' idea of methodological bracketing is just the sort of extremely useful generalising idea about the research process that his more sceptical persona seems to deny. The introduction of the two brackets of 'strategic conduct analysis' (in my terms, 'agent's conduct analysis' – see Chapter 3) and 'institutional analysis' are as far as he goes in this direction. I fully endorse the choice of this particular direction – and am greatly indebted to it – but believe that Giddens has only just begun to scratch the surface of possibilities. In the following section, I will attempt to: show more clearly the divergent fields of vision and empirical selection that strategic conduct analysis and institutional analysis direct one towards; increase the number of useful forms of bracketing; and also show how the technique of methodological bracketing makes it possible further to deconstruct the notion of empirical research into more types than were introduced in the player grid of the previous chapter. The idea is to allow for a greater latitude of perspectives while providing guidelines for each, guidelines that can be reflexively monitored with a sceptical eye by researchers and readers alike.

Four Forms of Methodological Bracketing
Agent's Conduct Analysis

I will first present Giddens' definitions of strategic conduct analysis and institutional analysis at greater length. In a glossary of terminology at the end of *The Constitution of Society* (1984) Giddens defines strategic conduct analysis as:

> Social analysis which places in suspension institutions as socially reproduced, concentrating upon how actors reflexively monitor what they do; how they draw upon rules and resources in the constitution of interaction (Giddens, 1984, p. 378).

In the main body of the text, he writes that strategic conduct analysis means giving analytical primacy to the consciousness of agents as expressed in their words (discursive consciousness) and in their capacity to do whatever they do (practical consciousness):

> and to strategies of control within defined contextual boundaries... it is to concentrate analysis upon the contextually situated activities of definite groups of actors. I shall suggest the following tenets as important in the analysis of strategic conduct: the need to avoid impoverished descriptions of agents' knowledgeability; a sophisticated account of motivation; and an interpretation of the dialectic of control (Giddens, 1984, p. 288).

We have already encountered the centrality of knowledgeability and motivation within Giddens' ontology, and a methodological focus that endows them with such importance fits well with the ontological stress on hermeneutics and contextuality. The link between the ontology and its methodological consequences is drawn clearly and coherently through the requirements of this form of analysis. By the 'dialectic of control', which we have not yet encountered, Giddens refers to the way in which any attempt to control others in social relations (from a teacher in a class to the SS in Auschwitz) will be influenced by the balance of power between the controller and the controlled.

Giddens' message is that, just as one should not underestimate the knowledgeability of social actors, so one should not underestimate the power of even the seemingly weakest members of society. The use of power is only very rarely one way: shop floor workers can throw a literal or metaphorical spanner in the works; toddlers, pupils or students can refuse to comply with requests from parents, nursery nurses, teachers or lecturers; local councils can refuse to implement central government directives; national governments can find ways to hinder international agreements on free trade; Lucinda can refuse to listen politely to a lecture on propriety from the Judds; the butler Stevens was physically, if not hermeneutically, in a position to pour the 'refreshments' down Mr Spencer's starched white neck. The dialectic of control only stops working at the extremes, when an agent has quite literally lost her agency – unconsciousness or incarceration in a strait-jacket would be examples. With anything less than this, a strategic conduct analysis of power relations would still have to take the dialectic, or negotiation, of power between actors into account, and here Giddens typically gives the example of a seemingly helpless prisoner exerting agency by going on hunger strike or committing suicide – the Bobby Sands case in Northern Ireland being a powerful example of the power of the ostensibly powerless. Like knowledgeability, the specifics of the dialectic of control are always contextual and strategic conduct analysis (in my terms, 'agent's conduct analysis') proposes to analyse them as such.

Institutional Analysis

On the other hand, the glossary account of institutional analysis presents it as:

> Social analysis which *places in suspension the skills and awareness of actors*, treating institutions as chronically reproduced rules and resources (Giddens, 1984, p. 375, my emphasis).

Thus, institutional analysis draws a methodological veil over the strategic conduct of actors and treats 'rules and resources as chronically reproduced features of social systems' (Giddens, 1979, p. 80). Now this is a major move by Giddens because it seeks to legitimise the removal of any concern with the hermeneutics of actors from a form of analysis. This means that the judgement of which rules and resources are being employed in the 'chronically reproduced', or long-standing, practices of institutions is the judgement of the sociologist. Indeed, the charac-terisation of the institutional practices being considered can be entirely in the language of the sociologist without reference to the language and consciousness of the actors involved. The reason that Giddens wants to do this is in order that he can get a longer-term, wider angle, view on the structuring of social systems than would be possible if he continually dwelt on the hermeneutics of lay actors. The reality that matters to Giddens from the perspective of this bracket has a certain scale: it is like a painting, to borrow a phrase from Albert Borgmann, that would vanish as such if viewed through a microscope (cf Borgmann, 1993, p. 118). In this he would seem to be moving onto the sort of terrain occupied by the grand narrativists who are so criticised by postmodernists. However, for similar reasons to those I offered in the last chapter in relation to dreamer analysis, I do not think that the use of institutional analysis need *necessarily* be tarred by the same brush as the reviled modernist grand narratives. In the course of this chapter, I hope to elaborate guidelines that, if carefully adhered to, can legitimise ways of looking at the large scale and the long term that are consistent with the demands of a sophisticated realism beyond modernism.

Much of Giddens' more substantive writing has been from the vantage point of institutional analysis, and he has used it for a range of tasks that include the following: to compare traditional, absolutist and modern nation-states in terms of the typical character of their boundaries (for example from no clear boundaries in the former to clearly defined and highly administered borders in the latter), the respective roles of violence in social relations, the scope and intensity of administrative control over populations, and the forms taken by their central internal conflicts (cf Giddens, 1981, 1984, 1985; and Jary, 1991, Figure 5.7, pp. 134–5); to compare tribal societies with 'class divided' (medieval or feudal) and class (capitalist) societies, including an emphasis on the degree and forms of 'stretch' and interdependence in the different ways they organised themselves over time–space (cf Giddens, 1981, 1984, 1985; and Jary, 1991, pp. 124–42); and to outline what he sees as the main institutional dimensions of modernity, namely *industrialism,* heightened *surveillance* (control of information and social supervision), the consolidation and *centralised control of the means of violence* in the context of the industrialisation of war, and *capitalistic enterprise.* In line with a consistent emphasis on multiple causality in his work, Giddens stresses that modernity should not be reduced to any one of these organisational clusters: they are all centrally involved in the formation of modernity (Giddens, 1990, pp. 55–78).

Systems Analysis

Cohen has done much to illuminate the logic behind Giddens' use of institutional analysis (Cohen, 1989, pp. 202–7 and 232–78), but he has also distinguished both institutional analysis and strategic conduct analysis from a new form of bracketing, which he himself introduces under the heading of systems analysis. Cohen argues that neither of these forms of bracketing make any provision for looking at the time–space configuration of reproduced social practices: what he calls 'system patterns' (see the postal system example in Chapter 2):

> To conceive the time–space patterning of interactions from the standpoint of the analysis of strategic conduct would entail the introduction of so many details of social *praxis* that the patterning itself would almost certainly fade from view. Institutional analysis, on the other hand, is intended to facilitate the apprehension of the interwoven rules and resources that 'bind' social systems (Cohen, 1989, p. 89).

Given Giddens' insistence that the time–space dimensions of social relations be emphasised as an important aspect of ontology, Cohen argues that there is every reason to give serious consideration to the methodological brackets required in order to analyse the time–space patterning of social systems:

> In what I term *systems analysis,* temporary brackets screen off structural properties of social systems and the contingencies of interactions that depart from institutionalised routines. What remains in view is the ordering and the articulations between interactions in time and space (Cohen, 1989, p. 89).

The Similarities between Systems Analysis and Institutional Analysis

While Cohen distinguishes this new form of analysis from both strategic conduct analysis and institutional analysis, he wants to pair it as a sister to institutional analysis, in that he believes they share much in common in their respective modes of analysis (Cohen, 1989, pp. 89–90; cf Stones, 1991, p. 675). That is, both institutional analysis and systems analysis bracket the hermeneutic moment, and both concentrate on chronically reproduced practices or routines, as opposed to practices that depart from institutionalised routines. For the purposes of constructing a clear set of reference points in order to sustain reflexive vigilance about the status of knowledge claims, it is worth lingering for a moment on the selectivity implicit in these two sets of brackets. First, along the lines outlined in the previous chapter, I think the fact that they both bracket the hermeneutic moment means that it is useful to characterise them both as subspecies of a more encompassing category, which I have called Theorist's Pattern Analysis

(TPA). The label is prompted less by what these forms of analysis include than by what they leave out. That is, they both place in suspension the motivations, skills and awareness of actors. They are not in the business of finding out what is going on 'inside the heads' or under the furrowed brows of the agents who create the patterns of social events that they study. The meanings and significances of events are interpreted from the 'outside' according to the lights (beliefs, prejudices, theoretical baggage, promptings of past experience) of the theorist or external observer (cf. Stones, 1991, p. 675).

Second, both forms of analysis focus upon chronically reproduced practices, on *routines* that persist in the long term, in the *longue durée* of institutional life. Moreover, the routine practices that are focused upon are those that play a role in the reproduction of institutions; the focus is not on the routine, '24 hour', everyday practices of the agents who undertake those institutional practices. The reason for this, as Cohen points out, is that in their day-to-day activities individuals will typically engage in a variety of interactions, which will temporarily intersect with a number of different institutional systems of interaction (Cohen, 1989, p. 92). Chasing the individuals through their day, tracing out their routine time–space paths in a variety of institutional settings, would deflect attention away from an analysis of the practices of specific institutions. Thus, in Cohen's words, '*Institutionalised interactions rather than individuals, appear as the constituent elements of social systems.* Thus it becomes possible to perceive patterns as involving only some of the encounters any individual maintains with others on a repetitive basis' (Cohen, 1989, p. 93, original emphasis).

We can summarise: both institutional analysis and systems analysis are: (1) from the vantage point of the theorist and are thus lacking an 'internal' hermeneutic dimension; (2) focused on chronically reproduced routines as opposed to nonroutine practices that depart from the usual round of things; and (3) interested in the routines of institutions rather than of individuals (Figure 4.1). A reflexive sociologist undertaking these forms of analysis, or anything akin to them, must be aware of what she is doing – TPA on the routines of institutions – and what she is not doing – investigating the hermeneutics of the social actors, either within or outside the institution, tracing the time–space paths and practices of relevant social actors outside specific institutional moments or noticing the practices within institutions that depart from (appropriately defined) routines. By virtue of the methodological brackets chosen, the knowledge claims of the sociological researcher are restricted from the outset to claims that fall within a theorist's pattern analysis of the routines of the institution(s) analysed. The researcher must remember that she is leaving a lot out of the picture and that claims must, accordingly, be attenuated and partial, respecting their own limitations.

| Theorist's Pattern Analysis |
| Chronically reproduced routines |
| Routines within institutions |

Figure 4.1 Focus of institutional analysis and systems analysis as defined by Giddens and Cohen.

Agent's Context Analysis

In a parallel move to Cohen's coupling of his notion of systems analysis with institutional analysis, I introduced the methodological brackets of strategic context analysis (what I would now call 'agent's context analysis'; see Chapter 3) as sister to strategic conduct analysis (Stones, 1991, pp. 673–95). I argued that insofar as Giddens' bracket of strategic *conduct* analysis drew upon the ontological category of knowledgeability, it did so in a way that leads us back to the agent herself, her reflexive monitoring, her motives and her desires. By way of contrast, agent's *context* analysis draws on the notion of knowledge-ability in order to lead us more clearly outwards into the social world, into the social nexus of interdependencies, rights and obligations, asymmetries of power and the social conditions and consequences of actions. Agent's *conduct* analysis would be used if the question, or problem-to-be-explained, called for a knowledge of the motives, knowledgeability, skills (beliefs, purposes, intentions and so on) of given actors, whereas agent's *context* analysis would be used where the problem being addressed called for a knowledge of the terrain (strategic, ethical, communicative, aesthetic) that faces or faced an agent and that constituted the range of possibilities and limits to the possible; among other things, such knowledge is necessary in order to develop counterfactual claims about strategic possibilities.

This institutional direction of vision is the first reason why I believe it is important to have the notion of agent's context analysis. It allows an explicit emphasis on the *agent's* awareness of the range of potential courses of action, choices, alternative strategies, or however one might want to express it, and of the probable consequences of such courses of action. The second reason for the notion, which follows on from the first, is that it allows the *social theorist* a perspective from which to assess the range of potential courses of action and probable consequences, and to judge this assessment against that of the lay actor.

The lay actor may be judged to be more or less knowledgeable, more or less ignorant of her social conditions. This 'corrigibility' of a lay actor's knowledge of the practical context is something that is repeatedly stressed by Giddens as being central to his notion of critical theory, and is a necessary precondition for a sociologist being able to point to unacknowledged conditions of action. The bracket of agent's context analysis makes it much easier to 'think' the relation between a lay agent's knowledgeability and the theoretical critique of this.

From this point on in the book, use of the acronym ACA will indicate a generic term to encompass both agent's conduct and context analysis. Where I wish to write specifically about one or the other I will use the terms in full. In many research situations requiring a hermeneutic dimension, one would indeed have to employ both agent's conduct analysis *and* agent's context analysis in order properly to focus the question at hand. Figure 4.2 provides a practically oriented conceptualisation of three spheres of analysis (within which both agent's conduct and agent's context analyses may be relevant), against which an account could be measured in terms of its approximation to, or distance from, the Utopian benchmark of exhaustive contextualisation. All three spheres are potentially relevant to an investigation of an individual agent's hermeneutic frame of meaning and its relationship to current structural context.

An attempt at an exhaustive reconstruction would involve:

1 Exploring the biography, the life-history, of the individual agents for any formative and enduring influences that are relevant to their present perspective on the issues at hand.

2 Focusing on the many (or few) different spheres of present everyday life in order to construct a frame of meaning that includes all relevant, influential aspects of this life. One would try to understand the interweaving of perceptions of the different spheres insofar as they impinged – in combination or in relative isolation, consistently or in logical contradiction – upon the reflexive awareness of immanent constraints and opportunities, of the immanent costs, risks and potential gains of creative resistance. One may well find, for example, a more or less well-defined hierarchy of priorities, in which desires or attachments in relation to one sphere of, for example, the 24-hour or weekly cycle, would be sacrificed – and therefore perceived as constrained – in order to safeguard a minimal satisfaction of wants in another sphere.

3 Analysing the individual's knowledge of the plural systemic conditions that combine to help produce any one of the various

spheres of everyday life. These conditions – social mechanisms and their interrelations – will provide the context in which the active resistance of individuals will produce certain consequences. We need to know the agent's perception of the likely consequences to follow from any attempt at resistance or creativity. Thus one would need to engage in an agent's *context* analysis of systemic interrelationships. The sociologist may also want to make an assessment of the extent to which the lay individual's assessment of the situation is accurate or inaccurate and, therefore, the extent to which an attempt at resistance and creativity would be likely to lead to intended or unintended consequences.

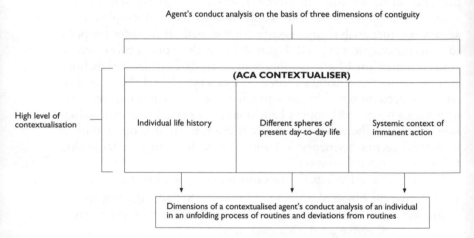

Figure 4.2 Relevant spheres of analysis for the contextualised reconstruction of an individual's frame of meaning in relation to a situated practice

A highly contextualised ACA of a situation, focusing on all three dimensions of an agent's frame of meaning, could thus allow one to ask questions about the duality of structure and agency that other forms of analysis could never reach. In this, there are points of great significance for sociology, which I can only signpost here. Many sociological studies are based upon aggregations of individual agents. Thus, surveys of more or less depth and complexity are conducted with a sample of, for example, 229 industrial workers, 40 chief constables, 42 readers of women's romances, or whatever the subject, and then the answers are coded and sorted into various categories. In terms of Figure 4.2, one of the consequences of this is that the process of coding tends to efface the specificity of the frames of meaning of individual actors. Even if all three dimensions are taken into account, the typical processes of coding tend to dismember the internal interrelationships of individual identities in order to compare elements abstracted from the whole frame of meaning. Thus, in Goldthorpe *et al.*'s celebrated study of the *Affluent Worker in the Class Structure* (1969) the particular method of aggregation that they use means that it would not be possible for a cross-questioning reader to look at the nuances of an individual frame of meaning, that articulates, for example, a prestige image of society with a white collar self-identification and a propensity to vote Conservative. It would be interesting to compare and contrast such a worker with one whose only category difference was to vote Labour. The explanation of this might lie in any one of the three dimensions of an agent's frame of meaning and would include both the relevant nuanced differences in social structural circumstances and the ways in which the individual agent responded to those circumstances. Goldthorpe *et al.* do, to be sure, use statistical methods to discern clusters of positions – for example '7 of the 19 men holding 'prestige' models were middle-class identifiers and… 5 of the 7 were Conservative or Liberal supporters' (Goldthorpe *et al.*, 1969, p. 176, footnote 3) – and these findings could be used as heuristic pointers as to what to look out for in the exploration of individual agent's frames of meaning. Such heuristic tools would, nevertheless, retain their quality of abstraction from the plural, interlocking and condensed nature of an individual's frame of meaning.

One aspect of this, that we shall return to in Chapter 7, is the loss of the specific texture and idiosyncrasies of an individual agent's use of, and experience of, language, symbolism, connotation, condensation and strength of emotion. In the 'affluent worker' study, this is certainly lost, in that there is hardly any presentation of the actual words of the individuals interviewed: they are virtually always pre-interpreted for us and presented in theorist's language. Robert Reiner's *Chief Constables*, as a contrasting example, is sprinkled liberally with direct quotations, which capture the varying argots, styles, palpable enthusiasms and dislikes of his subjects (Reiner, 1991). Even here, however, the words, the mimesis, are abstracted from any one individual's frame of meaning, and snippets of speech from a whole variety of chief constables is drawn on selectively in a series of chapters discussing, say, 'Chief Constables' Criminology' or 'The Social Philosophy of Chief Constables.' However, when in Chapter 12, Reiner constructs a series of ideal types of chief constable, which he labels Barons, Bobbies, Bosses and Bureaucrats, he presents 'four case-studies of individual chief constables in some detail, to make sense of their perspectives as a whole' (Reiner,

1991, p. 303). Reiner's study hints that the loss of individual agents' frames of meaning is not a necessary consequence of a study that includes some level of aggregation. It also brings to the fore what is lost in terms of the duality of structure and agency, perceptions of constraints and opportunities, in those cases that code on the basis of aggregations of elements abstracted from individual frames of meaning.

Limited Horizons: Giddens as a Certain Kind of Dreamer

How do we account for the seeming paradox of Giddens' introduction of the notion of methodological bracketing, on the one hand, and his dismissal of the importance of methodology, on the other? The careful distinction between institutional analysis and strategic conduct analysis suggests that while, for Giddens, structuration theory may not be intended as a methodological approach, he does regard certain methodological approaches as more consistent with structuration theory than others. This acknowledgement is significant because it shows that, in certain circumstances, Giddens can be drawn into seeing the significance of methodology. Apart from his tendency to present all generalising methodological rules as necessarily empiricist, the most sympathetic and, to my mind, probably the most plausible, explanation for the relatively dismissive attitude of Giddens towards method- ology is that his concerns – the sorts of question he has been interested in – have been relatively restricted. He has shown most enthusiasm for just one particular type of theory construction, with only two clear subdivisions: that is, the dreamer type of theory construction, using *either* an institutional analysis of routines *or,* in other cases, an agent's conduct analysis (both generally at the floater level) as illustrative examples. This enthusiasm has been paralleled by, on the one hand, a lack of critical engagement with questions concerning the translation of the structurationist ontology into the specific contextualised case studies which are the stuff of player theory, and, on the other, the absence of any exploration of a subject matter more accessible to other forms of methodological bracketing.

The suggestion that a restricted range of research concerns explains Giddens' downplaying of methodology, together with the associated observation about his predilection for dreamer theory, can help to shed some light on an intriguing ambiguity in the critical reception of Giddens' introduction of methodological brackets. It seems to me that both strategic conduct analysis and institutional analysis can be read as either dreamer or player methodological tools. Whereas Thrift clearly reads them as player tools – he wants to see Giddens contextualising in context, showing structuration in process in the arena of a particular place in a particular historical period of time – Giddens has generally seen them as aids in the construction of dreamer theory. Like, it seems, Thrift and Cohen, I always read Giddens' initial 1970s renderings of structuration theory (*New Rules of Sociological Method*, 1976, and *Central Problems in Social Theory*, 1979) as works inviting an orientation to contextualising in context, towards doing hermeneutically informed research of particular social processes in particular places. Like these authors I was disappointed – and somewhat perplexed – when Giddens did not seem to be interested in doing this. With the benefit of hindsight, it now seems likely that Giddens was much more interested from the start in providing the general sensitising ontological concepts, which would give him a licence to critique other grand sociological theories, and to produce some sensitised ones of his own.

Certainly if we look at the formal structure of Giddens' more substantive work, we can see that the emphasis is on dreaming, on large-scale generalising, rather than on contextualising, and the two subdivisions within this overall predilection for dreamer theory can be fairly clearly and simply discussed in terms of a division between his different books or parts of books. Thus, *Contemporary Critique of Historical Materialism, Nation State and Violence* (1981), Chapters 4 and 5 of *The Constitution of Society* (1984), and the bulk of *The Consequences of Modernity* (1991) are all written primarily using illustrations viewed from the methodological standpoint of institutional analysis at the floater level. These illustrations are then used as bases from which to make generalisations about extensive clusters of practices stretching way beyond the illustrative example. In shorthand, the floater illustrations are used as the basis for dreamer generalisations.

Giddens' claims in these works about class societies, class-divided societies, absolutist states, nation-states, the growth of cities, increasing surveillance and greater time–space distanciation are hypothetical projections – projections produced through illustrative examples, coupled together with a reworking of previous theories about traditional and modern societies on the basis of the structurationist ontology (see Figure 3.5). The claims made about the different aspects of society discussed by Giddens in these books are arrived at by his drawing on a variety (more or less) of illustrative examples, abstracting them from the specificities of their particular contexts – buffeted as these are by the contingencies and irregularities of open systems – and then imaginatively generalising them to other times and other places beyond the illustrative examples.

Turning to another set of texts. To the extent that they go beyond the level of ontology to more substantive claims, Chapters 1–3 of *The Constitution of Society* (1984), *Modernity and Self-identity* (1991) and *The Transformation of Intimacy* (1992), are all written primarily using illustrations viewed from the methodological perspective of agent's conduct analysis at the floater level of theory construction. In a parallel move to the one used in the works above, these illustrations are then used as bases from which to make speculative generalisations about the internal hermeneutics of huge numbers of social agents whose lives are lived far beyond the time–space locale of the illustrative example. As before, the floater illustrations are used as the basis for dreamer generalisations. Thus, *Modernity and Self-Identity* concentrates upon the way in which actors draw upon their structural context in their social relations. It places in suspension institutions as socially reproduced and concentrates upon how actors reflexively monitor what they do. Guided by the stratification model of the agent, and by way of theoretical hypothesis and illustrative examples, it shows an interest in the supposed actuality of agents' knowledgeability, develops a sophisticated account of generalised motivation, and includes a central role for the way in which modern individuals cope with the web of power relations in which they are enmeshed.

The dreamer model, as *Modernity and Self-Identity* shows, is able to take on board an agent's conduct approach. However, what it does not do is focus its analysis in a concentrated way upon the 'contextually situated activities of definite groups of actors', for the book's focus is provided by the archetypal dreamer concerns of abstraction and generalisation. The hermeneutic respect shown to agents here is derived from a combination of random illustrative example and metatheory, abstracted from context and then generalised to other agents on the basis of a hypothetical dream. The emphasis is on similarity rather than difference, and, to avoid the charge of despotism, such hypothesised generalisations must acknowledge themselves as, indeed, hypothetical and generalised beyond the evidence, as well as partial in intent.

In summary, it seems that Giddens has stuck pretty much to a fairly restricted range of research types. This is of no small import, for if one only travels along limited types of thoroughfare, say along motorways or expressways, there will most likely seem little need to develop the skills of sign or map reading into realms beyond those required for finding one's way along these familiar avenues. The problems of finding your way along unknown and differently marked (or unmarked) territory will not be yours. Not for you the need to be able to locate new routes for destinations not served by the major roads, to distinguish the appropriate route for your journey from the other tracks, routes, roads and byways. Acquaintance with the wider world of maps, the world beyond the thick blue lines you usually look for, with their manifold legends, abbreviations, boundaries, roads, paths, rights of way and orienting grid references, becomes necessary only as one strays beyond the known onto unfamiliar thoroughfares. The more varied the types of road and path, the greater the need for map-reading skills – for generalised knowledge to bear on the peculiarities of the local. The more varied the journeys one takes, the more need there will be for that generalised knowledge.

Likewise, with a myriad of different research destinations to choose from, a thousand and one possible questions to ask, calling for more or less contextualisation, more or less knowledge of actors' hermeneutics, more or less contiguity, more or less abstraction and generalisation, the greater the need will be to have been trained in the skills of method-ological orienteering, to be able to select the appropriate methodolog-ical route for the task at hand with the aid of the whole range of symbols, abbreviations, models and player grid references. Giddens' repetition of dreamer studies employing the institutional analysis of routines and agent's conduct analysis means that he need be acquainted with only a limited range of orienteering skills. He has not had need for the others and so, I suggest – with appropriate theoretical humility, of course – he has not understood the need for them. Figures 4.3 and 4.4 present elaborated versions of the player and dreamer grids, which – while by no means exhaustive – will allow us to see more clearly the relatively narrow focus of Giddens' work as compared with an expanded range of research possibilities.

Expanded Horizons Fit for a Rich and Complex Ontology

Figures 4.3 and 4.4 are in a sense purposefully dizzying in order to make the point, whereas the fact that they are by no means exhaustive marks a textual strategy whose aim is not to lose every reader at this stage. In thinking about particular research projects, the dizzying effect is much less than a first glance at the figures might suggest. For, with a project in mind, one is much more focused, not attempting to take in everything but, on the contrary, trying to limit one's focus in a system-atic, logical and methodologically consequential manner. Maps, too, are dizzying if one tries to take in everything, but less so as one homes in on a particular route.

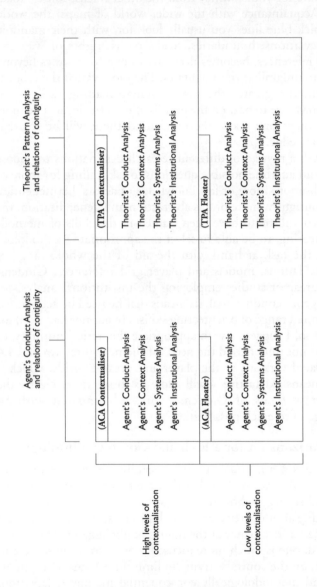

Figure 4.3 Elaborated version of player grid, including a wider range of methodological bracketing

Agent's Conduct Analysis and relations of contiguity

Theorist's Pattern Analysis and relations of contiguity

High levels of contextualisation

Low levels of contextualisation

(ACA Contextualiser)

Agent's Conduct Analysis
Agent's Context Analysis
Agent's Systems Analysis
Agent's Institutional Analysis

(TPA Contextualiser)

Theorist's Conduct Analysis
Theorist's Context Analysis
Theorist's Systems Analysis
Theorist's Institutional Analysis

(ACA Floater)

Agent's Conduct Analysis
Agent's Context Analysis
Agent's Systems Analysis
Agent's Institutional Analysis

(TPA Floater)

Theorist's Conduct Analysis
Theorist's Context Analysis
Theorist's Systems Analysis
Theorist's Institutional Analysis

The agent's conduct analysis side of the player grid includes both agent's conduct analysis and agent's context analysis, as one would expect. However, I have also included systems analysis and institutional analysis, and, given that Giddens' and Cohen's definitions of these brackets explicitly exclude agent's conduct analysis, my inclusion of them requires some explanation. My reasoning relates directly to the theme of the restricted nature of Giddens' research interests, and is simply that there is no need always to restrict the study of system connections or institutional practices to the perspective of an external theorist. If connections between practices within a system are produced in actuality by more or less knowledgeable agents, why not study the way the agents understand their own role in this process? The same goes for the analysis of the day-to-day, year-to-year, decade-to-decade practices within institutions. While it is evident that Giddens and Cohen have their own reasons for focusing on systems and institutions from the perspective of a theorist's pattern analysis, other researchers could well have their own reasons for looking at the production of the same sorts of practices from the perspective of an agent's conduct analysis.

On the theorist's pattern analysis side of the player grid, one has the expected brackets of systems analysis and institutional analysis, and also the rather counterintuitive brackets of theorist's conduct analysis and theorist's context analysis. The reason for the inclusion of these two categories is quite simply that social scientists do in fact very often make claims about the conduct and context analysis of social actors, either individuals or groups, even though they present no evidence of having undertaken any sort of agent's conduct analysis. The theorist decides for herself that a certain actor must have been thinking this or that, must have known this, been motivated by that, intended the other. Characterising labels are often attributed to individual agents, or to supposedly like-thinking cabals (aggregate groups), in order to fix the theorist's interpretation more firmly and to camouflage the lack of appropriate evidence. The dissembling associated with these strategies is not to be encouraged, but one can easily think of occasions – especially when evidence for an agent's conduct analysis is hard to come by – when one could see the heuristic value of using these brackets in a hypothetical and suggestive way, with appropriately acknowledged humility and provisionality.

Similar chains of reasoning have informed the methodological brackets laid out in the dreamer grid. The differences are that the methodological bracketing of focus will here be apparent, first, in relation to a question that is generalising in its scope and, second, in

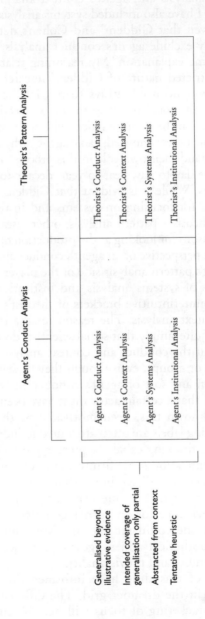

Figure 4.4 Elaborated version of dreamer grid, including methodological bracketings of focus

the bracketing of the illustrative examples that, necessarily, will be addressed at the player level (with more or less contextualisation and hermeneutic appreciation).

The range of possible research perspectives can be expanded also in another direction. Whereas both Giddens and Cohen designed their brackets of institutional analysis and systems analysis to be used specifically to look at practices and interactions that conform to institutionalised *routines,* they could clearly be used just as well as a means of identifying the contingent outcomes of interactions that depart from institutionalised routines. Thus, for example, the TPA Floater box from the player grid could be redrawn as in Figure 4.5.

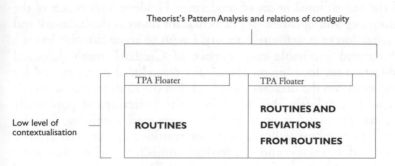

Figure 4.5 Focus on 'Routines' or on 'Routines and Deviations from Routines': illustrated in relation to the TPA Floater box

Imagine, for example, a weekly routine of a business person, working for a transnational company, which involves certain interactions and articulations in time and space: the business person disembarking from a train at Liverpool Street station, London, jumping into a taxi to take her to Heathrow and then catching a flight to Rome from Gate 7, Terminal 2. If this routine were suddenly broken because the taxi was involved in a crash on the way to the airport, or a bomb alert at Heathrow meant that the flight was diverted to leave from Gatwick, or a strike by Italian airport workers meant that the flight was cancelled at the last minute, the intrepid sociologist wanting to view the ordering of interactions in time and space would still have to play substantially the same game. The one difference would not be a change in the bracket that focuses the analysis but in the contingent departure from routine brought about by the articulation of the usual time–space routines and interactions of our traveller with other social processes beyond her control: another motorist's reckless driving; the strategic actions of a terrorist movement; or the industrial action of an Italian trade union. Whether one traces out the various parts of this time–space patterning of interactions from the standpoint of agent's conduct analysis or from a theorist pattern position will depend upon the specific question being asked and the practical difficulties of unearthing the relevant hermeneutic information.

Limited Horizons Shutting out Contingency and Openness

All these nuances of methodological focus can be used to shed light on another aspect of Giddens' project, which has received a good deal of critical comment. It is said that in his writings on historical sociology and the institutional nexus of modernity, Giddens loses much of the contingency and openness of praxis that for many is the hallmark and the attraction of structuration theory. I want to argue that this loss is a striking and inevitable consequence of Giddens' methodological predilection for focusing on chronically reproduced routines, and for doing so within the dreamer model, so that the routines are automatically and completely abstracted from the buffetings of potentially disruptive forces in open systems. As we have seen, within the dreamer model, these chronically reproduced routines are derived from a mixture of ontology and theoretical conjecture, with illustrative examples that seem to fit and to confirm. They are then generalised way beyond the fitting, confirming, illustrative example. There is not much room for contingency and openness here.

In addition, one other factor serves to deepen the trough of inevitability that Giddens ploughs. This is his predilection for using TPA Floater examples as illustrations for his dreamer theories of chronically reproduced practices. This means that not only have the cards been stacked against contingency and openness by the prior choice of chronically reproduced practices, but now the absence of ACA also means that there is no way we are able to get any sense of any agents who might want to change things – break the routines – but who feel that the constraints are too great. Thus, one is not only given chronically reproduced practices, but also a lack of differentiation between chronic routines which are reproduced owing to normative commitment and those that are reproduced due to pragmatic acquiescence, instrumental compliance or listless apathy (cf Held, 1984, pp. 301–2).

Such distinctions, resting as they do upon characterising the reactions of agents to their structural contexts, are the very lifeblood of structuration theory, of the duality of structure and agency. They are distinctions to which Giddens adheres at the ontological level but is unable to sustain as he follows this methodological strategy. Giddens' methodological approach makes it inevitable that he will treat his object of study as an already '*unfolded* causal process' rather than take up the perspective of someone looking at events 'as if' they were only just unfolding – treating the object of study as an '*unfolding* causal process'. His mode of analysis ensures that the chronic routines being studied are abstracted from two of the forces with the most power to disrupt the inference of inevitability joining the unfolding to the chronically reproduced unfolded – namely, open systems and agency choice.

These points can be expanded if we lay out four statements about contingency that structuration theory would endorse and then note their relationship to Giddens' writings on historical sociology and modernity:

1 Society did not have to turn out like this; there is nothing preordained about the historical development of societies.

2 As agents can always potentially 'choose to do otherwise', social routines or trends of societal development are always susceptible to the contingent, potentially deviant, choices of agents.

3 Social practices and their consequences at any one point in time are the product of open systems, in which many different social processes come together to create the final result. The particular form that is taken by interaction of these different processes is a highly specific and contextualised affair.

4 In many specific situations, agents do in fact 'choose to do otherwise', to deviate from 'chronically reproduced routines'. The sources of this openness are multiple and highly textured but they include instances in which agents have reflexively learnt from past mistakes or have acquired new information (for example from reading a book on divorce or self-therapy), which allows them to make a more informed, considered and perhaps more self-confident judgement.

The first two senses of contingency are maintained by Giddens in the studies using institutional analysis at the dreamer level. The first sense is a metatheoretical article of faith of the kind that lies at the core of structuration theory; it is part of what Cohen has referred to as the 'metaphysical core' of a theory (Cohen, 1986, pp. 123–4). It is thus unimpeachable, and it functions in Giddens' works of historical sociology as a reminder of the structurationist ontology and its insistence that nothing in social life is predetermined and inevitable. The second sense of contingency has a presence in these works only as a neglected opportunity because the definitional focus of institutional analysis, as directed towards chronically reproduced practices, rules out of court any attention to contingent deviations from those practices. The focus is on routines, rather than on deviation from routines. In this sense, the emphasis on ontological contingency is academic, because the analyst is only looking at cases in which the agent is 'choosing to do the same again' with monotonous regularity. As mentioned above, Giddens' use of institutional analysis (TPA, routine) renders the core ontological notion of the duality of structure and agency redundant for empirical purposes. If the absence of 'internal' hermeneutics means that we do not know how an agent draws on her structural context we will not know about her knowledgeability or intentions. It follows that we will not know which conditions of action are acknowledged and which are unacknowledged, which are intended and which unintended. All we have are conditions, behaviours and consequences that are identified from afar by the external theorist rather than by the lay agents involved.

By way of contrast, the third and fourth senses of contingency are absent from Giddens' dreamer works of institutional analysis. This is because these specifications of contingency are highly specific and contextualised; they refer to aspects of social reality that player theories are designed to address. The sources of the fourth sense of contingency would have not only to be investigated in the terms of the player model, but also to be informed by agent's conduct analysis within this model. The third sense, however, could be looked at from either a theorist pattern or a hermeneutically informed (agent's conduct) perspective. In relation to Giddens' large-scale works of institutional analysis, the important thing about the third and fourth meanings of contingency is that they do not make an appearance there. They are defined out of court by a combination of, on the one hand, a form of methodological bracketing that excludes both hermeneutics and departures from routines, and on the other hand, by his use of the dreamer model of theory building in a way that does not allow for the specificity and contextualisation that the analysis of these forms of contingency requires. To put this another way, institutional analysis in the dreamer model is geared to the generalisation of routinely reproduced practices inferred from theoretical reflection and/or from illustrative examples uninformed by agent's conduct analysis and without a high degree of specificity and contextualisation. The focus is on already unfolded routines chronically reproduced by agents who, from this vantage point, are totally predictable and one-dimensional. All this is a long way from the openness and contingency of unfolding processes in specific times and places mediated by reflexive, knowledgeable and motivated agents in conditions that are more or less acknowledged and more or less exposed to a number of intervening influences.

It is now very clear why it has been possible for Giddens' work to receive criticism for two seemingly opposed and contradictory excesses. On the one hand, structuration theory has been criticised for presenting a notion of agents and praxis that is far too open ended. In this view, it is said that one receives an image of people getting up in the morning and eating a hearty breakfast before going off to remake the world. All is creativity, possibility and contingency. On the other hand, Giddens' sociology of the *longue durée* has been criticised for not being open enough, for seeming inevitable and evolutionary despite protestations to the contrary. Craib comments that despite all the talk about the openness of praxis, the ability of agents to do otherwise, and the contingency of social life, all these aspects seem to disappear when Giddens actually begins to talk about phenomena belonging to the large scale and the long term. His actors now seem to be very boring people with very little thought of reshaping the world. Modernity, for example, appears to them as a juggernaut beyond their control (cf Craib, 1992a, p. 105–6, 179–80). The identification of Giddens' work on historical sociology as the product of a particular type of dreamer hypothesis, focused according to the methodological brackets of theorist's institutional analysis, explains quite precisely why social systems appear there as chronically reproduced and rather abstract juggernauts with very little room for contingency.

Limited Horizons Unaware of their Limitations: The Indeterminacy of Counterfactuals Formulated at Altitude

It will be useful at this point to bring back in a theme introduced earlier in the chapter, that is, the notion of a benchmark of a highly contextualised ACA of a situation. Such a notion can be used to shed much light upon the contingency of agency and open systems. It imposes an awareness of the heaviness (in Kundera's terms) of counterfactual questions, awareness of the detail relevant not only to the kind of questions that ask what would have happened if event X had not happened, but, also to those that ask whether it is realistic to suppose that X could possibly not have happened; what would have had to be different for this to be so? Could event Y have happened instead? What would have had to change for event Y to have happened? Is it realistic to suppose that these things could have changed? (cf Hawthorn, 1991, especially pp. 1–37, 157–87). Among the things that would have to change in virtually all counterfactuals concerning social relations are the ACA of strategic actors – whether these be micro-actors or those actors with the power to affect social relations over large tracts of time–space whom Nicos Mouzelis has usefully termed mega-actors (Mouzelis, 1991, p. 107).

It is with these points in mind, as salutary benchmarks, that I want to close this chapter by staying with Giddens' historical sociology – with the big sweep – in order, once more, to highlight the dangers of underestimating the complexity of the epistemological and methodological process. To this end, I want simply to note that here Giddens does, in fact, make the sorts of despotic claims about contingency that he has no means of substantiating at the theoretical and methodological level at which his analysis is pitched.

Both the instances I will refer to are cited by David Jary in a clear and insightful article whose title neatly evokes – lest we forget – the vastness of scale of Giddens' project in the realm of historical sociology, ' "Society as Time-traveller": Giddens on Historical Change, Historical Materialism and the Nation-state in World Society' (Jary, 1991, pp. 116–59). First, Jary notes Giddens' insistence that the development of capitalism and the nation-state respectively must be seen as interdependent phenomena, neither being the determining factor. Moreover, their mutual developments, together with the distinctively European site of their initial trajectories, were historically contingent. Contingency lay, not least, in the condition of a geopolitical context, in which, for the first time, Europe was no longer threatened militarily from the east, and in which it had attained worldwide naval supremacy (Jary, 1991, p. 130). Jary writes:

> That there was much that was not inevitable or 'evolutionary' about these developments, Giddens declares, is confirmed by noting how very different history might have been, for example, had Charlemagne succeeded in his goal of a new European empire or if the European powers had suffered lasting defeat at the hands of the Ottoman Turks in the seventeenth century (Jary, 1991, p. 130; cf Giddens, 1981, pp. 183–84).

The claim is informed, of course, by the first two, sensitising, notions of contingency (see above), but the reader is given no sense that a truly adequate, rather than gestural, demonstration that history could have been very different would require much more contextualisation of events and system interconnections than are available to Giddens from the dizzy heights of a Theorist's Pattern Floater analysis.

The same is true of the second example of counterfactual conjecture cited by Jary, in which Giddens, bringing things into the twentieth century, suggests that there was nothing inevitable about: the industrialisation of warfare; the triumph of sentiments of nationalism over internationalism; and the hegemony of the concept of the 'independent unity of each state' as against the 'older type of imperial system' and the more recent forms of European colonialism (Jary, 1991, p. 137). Giddens insists, for example, that:

> If the course of events in the Great War, including the participation of the USA in the hostilities and the peace settlement, had not taken the shape they did, the nation-state in its current form might not have become the dominant political entity in the world system (Giddens, 1985, pp. 234–5; cited in Jary, 1991, p. 137).

Again, there would be nothing objectionable about these claims from the perspective of a dreamer analysis based on TPA floater examples and staying loyal to the ontological precepts of the first and second notions of contingency. A convincing demonstration, however, would, at the very least, have to include an analysis of the third and fourth notions of contingency.

A Heightened Reflexivity Versus Defeatist Postmodernism

Bauman has argued that it is in Giddens' conceptual innovations in relation to the large-scale, long-term processes of society that his real importance lies. He judges Giddens' contributions in these areas to 'be among the most seminal developments in contemporary sociology' (Bauman, 1989b, p. 54). Bauman's admiration for Giddens' 'profound analysis' (Bauman, 1989b, p. 43) of modern society, its history and its tendencies so far way surpasses his view of Giddens the metatheorist. Bauman argues that sociology in general still has far too little to say about the crucial experience of our time; it has failed to come to grips with what is truly novel in the society of today. Its lack of self-confidence has led it to a self-justifying preoccupation with method and metatheory at the expense of a theory of contemporary society. This, says Bauman, is a great mistake, for sociology will stand or fall on its theory of contemporary society, rather than on its contemporary theory of sociology. He believes that Giddens the metatheorist's call for *New Rules of Sociological Method* is emblematic of sociology's misguided navel-gazing. There is no royal road out of the present crisis through

the devising and adoption of correct methods that can establish the
credentials of sociological activity:

> rules of method are an internal affair of sociology, part of its power
> rhetoric and of a pep talk turned upon itself; above all, this rhetoric is a
> manifestation of a crisis of confidence caused by uncertainty regarding the
> substance of the sociological project. 'Rules of method' tell us little about
> the subject-matter of sociology; moreover, in no way do they contain a
> guarantee that sociology would have something valid and relevant to say
> on this subject... to claim the right to speak with authority sociology
> would have to update its theory of society rather than its idea of social
> action. Let us concentrate on this central task (Bauman, 1989b, pp. 43–4).

Bauman is undoubtedly right to insist that a concern with
metatheory and 'scientificity' will not in itself lead to many insights
about the nature of contemporary society. He is also right to note the
crisis of sociological confidence and the need for a theory of contemporary society. However, as follows from what I have said so far, I think
that he overstates his case in a way that is damaging to the very
enterprise of creating convincing theories of contemporary society.
Bauman's argument has the effect of reinforcing a division, a duality,
between theories of society and sociological theory, which need not
and should not exist. I agree that this division has historically existed in
the way he portrays it, and that this division has been to the detriment
of theories of society, but I do not find convincing the implication that
somehow the creation of theories of society is incompatible with
metatheoretical and methodological concerns. In this respect, Bauman
either misperceives or overstates the contrast between Giddens as
theorist of society and Giddens the metatheorist, for Giddens as
dreamer, as the conceptual innovator in relation to the big questions of
modernity, its origins and the developments of world history, relies
very closely for his inspiration on the structurationist ontology that
formed the substance of *New Rules of Sociological Method*.

In my opinion, the rules for dreamer theory need *more* attention
paid to them, need to be developed more not less – we need, not least,
to know when we are dreaming and when we are playing. We also need
to know much more about how we are playing when we are playing.
The implied decoupling of theories of society from metatheoretical
and methodological concerns contained in Bauman's argument – or at
best the benign neglect of metatheoretical and methodological
concerns – would leave sociological theories of society wide open to a
gamut of postmodernist accusations: the privileging of the social
theorist in opposition to ordinary social players in the construction of

theory; the authoritarianism implicit in this; the scepticism about the validity of any particular theory of society; and the charge that there is little, if any, difference between theory and fiction except the former's claim to be true. I have tried to indicate already that the charge of authoritarianism or despotism levelled by postmodernists at the large-scale pretensions of the social sciences can be initially mitigated by a reflexive and open acknowledgement of the provisional and hypothetical nature of a dreamer theory of society or aspects of society.

The player and dreamer elements discussed in this chapter, including ontology, epistemological guidelines, theoretical categories and methodological brackets, are all involved in the construction of knowledge. Careful attention to them can provide a systematic means of focusing on specific aspects of the social. More than this, however, the development of detailed and explicit guidelines gears us to the extensive powers of a heightened reflexivity. They enable us to focus, with a much keener eye, precisely upon how we focus, so that we can have more awareness of what we see, what we do not see, and why.

Note

1 The major role that Giddens' ontology plays in the present book should make it clear that I do not agree at all with Gregson's argument that structuration theory is irrelevant to empirical research.

Chapter 5

Contextualising, Floating and Dreaming: Variations from the Sociologies of Politics, Culture and Ethics

An important precept of the past-modern sociology I am advocating is that 'anything goes but not any old how'. This is in contrast to the defeatist postmodernist position, which I take to be 'anything goes and just any old how'. To concentrate on the first half of the precept, for the moment, my attachment to it represents a desire – to milk the metaphors – to let a hundred flowers bloom, to let anything at all in to a sociological explanation or analysis that might help, might give us new angles, new perceptions, better knowledge and so on. The world is a rich and diverse place, and this should be respected by an appropriately rich and diverse epistemological outlook. In this respect, I am in agreement with the way in which Craib has interpreted and invoked the 'anarchist theory of knowledge' proposed by Paul Feyerabend in the mid-1970s. The central message that Craib puts across in this discussion is that too narrow and rigid an attachment to a particular perspective can blind you to things that are, so to speak, in front of your eyes:

> The history of X-rays, for example, shows how evidence need not be seen or can be discounted when it does not easily fit the prevailing theory... Feyerabend points out the necessity for science to resort, at times, to the irrational, to 'unreason', whether this be rhetoric or perhaps apparently crazy ideas. In *The Sociological Imagination*, C. Wright Mills suggests, as part of the research, throwing one's notes in the air and seeing if you can make any sense of the way they come down. Unthought-of connections, relationships or ideas can emerge in this way (Craib, 1992, p. 118).

This is not, however to neglect the role of epistemological and methodological guidelines, and debate about these guidelines, to aid the best translation possible of whatever ontology one chooses into the stuff of the real world conjuncture. There is a distinction to be made here between the improvisation possible as part of the *production of knowledge* – whether informed by the idiosyncrasies of personal or subgroup experience or by crazy creative ideas – and the necessarily more structured (although not unchanging or unchallengeable) sphere of the *assessment of knowledge*, the validation of knowledge.[1]

It is here that I part company with the defeatist postmodernists. Hence, the chastening 'not just any old how' pinned like a tail to the lively puppy of the 'anything goes'. Both ends of the homily are necessary. This is especially so given that, under the cover of 'just any old how', defeatist postmodernists are inclined to smuggle in an overly puritanical attitude to 'anything goes'. They tend to impose unnecessary restrictions on the range of possible research strategies. For example, postmodernists, as we have seen, have been against grand narratives. From an ontological perspective that pays due respect to the local, to differences and so on, one can understand and strongly support this critique. However, when this prevents any discussion at all of the bigger questions – the broad sweeps, the sense of generalised tendencies, a feeling for the *longue durée*, a further sighted perspective on systemic conditions of existence – the liberating qualities of the critique can turn into shackles. The categories of floater and dreamer construed within the reflexive frame of a realism beyond modernism are meant as devices that can unlock the shackles of – while retaining the integrity of and the respect for – the liberating ontology. In this chapter, I want quite simply to begin to show the many variations and cross-fertilisations that are possible for a sociology whose practitioners do not just dismiss studies that do not do their favourite thing of the moment but, rather, can be reflexive about what a particular study at hand is doing and appreciate it for what it is (not necessarily what it purports to be) – no more and no less.

Political Sociology: Placing Zygmunt Bauman's *Modernity and the Holocaust*

Five Conditions for the Holocaust: Part Dreamer, Part Floater

Zygmunt Bauman, in *Modernity and the Holocaust*, names five factors that 'had to come together to produce the Holocaust':

1 A radical antisemitism of the Nazi type, which Bauman characterises as definitively 'modern': racist and exterminatory, in the sense that prejudicial sentiments are combined with rationalising, social engineering, strategies best captured by the metaphors of architecture, gardening (weeding) and medicine (surgery). These strategies

are put in 'the service of the construction of an artificial social order, through cutting out the elements of the present reality that neither fit the visualised perfect reality, nor can be changed so that they do' (Bauman, 1989, p. 65).

2 The transformation of this radical antisemitism into the practical policy of a *powerful centralised* state.

3 That state being in command of a huge efficient bureaucratic apparatus.

4 An extraordinary wartime situation – a 'state of emergency' – which allowed the government and the bureaucracy it controlled 'to get away with things which could, possibly, face more serious obstacles in time of peace'.

5 The noninterference, the passive acceptance of those things by the population at large (Bauman, 1989, p. 94).

Bauman argues that conditions 1 and 4 can be seen as non-necessary attributes of a modern society, of modernity. The other three conditions, however, are 'fully normal. They are constantly present in every modern society' (Bauman, 1989, p. 95). The Holocaust brought together some ordinary factors of modernity that are usually kept apart. It is only the combination of factors that is unusual and rare, 'not the factors that are combined' (Bauman, 1989, p. 94). Bauman takes to task those interpreters of the Holocaust who consider it to be a product of deep and dark uncivilised forces, of a resurgence of a premodern barbarism not yet tamed, not yet brought under the sway of reason, science and civilisation. On the contrary, he says, the Holocaust was the product of bureaucracy and science, of an instrumental reasoning that instituted systems with a meticulous functional division of labour; a correlative distancing – spatially, perceptually and psychologically – of one single functional task from the consequences of that task; a substitution of immediate employment and technical responsibility for moral responsibility (I'm doing my small task well: managing a regular steel supply in a bomb factory, producing napalm in a chemical factory); and a rationalised language that dehumanised the objects of bureaucratic operations (Bauman, 1989b, pp. 12–18, and 96–104).

The concern with inherent potential tendencies is, at root, a realist one, and Bauman's five conditions of existence are, in Bhaskar's terms, five differentiated power mechanisms whose interactions with one another are said to produce the Holocaust. Bauman himself uses a strikingly realist metaphor to invoke the hidden potential normally lying dormant within these real structures of modernity. He writes: 'Separately each factor is common and normal. And the knowledge of saltpetre, sulphur or charcoal is not complete unless one knows and remembers that, if mixed, they turn into gunpowder' (Bauman, 1989b, p. 94).

Bauman's Partial Take on the Fifth Condition: How Much Does He Tell Us about the Passivity of German Citizens in the Face of Evil?

Bauman's analysis is part dreamer, part floater, directed here towards the analysis of systems. It is produced through a combination of sociological theories of modernity and specific historical studies of the Holocaust. On the one hand, it is an extrapolation to the time and the place of Nazi Germany of generalised and abstracted theoretical insights about the workings of modern societies. On the other, it is a use of the Holocaust to illustrate the generalised dangers of modernity. Conditions 1 and 4 are floater observations about Nazi Germany; conditions 2, 3 and 5 are dreamer theory observations about modernity in general, which are judged to fit the Nazi case.

From the latter three let us take, as an example, the fifth condition: the noninterference, the passive acceptance of all the stages and paraphernalia of Nazi genocide by the population at large. Such passivity is portrayed by Bauman as a normal aspect of modern societies. In the final chapter of the book, he provides what is, in effect, a generalised dreamer analysis of those social mechanisms of modernity that 'silence or neutralise moral inhibitions and, more generally, make people refrain from resistance against evil' (Bauman, 1989b, p. 95, cf pp. 169–200).

This analysis generalises about agent's conduct analysis and agent's context analysis in a way that abstracts the individuals from their very specific, local, contextual milieux. The illustrations used emphasise the similarity of response, the uniform passivity, of agents. Even if the quality of motives differ – with more or less normative commitment – the passivity and complicity is the same. Thus, for example, Bauman quotes Christopher Browning's investigation of the four officials manning the notorious Jewish Desk (D III) within the German Foreign Ministry, noting the importance of loyalty to the organisation, the moral responsibility only to one's fellow workers or immediate employer who fall within one's circle of proximity. Even where the job is perhaps disapproved of, secretly abhorred, it still tends to get done, and done well under the aegis of such injunctions. Two of the four officials were satisfied with their jobs while the two others preferred transfer to other tasks:

Both were successful in eventually getting out of D III, but while they were there they performed their duties meticulously. They did not openly object to the job but worked covertly and quietly for their transfer; keeping their records clean was their top priority. Whether zealously or reluctantly, the fact remains that all four worked efficiently... They kept the machine moving, and the most ambitious and unscrupulous among them gave it an additional push (Browning, 1980, p. 190, cited in Bauman, 1989b, p. 196).

This emphasis on uniformity, on the similarities in outcome that exist, on the elements of specific practices that have similarities with each other, seems to me to be perfectly legitimate and illuminating. There is a place for this kind of big theory as long as, among other things, its generalising claims are not read as exhausting all instances, either in breadth of number or in complexity of each instance. On the other hand, the need to be aware of the limitations of dreamer theory places a premium upon a highly tuned reflexivity towards the structure of one's analysis and knowledge claims. Reflexivity would, for example, bring to the fore the limitations involved in stressing similarities at the expense of contextual differences of content and outcome.

When Bauman uses a dreamer theory of modernity to discuss the passivity of the German population in the face of genocide, he subsumes the specificities of the German case. There are many significant aspects of the German case towards which he does not turn his lens. We can see this if we look at, for example, Robert Gellately's *The Gestapo and German Society* (1990) which is an account of the enforcement of racial policy with particular reference to Lower Franconia, Bavaria, between 1933 and 1945. Gellately tells us about those who did resist and the conditions under which they did this, and he also gives us details, likewise missing from Bauman's account, of the particular ways in which the state/police interacted with, and infiltrated, civil society to provide a network of informers who were able to pass on information about noncompliance with Nazi racial policy in even the most private spheres of social, family and sexual life. These networks:

eliminated the 'more or less protected enclaves' required for people to gather, mobilise, and give expression to disobedience. In spite of the odds, however, some refused to comply with Nazi teaching on race, kept up contacts, and offered help even when it became life-threatening to do so. False accusations, including the exploitation of the situation for private purposes, helped to build barriers between the Jews and everyone else in the country (Gellately, 1990, p. 184; cf Chapters 5 and 6, pp. 129–84).

The Lightness of Unfolded Routines versus the Heaviness of Being There

If three of Bauman's five conditions are construed at the dreamer level of modernity, the idea of the five different conditions coming together to produce the Holocaust is then pitched, at best, at a level that is itself a combination of floater and dreamer. We are, therefore, given no detail about how they came together (how could we be?), what specific forms they took in coming together, whether they did in fact come together at one or more specific moments, or whether this is too simplistic a rendering of what Bauman has in mind. Neither are we told whether these are necessary and sufficient conditions for the Holocaust to happen, or are just five out of many conditions that were needed to produce it. The level of detail we are given is very low and is not harnessed to attempts to trace through any relations of contiguity in their historical specificity. The focus on the bureaucratic system is not a historically specific one; it is an ideal type, dreamer focus. It is also directed very definitely towards routines and not towards deviations from routines. Where the sense of a definite time and place are in fact introduced into the discussion of bureaucracy, the reference points are given fleetingly and without context, and this is combined with a theoretically driven sense of inevitability and inexorability about its workings:

> Hilberg has suggested that the moment the first German official had written the first rule of Jewish exclusion, the fate of the European Jews was sealed. There is a most profound and terrifying truth in this comment. What bureaucracy needed was the definition of its task. Rational and efficient as it was, it could be trusted to see the task to its end (Bauman, 1989b, p. 106).

The unfolded process is looked upon as an unfolded process. While there is, with little doubt, something of the ethic of the myth of eternal return in Bauman's own *motivation* to pursue this subject (cf Bauman, 1989b, pp. vii–xiv, 1–6) – he wishes us to see the dangers inherent in modernity, to see the possibility and to fear the return of that weight – his actual analysis gives us little real sense of that weight, of an unfolding reality, such as is given, for example, in Primo Levi's *If This Were A Man*, or Gitta Sereny's *Into That Darkness*, an exhausting biography of Franz Stangl, the Commandant of Treblinka, or in Christopher Browning's *Ordinary Men*, a harrowing 'thick description' of the role played by Reserve Police Battalion 101 in the Final Solution in Poland (Levi, 1987; Sereny, 1974; Browning, 1992). In these testaments, we have, in addition to the experiential heaviness of the hermeneutic dimension, the sense also of contingency embedded within both this and other dimensions. The latter takes in, not least, the contingency of *the system* and its functions, extending the boundaries of Bauman's very specific perspective. Browning gives us glimpses beyond the unstoppable machine, smooth and perfectly integrated in its mechanistic functionality. He cites in full a report from mid-September 1942, written by an Order Police captain of Reserve Battalion 133 in Police Regiment 24, relating the experiences of one week of operations guarding the deportation trains to the east. In his commentary on the account, Browning notes a combination of factors that direct us more to the chaos and confusion of the events than to any preconceptions about the smooth and immutable self-reproduction of bureaucratic routines:

> This document demonstrates many things: the desperate attempts of the deported Jews to escape the death train; the scanty manpower employed by the Germans (a mere 10 men to guard over 8,000 Jews); the unimaginably terrible conditions – forced marches over many miles, terrible heat, days without food and water, the packing of 200 Jews into each train car, etc. – that led to fully 25 percent of the deported Jews dying on the train from suffocation, heat prostration, and exhaustion (to say nothing of those killed in the shooting, which was so constant that the guards expended their entire ammunition supply as well as replenishment) (Browning, 1992, p. 36).

A short extract from the shockingly impersonal (bureaucratic, dehumanised) report itself – written by the captain after the completion of the journey – compounds the sense of muddle and improvisation that accompanied the barbarity of the operation:

> Given the already described strains on the Jews, the negative effects of the heat, and the great overloading of most of the cars, the Jews attempted time and again to break out of the parked train cars, as darkness had already set in toward 7.30 p.m... Breakout attempts from the parked train could not be prevented in the darkness, nor could the escaping Jews be shot in flight. In all train cars the Jews had completely undressed because of the heat... Throughout the entire trip the policemen had to remain in the cabooses, in order to be able to counter the escape attempts of the Jews. Shortly into the journey the Jews attempted to break through the sides and even through the ceilings of certain train cars. They were partially successful in perpetrating this scheme, so that already five stations before Stanislawow, Corporal J. had to ask the stationmaster in Stanislawow by telephone to lay out nails and boards in order to seal the

damaged cars as required by orders and to request the station guard to watch the train... The work took one and one-half hours. When the train subsequently resumed its journey, it was discovered at the next stop some stations later that once again large holes had been broken by the Jews in some of the train cars and that for the most part the barbed wire fastened on the outside of the ventilation windows had been torn off. In one train the Jews had even been working with hammer and saw... (cited in Browning, 1992, pp. 33–4).

The weight of an unfolding process is intimately related to the sense of being there, of the sense of being in the situated context of the agents involved. Part of this involves an appreciation of motivation, whether it be the impulse to control or the desperation to be free. Part involves – starkly so in this situation, wherein by 1942 deportations no longer entailed an unknown fate for many of the victims (Browning, 1992, p. 31) – some sort of understanding of the immediate social context. Closely related to this is an agent's context analysis of alternatives, possibilities and constraints, the stubborn sense that things might be different filtered through one's knowledgeability of immediate circumstances. We have seen that, as is likewise the case for Giddens in his historical sociology, this is not a focus for Bauman in his account of the Holocaust. In this respect, it is also noteworthy that he mentions the intense, prolonged and continuing debate among so-called 'intentionalist' and 'functionalist' historians of the Holocaust, only to dismiss its relevance to his own thesis. This is noteworthy because Bauman is right, and the fact that he is right throws light (as does Browning's research) on the limitations, as well as the strengths, of his theoretical and methodological approach.

How Much do we Know about the Holocaust System?

This intentionalist/functionalist debate revolves around the role of state élites, some of Mouzelis' mega-actors, whose power to alter things, to radically change and disrupt the breadth and depth of routines, can be enormous. As Mouzelis puts it:

individual occupants at the top of bureaucratic and non-bureaucratic hierarchies are mega or macro actors, in the sense that their positions enable them to mobilise considerable resources and that their interactions and decisions can dramatically affect a large number of people. Therefore, *macro* does not always imply a great number of individuals involved in decision-making; it may also refer to decisions by a few or a single powerful actor. This means that macro in terms of the *origin* of strategies or decisions may imply a single person or a few individuals; whereas macro in terms of the *consequences* of implemented strategies or decisions always involves a great number of actors (Mouzelis, 1991, p. 109, original emphasis).

The intentionalist/functionalist debate is about powerful people, and about whether they exerted that power contingently and pragmatically according to changing circumstances, with the Final Solution emerging through improvisation rather than deliberate planning (functionalists), or whether they – Hitler in particular – had a blueprint for extermination that was just waiting for the right time and the right conditions to arrive before it was duly put into action (intentionalists).

There are, by now, many subtle variations on these themes, which highlight many contextualised factors and fragments of documentary evidence about these factors. Sorting through the historical record, trying to fathom the real processes, is of great significance for our view of the specific role of the bureaucracy, about whether we are to perceive it as more or less autonomous from, more or less directed by, Hitler and others in the Nazi government. Should we view the bureaucracy as directive and highly integrated, or as responding to crises in a rather *ad hoc* and reactive manner? For example, the functionalist argument of Hans Mommsen emphasises the chaotic structure of the Nazi regime, with office piled upon office with 'underlings... left to find their way in a bureaucratic and administrative jungle' (Mommsen, 1983; Marrus, 1993, p. 42).

Canadian historian Michael Marrus[2] notes the position of another functionalist, Uwe Adams, who argues against the view that a course was set for European-wide mass murder from a very early point. Rather, one decision led to another in a very piecemeal fashion, with orchestrated genocide emerging as the only perceived way to resolve a hopeless mess. The final decision was not taken, according to Adams, until September or November 1941. He suggests that the Nazis had set in motion deportations from the west and that when the 'territorial' option in Russia was foreclosed by the stalling of operation Barbarossa, the Nazis had to do something with the Jews accumulating in Poland: 'Hitler and his relentless anti-Jewish ideology were the dynamic element, pressing for a solution to the 'Jewish question'; policy evolved, however, in the chaotic institutional environment of the Third Reich, where planlessness and internal contradictions were the norm' (Marrus, 1993, p. 43).

In turn, Adams has been criticised by Browning and others for, among other things, overestimating the degree of disorder and improvisation involved in the ultimate decision to implement the Final

Solution. Browning argues against the view of great masses of Jews accumulating in Poland, as no evidence of concrete preparations for such a massive deportation before the summer of 1941 have ever been discovered. He suggests that Adams's misunderstanding stems from his misinterpretation of Göring's documented authorisation to Heydrich on 31 July 1941 to prepare a 'total solution'. This, on Browning's reading, could not have referred to the expulsions that Adams speaks of because Heydrich already had such authority and had been expelling Jews on a smaller scale since the beginning of 1939. Rather, 'Seen in the context of the furious killings then under way by the Einsatzgruppen (author's note – killing teams of motorised SS troops working alongside the Wehrmacht as they pushed forward into Russia in the summer of 1941; they were responsible for more than two million deaths), Göring's communication appears rather like a warrant for genocide' (Marrus, 1993, p. 44; cf Kershaw, 1989, p. 105). Thus, this argument goes, the decision for the Final Solution seems to have been taken in the early months of 1941, and by the summer at the latest, with more direction from the Nazi élite than Adams allows for and with less of a sense of *force majeure*. Browning still, however, considers himself to be a 'moderate functionalist' and suggests a partially *ad hoc* and reactive, partly co-ordinated narrative of escalation (cf Browning, 1993, pp. 211–26).

Many aspects of the debate are probably irresolvable, as the documentation available in relation to crucial junctures is just not available (cf Kershaw, 1989, pp. 82–106; Marrus, 1993, pp. 40–6; Burrin, 1994, p. 115). The point is that the debate is about the specificities of what really happened. It is about giving weight to these processes, the possible alternatives, the detail of agency, constraint, contingency, intentional order and unintended emergent outcome, that are necessarily implicated in any 'experience-near' assessment of whether or not the whole thing could happen again. Contrast this with the complete absence of contingency, and the deflection from any specifics, in Bauman's assessment of the intentionalist and functionalist split:

> Whatever the ultimate outcome of the debate… there is hardly any doubt that the space extending between the idea and its execution was filled wall-to-wall with bureaucratic action. Neither is there any doubt that however vivid was Hitler's imagination, it would have accomplished little if it had not been taken over, and translated into routine process(es) of problem-solving, by a huge and rational bureaucratic apparatus (Bauman, 1989b, p. 105).

Bauman is not involved in a process of inquiry: he has a thesis to outline. He is looking from afar and with a partial eye towards already unfolded routines that he knows must have been there, even though he does not always look too closely at where and how. The particularities of the unfolding of history in Nazi Germany do not affect Bauman's argument here, because, to repeat, it is essentially a dreamer argument about modernity. Thus, to successfully annihilate more than 20 million people, 6 million Jews among them, required a huge and rational bureaucratic apparatus. The enormity of the figures reflects the difference between an unco-ordinated, heterophobic, impulsive pogrom, and a massive industrial killing operation that co-ordinated and drew together transport, scientific know-how, resources and people across vast geographical areas. Given the most rudimentary – if most essential – facts about the Holocaust, the numbers who were killed, Bauman can apply what he knows about modernity in general to speculate upon the existence, the nature and the necessity of a huge and rational bureaucratic apparatus. His discussion of the nature of bureaucracy can be illustrated with examples from the Vietnam War just as well as from Nazi Germany.

A Perspective on the Real is a Perspective on the Real is a Perspective...

The particularity of Bauman's choice of theoretical and methodological perspective can be thrown further into relief when it is contrasted with another of his own perspectives, adopted in relation to a different subject matter, and (possibly) with a different audience in mind. Bauman presents rather different theoretical and methodological injunctions in *Intimations of Postmodernity* (1992), which were briefly reviewed in Chapter 2. There we have a focus, an emphasis, on randomness rather than inexorability and routine. The heuristic starting point – and we shall kindly assume that this is what it is – is completely different. The totality is viewed here:

> as a kaleidoscopic – momentary and contingent – outcome of interaction…; any pattern that may temporarily emerge out of the random movements of autonomous agents is as haphazard and unmotivated as the one that could emerge in its place or the one bound to replace it, if also for a time only. All order that can be found is a local, emergent and transitory phenomenon (Bauman, 1992, p. 189).

Against the sociological modernist complicity, as Bauman sees it, with modernity's promotion of pattern monotony, predictability and manageability of conduct, he advocates a focus on the habitat in which agency operates and which it actively produces in the course of operating (Bauman, 1992, pp. 190–1). The postmodern Bauman presents a heavier, more unfolding, less routine and orderly, more contextual perspective on theory and its role. One can see that Bauman's theoretical choices are guided by his normative attitudes to the contrasting projects. In looking at the Holocaust, he is seeking to expose the tendencies and dynamics of modernity; in advocating his brand of postmodern theory, he is wanting to guard against the evils of modernity, to accentuate the local, the diverse and the unpredictable through the promotion of a state of mind – of a phylactery perspective. My point is that the choice is a choice, a perspective is a perspective. It would have been possible for Bauman's study of the Holocaust to focus upon the contingencies, the unpredictabilities, the deviations from routines, the conjunctures at which things could have turned out differently. There are certainly many Holocaust scholars who have done this. It is the desire to spread the specific message about the broad inherent potential tendencies within modernity that leads Bauman to theorise in the particular way he does. Specific projects, specific questions, specific methodological brackets, specific claims.

The Sociology of Ethics: Stealing Medicines and the Fear of Being Cruel

An Appreciative Look at Carol Gilligan: Between Contextualiser and Grand Narrativist

From Bauman's dreamer/floater analysis to Carol Gilligan's player study. The issue of perspective is central to the adequate handling of player studies and to the development of player theory. And, within a perspective, the issue of the specific question that is asked is, in turn, equally crucial. Take, for example, the case of Gilligan's book *In a Different Voice: Psychological Theory and Women's Development* (1982), 'one of the most widely quoted and influential feminist works of the eighties' (Faludi, 1992, p. 361). I want to present certain aspects of this book in some detail because it has been criticised by those sympathetic to postmodernism – see among others, Nancy Fraser and Linda Nicholson's, 'Social Criticism without Philosophy: An Encounter between Feminism and Postmodernism' – for not asking specific enough questions and hence veering towards a false generalisation about the nature of women's moral thinking and development (Fraser and Nicholson, 1990, pp. 32–3). While I think that the criticism, which I will come to in a little more detail later, makes an extremely important point as far as player theory is concerned, I want to try to present something of the texture of Gilligan's argument in order that its strengths too can be appreciated.

In the course of teaching developmental psychology and moral reasoning, Gilligan was struck by the fact that all the available theories, especially the most influential work of Lawrence Kohlberg, rested on interviews with, and analyses of, *male* respondents. Kohlberg had produced a stages model of moral development on a scale of 1 to 6 with the highest level constituted by moral reasoning according to abstract principles such as equality, justice and fairness. Helping and pleasing others was placed at level 3. Gilligan set out to challenge this model on the grounds of its gender bias. On the basis of three pilot studies, two with both male and female participants and one, on the moral reasoning involved in the decision whether or not to have an abortion, comprising solely women, Gilligan argued that the empirical evidence from her limited studies was that women's moral reasoning was closer to Kohlberg's level 3 than to his male inspired level 6. Gilligan insisted that this was not a sign of moral immaturity on the part of women but, rather, a sign of difference – the different voice of her title. Whereas men tended to think in terms of abstract principles, women are more likely to make moral choices in a given context out of a concern for particular individuals.

Each of Gilligan's studies relied on interviews and asked the same set of questions about conceptions of self and morality, and about experiences of conflict and choice. These questions included moral dilemmas that the interviewees were asked to resolve. For example, one was from a series devised originally by Kohlberg, in which a man named Heinz considers whether or not to steal a drug that he cannot afford to buy in order to save the life of his wife. The description of the dilemma itself, which involves Heinz's predicament, the wife's disease and the druggist's refusal to lower his price, is followed by the question, 'Should Heinz steal the drug?' The reasons for and against stealing are then explored through a series of questions that seek to reveal the underlying structure of moral thought (Gilligan, 1982, pp. 25–6). The answers to this and other questions and dilemmas suggested strongly to Gilligan the thesis, just noted, that whereas men tended to think in terms of abstract principles, women are more likely to make moral choices in a given context out of a concern for particular individuals.

Thus of two 11-year-olds, Jake and Amy, who were asked to consider Heinz's dilemma, Jake sets up the dilemma as one between the principles of life and property, in that he decides that Heinz should steal the drug because 'a human life is worth more than money... the druggist can get a thousand dollars later from rich people with cancer, but Heinz can't get his wife again' (Gilligan, 1982, p. 26). As Gilligan comments, Jake sees the dilemma as a 'math problem with humans... he abstracts the moral problem from the interpersonal situation' (Gilligan, 1982, pp. 28, 32). Amy, on the other hand, responds by challenging the question in the form in which it was intended. She begins to imagine Heinz's real lived context and considers not *whether* Heinz should act in this situation ('Should Heinz steal the drug?') but rather *how* Heinz should act in response to his awareness of his wife's need ('Should Heinz *steal* the drug?') (Gilligan, 1982, p. 31):

> I think there might be other ways besides stealing it, like if he could borrow the money or make a loan or something, but he really shouldn't steal the drug – but his wife shouldn't die either... If he stole the drug, he might save his wife then, but if he did, he might have to go to jail, and then his wife might get sicker again, and he couldn't get more of the drug, and it might not be good. So they should really just talk it out and find some other way to make the money (Amy, quoted by Gilligan, 1982, p. 28).

Gilligan notes that Amy focuses the dilemma on the failure of the druggist to respond to the wife's need. She finds this a puzzle and assumes that if the druggist were to see the consequences of his refusal to lower his price, he would then realise that 'he should just give it to the wife and then have the husband pay back the money later'. Gilligan tells us that Amy considers the solution to the dilemma to lie in making the wife's condition more salient to the druggist or, failing that, in appealing to others who are in a position to help (Gilligan, 1982, p. 29). Gilligan concludes that:

> Her world is a world of relationships and psychological truths where an awareness of the connection between people gives rise to a recognition of responsibility for one another, a perception of the need for response. Seen in this light, her understanding of morality as arising from the recognition of relationship, her belief in communication as the mode of conflict resolution, and her conviction that the solution to the dilemma will follow from its compelling representation seem far from naive or cognitively immature. Instead, Amy's judgements contain the insights central to an ethic of care, just as Jake's judgements reflect the logic of the justice approach (Gilligan, 1982, p. 30).

This proclivity to see moral choices in terms of caring and protecting in situations embedded in the web of real relationships appears over and again in the interviews. The women would repeatedly contextualise the rather abstracted moral scenarios, requesting or supplying missing information about the nature of the people and the places where they lived. In turn, the dilemmas intended by the interviewers were repeatedly recast in a similar manner to the way in which Amy had done so. Thus, women in the abortion study recast their dilemma 'from a consideration of the good to a choice between evils' (Gilligan, 1982, p. 101), in which the violence and suffering inherent in any real world resolution of the dilemma compromised any notion of justice. One of these women, Ruth, seemed to draw a parallel between her conflicting wishes to become a college president or to have another child, and Heinz's dilemma. If Heinz did not steal the drug he would be selfish in the extreme; if he did, he would be making the most enormous sacrifice. This conclusion was drawn by Ruth on the basis of her imputations from the information provided of the real world consequences of the theft for a man of limited means and little social power:

> Considered in the light of its probable outcomes – his wife dead, or Heinz in jail, brutalised by the violence of that experience and his life compromised by a record of felony – the dilemma itself changes. Its resolution has less to do with the relative weights of life and property in an abstract moral conception than with the collision between two lives, formerly conjoined but now in opposition, where the continuation of one life can occur only at the expense of the other. This construction makes clear why judgement revolves around the issue of sacrifice and why guilt becomes the inevitable concomitant of either resolution (Gilligan, 1982, p. 101).

I hope it is clear enough from this brief account of Gilligan's work that she makes a powerful case for a restrictive male bias in Kohlberg's model of moral development. In terms of questions and answers, she shows, as Fraser and Nicholson are quick to acknowledge, that mainstream psychology's exclusion of the lives and experiences of women from its models means that it has been claiming a universality it does not possess. The mainstream theories have been, in effect, about male moral development. Mainstream developmental psychologists never thought to ask questions about the differential moral voices of gendered men and women. New questions are needed in order even to begin the process of revealing new answers about the world. However, Fraser and Nicholson object not to the fact that Gilligan has asked a new question: they agree with her that its introduction was not a moment too soon. Rather, they feel that the way in which Gilligan has *answered* the question invites the same charge of false generalisation –

this time as to the voice of *all* women – which she levelled at Kohlberg. Just as Kohlberg did not consider the differences between male and female development, Gilligan's failure to consider variations in perspectives *between* women involves the silencing of differences to do with class, sexual orientation, race and ethnicity. Fraser and Nicholson write:

> Gilligan's disclaimers notwithstanding, to the extent that she described women's moral development in terms of *a* different voice; to the extent that she did not specify which women, under which specific historical circumstances have spoken with the voice in question; and to the extent that she grounded her analysis in the explicitly cross cultural framework of Nancy Chodorow, her model remained essentialist. It perpetuated in a newer, more localised fashion traces of previous more grandiose quasi-metanarratives (Fraser and Nicholson, 1990, pp. 32–3; cf Faludi, 1992, pp. 358–66, on the popular reception of Gilligan's work).

In other words, although Gilligan asks about gender, she does not ask about all the other contextual features that can make a difference to the voice of women (and men). Her perspective does not really begin to acknowledge the fragmentation of contexts and identities that are said to characterise modern life.

The criticism is a potentially powerful one, but we can still gain a lot from Gilligan's work, and it is important to find a theoretical outlook that is able to hang on to the good as well as throwing out the bad. It is a waste to dismiss Gilligan's book *in toto* as essentialist or as an illegitimate grand narrative. Thus, I think it is useful to look at Gilligan's findings from both player and dreamer perspectives.

First, in falsifying the claim of malestream developmental psychology to be a universal model, Gilligan's work is wholly successful. Here, it can be fruitfully treated as a player analysis that, while clearly limited in scope to three groups of women, is, still, asking them what they think in order to introduce the question of gender into the discipline's analysis of the real world. If the object of the exercise is quite simply to show that one can find a different voice out there, without any claim either to universal generalisation or to specific contextualisation in terms of other factors, Gilligan's analysis works. In my terms, a reflexive awareness of the limitations as well as the strengths of the study would underpin its legitimacy. Gilligan's successful use of the player perspective – to establish the existence of another voice – can be characterised as an ACA Floater analysis in terms of the player grid (see Figure 3.2). It is an ACA Floater analysis, moreover, which is entirely minimalist in terms of the contextualisation of all three aspects of an agent's frame of meaning (see Figure 4.2). The subjects of the research do, it is true, undertake an analysis of the systemic context of their moral choice – Amy does this when she considers the possibility of Heinz going to jail, of the possibility of taking out a loan to pay for the drugs, or of persuading the druggist to see the consequences of his actions – but this is both in relation to a hypothetical, rather than a real, context, and it is also abstracted from the current day-to-day and biographical contextualisation of the subjects' frame of meaning. However, insofar as the task can be accepted as the one of identifying the existence of a different voice, Gilligan is not required to do any more than this. Gilligan's objective here, the question she is posing, calls for no more than this low level of contextualisation. Her questioning of the existence of only one (male) voice is a desire to falsify the universal claims made by the tradition of developmental psychology built upon the work of Kohlberg, and her success in falsifying its universal claims comes from her ability to present convincing (albeit partial and Floater ACA) evidence of another, different, form of moral thinking and development. Fraser and Nicholson's objections only come into play beyond this point, when they believe that Gilligan does not guard adequately enough against the impression that she is herself making a universal claim for her other voice. But this is to move on to a different question. It is important to keep the two problematics, and their claims, separate.

A very closely related issue at the player level is whether, and how, one could *extend* Gilligan's type of investigation, through further more specific case studies, to take account of the diverse influences of ethnicity, class, sexual orientation, spatial location and a whole host of other possible factors. Gilligan's own subsequent work, and that of her co-researchers, has suggested that this can be done quite easily using the initial research as a heuristic starting point (cf Gilligan et al., 1988, 1990). It is certainly important to beware of the flattening tendencies of metanarratives, but, equally, it is important not to allow a sturdy vigilance in this respect to intimidate and prohibit the production of heuristics that can, among other things, act as an orienting (and corrigible) resource for the production of just those highly contextualised accounts that the less defeatist postmodernists wish to produce. Gilligan's player research could thus be used as the basis for a dreamer model, wherein her interviews could be used as illustrative examples from which it would be possible to generate hypotheses about generalised trends, which may or may not be present in particular places at particular times but, the suggestion would be, are likely to exist in a range of places within a given span of time. Like Giddens' notion of the self in late modernity (see Chapter 3), the idea of the distinctiveness of women's gendered moral thought could be elaborated upon in dreamer theory while remaining agnostic on how far the descriptions were accurate in relation to specific contexts, 'or what exceptions and countertrends to them exist'. Such abstracted, generalised, and above all tentative, theory could then be used as a resource from which to draw in generating more grounded and specific player hypotheses.

The Communicative Turn in Ethics: Between Atomism and Universalism

The relative importance of analyses that contextualise and pay attention to the hermeneutic dimension depends on our purposes. Faced with the task of acquiring knowledge for ethical purposes, in relation to a particular situation or dilemma, we might require certain information in order to know better how to acquit ourselves in a manner that is not totally self-interested or instrumental.

A debate has been raging in recent years about the extent to which the information one needs here is of the universal or the contextual kind. Universalistic theories of ethics, the products of the Enlightenment and modernity, which argue for universal rights to life, freedom of expression, freedom of movement and association, the obligation not to interfere with another's liberty and so on, typically abstract from individual cases and are often understood (rather crudely, it must be said[3]) as always being meant to apply in a uniform manner to everyone, irrespective of the particularities of context and the idiosyncrasies of the individuals or groups involved. Their application to particular cases is thus said to be algorithmic: there are rules that should be applied. This is the way in which the boys in Gilligan's initial study responded to the cameo dilemmas presented to them; as we have noted, the girls tended to want to be more flexible, to find out more information about the situation, about the people involved, about the possibilities of getting a loan or of paying the stolen money back later in order to save a life. One of the biases in universalist theories that Gilligan found exposed in her work was their overly rationalistic bias, downgrading the emotive, caring side, which, Gilligan argued, the women she studied would be more likely to put in the balance alongside the formal rationalistic rules. The response of Amy, cited above, in Gilligan's book is a clear example of thinking in terms of bonds of solidarity and care within interdependent relationships, and of using the resources of this type of thinking to question a colder notion of justice as a set of formal rules handed out to autonomous men construed as islands unto themselves in a sea of similar islands (cf Benhabib, 1992, p. 51 and *passim*).

A growing number of other writers who have been influenced by contemporary social theory's turn to contextualism, including Richard Rorty, Jürgen Habermas, Seyla Benhabib and Steven White, have, whatever their other differences, been concerned to acknowledge that moral selves are not abstract individuals but, in Benhabib's words, 'embedded, finite, suffering and emotive being[s]... [with a] variety and richness... of emotional and character development' (Benhabib, 1992, p. 50). There is a keen emphasis on the differences between moral selves, the multiplicity of value-perspectives and the diverse contexts within which they are formed. Also, in line with both feminist critiques and the growing interdependency of late-modernity, there is an emphasis on solidarity, mutual care and interdependency. These two sets of emphasis have combined to produce a distinctive form of ethical thinking, which highlights the need to break down communicative barriers – a 'communicative ethics'. Thus, even in the works of those writers who will accede to only the most minimalist place for universal precepts (that is, in those writers who reject or steer clear of any discussion of the general forms of moral argumentation that might be adopted in the search for practical agreement), there still exists a formal universalist injunction, a badgering, to try to create the optimum conditions under which diverse real individuals or groups can virtually or actually engage in an ethically adequate intersubjective dialogue about issues of solidarity, mutual care and responsibility in conditions of interdependency.

Richard Rorty as a Dreamy Underlabourer for Ethical Sensibilities in a Rich and Complex World

Rorty's is the least formalistic of all the formulations of the writers I have cited, but his particular gloss on contextualism brings out well the texture of the shared emphasis that they each construe in their own subtly different ways. For Rorty, the intersubjective dialogue and/or agreement he speaks of is a self-consciously loose construction. The historically contingent but pragmatically universal imperative involves striving to expand the circle of those we allow to be members of what Rorty – following Habermas in this at least – calls our 'communicative community'. Moral obligations are understood to be attached to our contingent sense of solidarity with other members of such a community, a sense of solidarity that may give rise to actual intersubjective agreements to jointly want X or Y, or, at least, just holds out the generally accepted conceivability of intersubjective agreement (or, perhaps, the solidarity-inspired *desire* for agreement whether or not it is, or would be, actually forthcoming).

Accordingly, we are urged to 'extend our sense of "we" to people whom we have previously thought of as "they"', to 'keep trying to expand our sense of "us" as far as we can', to stay on the lookout for people we marginalise – 'people whom we still instinctively think of as "they" rather than "us". We should try to notice our similarities with them... to see more and more traditional differences (of tribe, religion, race, customs, and the like) as unimportant when compared with similarities with respect to pain and humiliation'. This 'we' or 'us', which we should strive to expand, should be given 'as concrete and historically specific a sense as possible'; its facilitation requires a recognition of 'the importance, for moral progress, of... detailed empirical descriptions' (Rorty, 1989, pp. 192, 196). Rorty's imperative is based, contingently, on being the kind of liberal who is 'more afraid of being cruel than of anything else' (Rorty, 1989, p. 192).

The idea is to understand other people's, other groups', hermeneutic views of the world to such a depth that one can grasp their myriad and particular varieties of pain and humiliation. This obviously requires contextualisation and hermeneutics, and Rorty, accordingly, suggests that the novelist's and the ethnographer's 'detailed descriptions of varieties of pain and humiliation... [are] the modern intellectual's principal contribution to moral progress' (Rorty, 1989, p. 192). He believes that such descriptions are likely to be the most effective way of expanding our sense of 'us', of including more and more groups in the category of 'we', 'one of us', as opposed to the 'them', which is also made up of human beings, but the wrong sort of human beings. Rorty's argument rests on the belief that more local, contextualised and richly imagined human beings are more likely to elicit a moral response of solidarity, more likely to provide the basis for intersubjective agreement, than are abstractly conceived human beings. He asks why gentile Danes and Italians were more likely to hide their Jewish neighbours from the authorities than were Belgians in the times of the concentration and extermination camps. In writing about the Danes and Italians he says:

> Did they say, about their Jewish neighbours, that they deserved to be saved because they were fellow human beings? Perhaps sometimes they did, but surely they would usually, if queried, have used more parochial terms to explain why they were taking risks to protect a given Jew – for example, that this particular Jew was a fellow Milanese, or a fellow Jutlander, or a

fellow member of the same union or profession, or a fellow bocce player, or a fellow parent of small children (Rorty, 1989, pp. 190–1).

Rorty has produced here a dreamer hypothesis based upon a rich, complex ontology. It contains a contingent normative starting point – that of a certain kind of liberal – but it also contains a certain perception of human capacities and the conditions under which these potentials tend to be actualised. It is an important generalised theory, with clear and wide practical implications if it is right. The value of retaining such 'grand' theories – and I dwell on the irony with purpose – should be clear, as long as they are seen for what they are. In Rorty's case, the illustrations used for the dreamer hypothesis seem to be pitched at the TPA Floater level: data about numbers of helpers in Italy, Denmark and Belgium respectively, are used to speculate upon the reasons behind the data, and this speculation is simultaneously coupled with the more generalised theory about why people act in the ways they do. Rorty's player level research grounding of his dreamer hypothesis is thus much weaker and more suppositional than Gilligan's. On the other hand, he is acutely sensitive to the potential power of local and contingent situations, of the significance of, and the idiosyncratic significations involved in, playing down there at the level of real life, in a context of cultural and personal resonances. This is clearly what his hypothesis is about.

In sum, the universalist injunction in his view of ethics is sustained by a generalised and tentative dreamer theory, which is buttressed at the TPA Floater level but which ideally requires a much greater contextualisation (including ACA), both for its epistemological substantiation and for its practical adequacy in an unfolding process of, sometimes quite literally, life and death.

Cultural Sociology: From Dallas to Heaven and Back Again

Comparisons and Compatibilities between More and Less Contextualised Analyses of the Consumption of Popular Culture

Ien Ang's *Watching Dallas: Soap Opera and the Melodramatic Imagination* (1985) is an example of research in the field of cultural sociology that, like Gilligan's *In a Different Voice*, is pitched at the ACA Floater level. They both lie in what might be thought of as a *demi-monde* between the grand narrative and the highly contextualised, and looking more closely at this half-way world can help us to bring home both the importance of reflexivity and the diversity of research possibilities lying in wait for a more ecumenical, less peevish and more adventurous discipline. In the present section, I want to pursue this goal through drawing out some of the differences in works of cultural sociology between those hermeneutically informed player analyses that have a low level of contextualisation and those which have a higher level. As we shall see in Chapter 7, these differences in the intensity of the analysis are likely to be combined with differences in textual presentation. In this chapter, I will focus mainly on a comparison of Ang's minimally contextualised *Watching Dallas* and Janice Radway's more contextualised and finely grained *Reading the Romance*. Both of these, in turn, can be compared with the even greater contextualisation of Judith Stacey's ethnographic study of two extended 'postmodern' families of Silicon Valley in California, *Brave New Families: Stories of Domestic Upheaval in Late Twentieth Century America*, which I will discuss in Chapter 7.

Dallas *Viewers and the Pleasures of the Tragic Structure of Feeling*

Ang states her objective as being to explore *how* viewers experience *Dallas*, 'what it means when they say they experience pleasure or even displeasure, how they relate to the way in which *Dallas* is presented to the public' (Ang, 1985, p. 11). She received 42 replies to an advertisement she placed in a Dutch women's magazine, *Viva*, which asked *Dallas* watchers to write to her and say why they liked, or disliked, watching it. The replies varied in length from a few lines to around ten pages. We receive very little information about the characteristics of the 42 respondents. We have the observation that all of the letters except three were written by single individuals. Of the three, one letter was written by two boys and two girls, and two letters by two girls. From the names of respondents, it emerged that only three letters were written by boys or men. The rest were written by girls or women, which is not surprising given that the advertisement appeared in a women's magazine. This is all we have to go on in terms of the social background of the viewers. I will return later to some of the detail that arises from this research strategy.

Ang is aware of the limitations of her knowledge about her correspondents and their lives. Her data are limited, in that she has only the letters without even formal biographical details such as age, sex and race, or answers to questionnaires. Ang did not have the resource open to Gilligan of the face-to-face dialogue with respondents. Ang is restricted to letters that are 'disembodied'. Her study is virtually at the bottom of the ACA Floater grid and, as such, is veering close to the boundary between player and dreamer analysis. This is because the more disembodied or decontextualised a player study is, the more abstracted it is from specific circumstances – which is one of the defining features of dreamer theory. In fact, Ang's work is ultimately a combination of the floater player analysis of the letters of her 42 respondents together with a dreamer theory about what she calls the 'tragic structure of feeling' that is experienced by *Dallas* fans. Ang derives (and invokes) this structure of feeling from accounts recorded in their letters by *Dallas* viewers, but she then hypothesises it as a generalisation that stretches some way beyond this player evidence.

Ang argues that the tragic structure of feeling is produced jointly by the narrative structure of the soap opera and the melodramatic imagination that responds to elements of melodrama within the text (Ang, 1985, p. 78).[4] It is 'tragic' because of the idea that happiness can never last for ever but, quite the contrary, is precarious. In the tragic structure of feeling emotional ups and downs occupy a central place:

> 'All that rowing and lovemaking I find marvellous to watch' (Letter 9). Isn't it precisely the radical contrast between the emotional associations of quarrelling and lovemaking that is so fascinating for her? (Ang, 1985, p. 46).

Ang argues that an 'experience of reality' expressed by many of her letter writers is not linked to a straightforward social realism of external realities. Rather, it is an emotional and psychological reality in which the concrete situations and complications confronted by the *Dallas* characters are seen as symbolic representations of more generalised life experiences of intrigues, rows, problems, happiness and misery. Miss Ellie's breast tumour and Sue Ellen's marital problems, for example, are situated in particular circumstances, but many aspects of these experiences can clearly be appreciated in abstraction from these circumstances and generalised through close analogy. This is so notwithstanding the very different life circumstances and class, race, cultural and biographical backgrounds of viewers. Many of the letter writers who like *Dallas* seem to recognise themselves in situations and can identify with characters, their dilemmas and their problems, and they therefore experience the programme as, in this sense, 'real'. Ang argues that the letters suggest that it is often precisely this recognition that arouses pleasure:

> I myself enjoy *Dallas* and the tears start to flow when anything tragic happens (in nearly every episode then) (Letter 14, Ang, 1985, p. 47).

> Do you know why I like watching it? I think it's because those problems and intrigues, the big and little pleasures and troubles occur in our own lives too.

You just don't recognise it and we are not so wealthy as they are. In real life too I know a horror like J.R., but he's just an ordinary builder. That's why I see so many aspects and phases of life, of your own life, in it. Yes, it's really ordinary daily problems more than anything that occur [*sic*] in it and that you recognise. And then it's so marvellous the way they solve them better than you've solved your own problems (Letter 4, Ang, 1985, p. 43).

You have to see the reality of life, and reality occurs there the way it is in real life too, the intrigues, especially with people living together in the same house. The wealth is the only difference, I'm not rich (financially, materially speaking) (Letter 6, Ang, 1985, pp. 43–4).

The pleasure, Ang suggests, comes from a mixture of recognition, emotional identification with the characters and an ability to play imaginatively with the line between reality and fantasy. Viewers who would not break down and sob uncontrollably in public or turn to drink as a means of solace can put themselves in Sue Ellen's shoes, and cry with her, giving way to the frustrations, impotence and fatalism that dominate her life. They can do this while knowing that the consequences that would flow from such behaviour in real life will not follow from behaving like this in fantasy:

The reason I like watching it is that it's nice to get dizzy on their problems. And you know all along that everything will turn out all right. In fact it's a flight from reality. I myself am a realistic person and I know that reality is different. Sometimes too I really enjoy having a good old cry with them. And why not? In this way my other bottled-up emotions find an outlet (Letter 5, Ang, 1985, p. 49).

Ang argues that the melodramatic imagination that drives this sort of pleasure is a semi-desperate attempt to bring the higher drama of moral forces to bear on everyday humdrum existence. Quoting Peter Brook, she characterises the melodramatic as 'a form of the tragic... for a world in which there is no longer a tenable idea of the sacred' (Brook, in Ang, 1985, p. 81). In a life in which every belief is open to question and there are no firm values to be derived from tradition, the 'larger than life' emotions evoked by melodrama's tendency to sentimental exaggeration offer an anchor:

The melodramatic imagination is therefore the expression of a refusal, or inability, to accept insignificant everyday life as banal and meaningless, and is born of a vague, inarticulate dissatisfaction with existence here and now (Ang, 1985, p. 79).

In the particular narrative structure of *Dallas,* it has been argued, the most important motor that propels the story onwards is the conflict between family-strengthening and family-undermining forces (Swanson, 1981, cited in Ang, 1985, p. 70). Coupled with the genre characteristic of soaps to be infinite (not to come to an end – in the medium-term at least!) and thus to resist the ultimate 'happy ending', the text of *Dallas* continually points to the gap that exists between desire and reality and the impossibility of reconciling them once and for all. All it can do here, and what it does do, is to raise problems that are known and recognisable, offering, in the words of Laura Mulvey:

> a personal escape similar to that of a daydream: a chance to work through inescapable frustrations by positing an alternative ideal never seen as more than a momentary illusion (Mulvey, 1978, p. 30, cited in Ang, 1985, p. 72).

Intriguing though it is, Ang's player evidence for this theory about the tragic structure of feeling is, one feels, rather thin. It is woven as much from the insights of other theorists than from the responses of viewers. Nevertheless, although one gets the sense that a meagre point in the letters is sometimes being pounced upon and squeezed for all its worth, the theory seems to be consistent with the meanings conveyed in the letter excerpts – as far as one can tell from such decontextualised documents. The low level of contextualisation of Ang's study makes it difficult to say too much about the players, or to talk with them and question them, and, accordingly, Ang's textual presentation is dominated by *diegesis* (see above). That is, the direction and pace of the argument, the conceptual paradigm and the descriptive language that sums up the player's experience all come primarily from Ang. Although the excerpts from the letters are themselves clearly examples of *mimesis,* the words of the letter writers are still selected and edited according to the pace and the rhythm of Ang's thesis. As the postmodern novelists discussed in Chapter 3 have shown, by popping up in the text here, there and everywhere and when you least expect them, it is impossible to ever get rid of some sort of diegetic control of mimesis. However, because the chosen research method does not allow the *Dallas* viewers to respond to Ang's diegetic control of their words – neither in the text itself nor in the process of the analysis upon which it is based – the control is more than it would otherwise have to be. Moreover, the diegesis itself, as we have noted, is particularly ill-informed about the context of the lives of the people whose words it is controlling.

Notwithstanding these negative comments, if that is what they are, Ang's work is still extremely valuable, that is, as long as it is acknowledged as a minimally contextualised player analysis used to inform a more general, tentative and partial dreamer analysis of, among other things, the 'tragic structure of feeling'. The crucial thing is that we know which rules researchers are playing by, what the status of their claims is: how near to reality do they think they have come, how exhaustively do they think they have covered that patch of the real?

Romance Readers and the Pleasures of Vicarious Tenderness

It is instructive to compare *Watching Dallas* with more highly contextualised player studies of similar phenomena. The plausibility of at least some parts of Ang's dreamer theory is reinforced by studies of other groups whose experiences of popular cultural forms seem to closely parallel Ang's interpretation and gloss on the experiences of her letter writers. However, there are also suggestive differences of emphasis and seeming contradictions, which could open up new vistas for further player analyses.

An impressive example of such a work is Janice Radway's study of women readers of romantic fiction in the midwestern community of Smithton, USA, *Reading the Romance: Women, Patriarchy and Popular Literature* (1987). Radway's methodological approach and the methods used to try to answer her questions are set out in great detail in both the main body of the text (cf Chapter 2, pp. 46–85) and in appendices (pp. 223–40). They include a combination of long, open-ended and general discussions, of up to four hours at a time, with 16 regular customers of one bookstore in Smithton; individual taped interviews with five of the most articulate and enthusiastic readers – these were followed up six months or so later with further interviews in which Radway 'checked points about which I was uneasy, and tested the hypotheses I had formulated already' (Radway, 1987, p. 48); long discussions with the owner of the bookstore, Dot Evans, whose review newsletters of the 'best buys' of the month had enabled her to amass a loyal following of customers and had established for her a national reputation; participant observation for three full days at the bookstore, watching Dot's interactions with her customers and talking informally with them herself; five more formal interviews with Dot; 41 pilot questionnaires, which were subsequently redesigned after 'it became clear that I had neither anticipated all of the potentially meaningful questions that might be asked nor had I always included the best potential answers for the directed-response questions' (Radway, 1987, p. 48); and 42 completed questionnaires of the redesigned variety. Importantly, also, between her first and second visits to Smithton,

Radway also read many of the specific titles of romances that had been mentioned during the discussions and interviews.

Radway is interested not only in the meanings of the romances conveyed to her by the readers, but also in the ways in which the women use romantic fiction, that is the role it plays in their everyday lives. This gives her a certain sensitivity to context. The women respondents, she found, were a relatively homogenous group in terms of education, social role and class position. Most were married mothers, living in single family homes in a sprawling suburb of a central midwestern state's second largest city (population 850 000 in 1970). The Smithton suburb itself had a population of 112 000 in 1970, which was a 70 per cent increase over the 1960 figures:

> during the early group discussions with Dot and her readers I was surprised to discover that very few of her customers knew each other. In fact, most of them had never been formally introduced although they recognised one another as customers of Dot. I soon learned that the women rarely, if ever, discussed romances with more than one or two individuals. Although many commented that they talked about the books with a sister, neighbor, or with their mothers, very few did so on a regular or extended basis. Indeed, the most striking feature of the interview sessions was the delight with which they discovered common experiences, and distastes (Radway, 1987, p. 96).

Radway cites Nancy Chodorow in noting the increasingly resolute isolation of women that has come along with the suburbanisation and secularisation of society. In preindustrial societies, women are said to have turned to local church and informal neighbourhood societies as means of temporarily abandoning their identity as the family's self-sufficient emotional provider. They could then adopt a more passive role, through which they received the attention, sympathy and encouragement of other women (Chodorow, 1978, p. 36, cited in Radway, 1987, p. 96). Chodorow argues that what is often hidden in generalisations about conventional contemporary families as places of emotional refuge is that 'no one supports and reconstitutes women affectively and emotionally – either women working in the home or women working in the paid labor force' (Chodorow, 1978, p. 36, quoted in Radway, 1987, p. 94).

Now, while we have seen that Chodorow has been criticised from a postmodern perspective for a cross-cultural approach that is overgeneralised, if we think of this particular insight as being a tentative and partial dreamer hypothesis (whether or not it was intended this way), we can recover its worth instead of just writing it off. As such, it would seem not only to have informed the interpretative framework of Radway's player analysis but to have been (provisionally) validated as a heuristic in the specific context of Smithton. For Radway's women quite strategically use romance reading as an available 'private' way of taking themselves away from the psychologically demanding and emotionally draining task of attending to the physical and affective needs of their families, a task that is allotted to them alone (Radway, 1987, pp. 90–5). Radway argues that the women's intense reliance on the romances 'suggests strongly that they help to fulfil deeply felt psychological needs' (Radway, 1987, p. 59). Thirty-seven of the 42 respondents indicated that they read religiously every day, with 22 reporting reading more than 16 hours a week and another 10 between 11 and 15 hours weekly (Radway, 1987, p. 59) – even the latter, I would guess, is about 3 times the weekly average amount of time spent reading by the typical undergraduate. Although they read to 'escape', they do not feel that they are rejecting their husbands and families – they loyally refuse any such suggestion – but they do admit the emotional necessity they feel of 'escaping' for a time. This escape has two dimensions to it. On the one hand, it allows them to:

> deny their physical presence in an environment associated with responsi-
> bilities that are acutely felt and occasionally experienced as too onerous to
> bear. Reading in this sense connotes a free space where they feel liberated
> from the need to perform duties that they otherwise willingly accept as
> their own. At the same time, by carefully choosing stories that make them
> feel particularly happy, they escape figuratively into a fairy tale where a
> heroine's similar needs are adequately met... The[ir] feeling of pleasure
> seems to derive from their identification with a heroine whom they believe
> is deeply appreciated and tenderly cared for by another. Somewhat
> paradoxically, however, they also seem to value the sense of self-sufficiency
> they experience as a consequence of the knowledge that they are capable of
> making themselves feel good (Radway, 1987, p. 93).

Radway's analysis is unusual in cultural studies because it combines a close reading and analysis of the relevant romance texts with an ethnographic engagement with the readers and the meanings with which they come away from the text. What she does is similar to Ang, but it is more detailed and contextualised.

There is an important difference in genre between *Dallas* and romantic novels, which possibly provides a key to differences between Ang's letter writers and Radway's readers. The soap narrative is infinite, so that intertwining plots will perpetually cross each other at various heights of happiness and despair, with the final dénouement always postponed and never expected. Ang's viewers play with the line between fantasy and reality to indulge in the tragic structure of feeling on the basis of secure expectations about the genre. They expect futility, frustration and unhappiness to be punctuated by only temporary resolutions of harmony and happiness. Romances, by way of contrast, have a back cover, and for the romance readers of Smithton, the happy resolution of the story, the heroine living happily ever after under the gaze of a caring, sensitive and emotionally supportive hero, is all important.

It seems that there is a *prima facie* disparity between Ang's belief that *Dallas* watchers have a propensity to take pleasure from the tragic structure of feeling and Radway's insistence that the 'happy ending' is imperative for a romance if it is to be successful among the Smithton women. Radway goes to a lot of trouble to distinguish successful 'ideal romances' (Chapter 4, pp. 119–56) from 'failed romances' (Chapter 5, pp. 157–85), which can even degenerate at the bottom end of the scale into what Dot labels 'garbage dump romances'. The happy ending is an essential, if by no means sufficient, ingredient of the ideal romance for the great majority of the Smithton women. In addition to this *sine qua non*, the three most important aspects to a story that determine its relative excellence are said to be the personality of the heroine, the character of the hero and the particular manner in which the hero pursues and wins the affection of the heroine (Radway, 1987, p. 77):

> the most obvious difference between the failed romances and those considered ideal by the Smithton women is that the former do not focus on the developing relationship between a woman and a man who alternately pursues her and resists the attraction she has for him. The failed romances, indeed, consistently fail to satisfy the Smithton readers' primary stipulation that the romantic fantasy focus only on 'one woman – one man'. These are not stories where narrative tension increases gradually and inexorably as the heroine and hero spend more time together, grow emotionally dependent on each other, and yet still resist giving total consent to their impending union. Rather, they are characterised by a rising and falling action that seems to parallel the couple's alternating connections and separation. Where the ideal romance appears to be about the *inevitability* of the deepening of 'true love' into an intense conjugal commitment, failed romances take as their principal subject the myriad problems and difficulties that must be overcome if mere sexual attraction is not to deteriorate into violence, indifference, or abandonment (Radway, 1987, pp. 161–2).

Radway's women willingly acknowledge that what they enjoy about romance reading above all else is the opportunity to identify with a woman, the heroine, who becomes so loved, valued and cared for by the hero. From within this frame of meaning, Radway's interpretation of the women's response to male violence in the romances is particularly interesting. She notes that although the issues of misogynistic attitudes and violence towards women are broached in many ideal romances, a sure way for a romance to fail or to be tossed onto the garbage dump is for it to exceed the bounds of what is considered acceptable to a reader identifying with the heroine. Radway argues that, even in ideal romances, the possibilities of male brutality of varying degrees are always evoked as a potential threat to female integrity, not because women are magnetised or drawn to it as some commentators have suggested (cf Douglas, 1980), but because they find such behaviour 'increasingly prevalent and horribly frightening' (Radway, 1987, p. 72). Women need to explain the situation to themselves and arrive at some sort of *modus vivendi*, some means of dealing with it. The bounds of acceptability are transgressed when the 'art form's role as *safe* display is violated' (Radway, 1987, p. 72). As these women would not tolerate certain behaviour in their own lives, vicarious witnessing and experiencing of it prompts such strong reactions of fear and anger that they cannot be explained away merely by a happy ending (Radway, 1987, p. 169). Every one of the titles in the sample relegated to the garbage dump had a 'happy ending', but the Smithton readers found these endings 'unconvincing and ludicrous' in the face of the degradation, brutality or violence that the heroine had earlier had to endure.

The heroes in both ideal and failed romances are stereotypically masculine. They are ruggedly handsome, emotionally reserved, controlled, independent, aggressive and scornful of feminine weakness (Radway, 1987, p. 168). The stereotype is not brought into question. The general parameters of the masculine character and the power it represents and wields are taken as given. There is a certain facticity and inevitability about them. In this sense, Radway comments, the Smithton women 'are significantly more inclined than their feminist critics to recognise the inevitability and reality of male power and the force of social convention to circumscribe a woman's ability to act in her own interests' (Radway, 1987, p. 78).

The difference between ideal and failed romances is about margins and potentials. Ideal romances are not about changing men's characteristics but about nurturing and easing out the more gentle and caring aspects of a given masculinity's potential. As Radway notes, the narrative structure of the romance places ultimate responsibility for this flowering on the heroine. Both writers and readers clearly desire to believe in the possibility of the transformation of the hero from the heroine's cold, insensitive and distant superior into her expressive intimate. Radway argues that this narrative strategy works only by side-stepping the 'crucial issue of whether the traditional social construction of masculinity does not rule out the possibility of nurturant behavior in men' (Radway, 1987, p. 216). The fear of the consequences of masculinity is dealt with by evoking male power and aggression, and then by demonstrating that while these are not illusions, they can be tamed and mellowed. The Smithton women receive the emotional refreshment they are looking for in a narrative of romantic love in which they become, for once, the centre of attention, in which they are reassured that it is possible for them to awaken the sleeping sensitivity in their own partner, and in which it is insisted that marriage is 'not an economic or social necessity or a purely sexual affiliation but an emotional bond freely forged' (Radway, 1987, p. 170).

Compatible or Incompatible Pleasures?

The significance of the happy ending for romance readers can be grasped quite easily once one understands something about the typical plot lines and narrative structures of romances. However, we have seen that even in ideal romances, there is room for something akin to Ang's tragic structure of feeling in the heroine's initial inability to pierce the cold, aloof and insensitive side of the later-to-be-transformed hero. The main difference is that an ideal romance must be able to find a convincing pathway out of tragedy and into a satisfactory union between hero and heroine, the latter's intelligence, humour and independence of mind successfully nurturing the potential that was always waiting there. In terms of constructing an interrelated, relatively autonomous, but mutually informing, set of player theories of women's consumption of popular cultural forms, we need to understand that different expectations are built into different genres.

Also, however, we need to understand the extent to which the different genres provide different sorts of pleasure. Do Ang and Radway's accounts suggest that the pleasures provided by soaps and romance novels, respectively, are markedly different? It is imperative that we look very closely at the two accounts before answering this. Even if we were to ignore the difference of genres for the sake of argument, it is also the case that the two authors are, up to a point, focusing on different questions. Ang is asking how it is possible to receive pleasure from experiencing the tragic structure of feeling, whereas Radway is focusing on *both* the pleasures *and* the negative experiences of her avid romance readers. However, where the questions do overlap, in the shared focus on experiencing the tragic in *Dallas* or in romances respectively, the answers seem to be very different in some respects but similar in others. In Ang, the dominance of the tragic appears as pleasurable, but in Radway it is more ambiguous. We have seen that the romance readers are repelled and nauseated by the violence and sexual domination of the garbage dump novels. However, it is quite possible that what Ang presents as the tragic structure of feeling is often, in fact, incorporated into ideal romances. The tragic elements in the latter are clearly circumscribed by boundaries that contain the reality and inexorability of male power and domination within 'acceptable' limits. Looked at in this light the pleasures provided by the different genres with respect to the tragic appear to be very similar, for it is the case that the tragic in *Dallas* is also kept within similarly attenuated boundaries. There is certainly nothing on prime-time soap operas to compare with some of the (studiedly limited) excerpts from garbage dump romances that Radway provides us with.

In principle, Ang and Radway's analyses respectively could be extended to look more closely at the other's questions in relation to their own subject matter, in a way that broadened our appreciation of the experiences of viewing soaps and reading romances. How important is the tragic structure of feeling to the enjoyment of romances? How do *Dallas* viewers reconcile themselves to a narrative structure that continually subordinates the happiness of the characters with whom they identify to a merry-go-round of problems, double-crosses, frustrations, tears and drink? If viewers who identify with Sue Ellen can find pleasure in her well-nigh perpetual pain, why do romance readers find such a prospect for their heroines insupportable? Are the answers to be found in reader/viewers' expectations of genre or in the social contexts they inhabit (we know little about Ang's respondents, and we could certainly know more about Radway's), or is there another explanation?

Although conjectures of the kind I have been spinning over the last page can work out points of possible coherence or contradiction between player analyses, and even build them into a dreamer theory that aims to generalise beyond the specific cases at hand, it is not possible to answer the resulting questions except through further player studies that extend the initial analyses. We shall see in the chapters that follow that there is virtually always room for extension, and for more contextualisation, and that the more we extend and contextualise, against our intuitions, the more we are able to respond to the postmodern exhortation to exercise scepticism. The more we have of substance, the more we have to doubt.

Notes

1 Thanks to Ted Benton for prompting me to express this point in these terms.

2 My account of the positions of, and differences between, Adams and Browning in relation to the Final Solution relies heavily upon the review provided by Marrus in The Holocaust in History, 1993, pp. 42–5.

3 This understanding, while common, is in fact an oversimplification and not a necessary consequence of taking universal principles seriously. See, for example, Ronald Dworkin, 1978, Chapter 9, 'Reverse Discrimination', pp. 223–39 who argues quite clearly that a judgement about the application of universalist precepts can rely very much on the specifics of sociological and empirical realities.

4 Ang defines *Dallas* as a prime time soap opera – cf Allen, 1983, on TV genre distinctions.

Chapter 6

A Positive Scepticism Towards Claims about Empirical Evidence

It is no coincidence that the examples used in Chapter 2 to illustrate ontological complexity were for the most part taken from novels and not from sociological studies. The novelist has the great advantage over the sociologist of being able to follow her characters anywhere and everywhere, into all the secret places of their lives, behind a multitude of closed doors. A lot of what happens in the real world happens out of sight of the sociologist – many actual events never becoming *empirical* events for her. And when things do happen within her sight, there is no guarantee at all of access to the thoughts of the characters involved. The novelist has the capacity, in principle, to produce a thoroughly contiguous, thoroughly hermeneutically informed, account of a given part of reality.

The sociologist must be less ambitious, must equip herself with the intellectual resources to be just as aware of what she has left out of an account as of what she has put in, just as aware of the limitations of her knowledge as of its substance. Sociologists do not usually want to do this. The culture of the academy militates against it. Acknowledging blank spaces in what we know seems to threaten our claims to expertise, to a superior voice. It seems to be the first step on the road to ruin and *relativism*. If we accept that we do not know everything, perhaps we do not know anything more than the next person. If we are not sure, not for certain, perhaps we should then confine the whole notion of truth, and its first lieutenant 'the superior argument', to the proverbial dustbin. Perhaps the defeatist postmodernists are right, and we would thus do better to concentrate on brushing up on the ballistic skills of rhetoric and persuasion needed to sell our own piece of fiction to the world.

Distinguishing between Relativisms on the Basis of Levels of Indeterminacy

Whether it be as accusation or proud boast, the label of 'relativism' is one that figures prominently in debates around postmodernism. As probably befits the notion, the meaning that is attached to its signifier is usually not very well defined and seems to cover a myriad of sins – or virtues, depending upon where you stand. In this chapter, I want to: (1) distinguish between two meanings of relativism; (2) show how a past-modern realism would naturally embrace only one of these kinds of relativism; and (3) indicate the role that empirical evidence must play in the rejection of extreme forms of relativism. Then, having established (1)–(3) as the reference points, I want to go on to reverse the emphasis by: (4) suggesting some practical guidelines that can be used to heighten our scepticism about the empirical evidence we are presented with. These are guidelines that can help to fine tune our sensibilities to the silences and blank spaces in the evidence, and make the underscoring of ambiguity and indeterminacy in an account as much an instinct for past-modern sociology as the urge to deny ambiguity and indeterminacy was for sociological modernism.

As a graphic means of introducing the issues at stake, I will quote a passage from Julian Barnes' novel *Talking it Over* (1991), in which the rather irritating Oliver is watching his best friend's wife, and own new love, Gillian, exercising her professional skills in restoring a painting:

'Oh, this should take me about another fortnight.'

'No, I mean how can you *tell* when you've finished?'

'You can sort of tell.'

'But there must be a point . . . when you've hosed off all the muck and the glaze and the bits of overpainting and your musks of Araby have done their work and you get to the point when you *know* that what you see before you is what the chap would have seen before him when he stopped painting all those centuries ago. The colours just as he left them.'

'No.'

'No?'

'No. You're bound to go a little bit too far or not quite far enough. There's no way of knowing *exactly*.'

'You mean, if you cut that picture up into four – which would be a distinctly pro-life act if you want my opinion and gave it to four different restorers, they'd each stop at a different point?'

'Yes. I mean obviously they'd all get it roughly back to the same level. But it's an artistic rather than a scientific decision, when to stop. It's something

you feel. There's no 'real' picture under there waiting to be revealed, if that's what you mean.'
'It is, oh it is. Isn't that wonderful? Oh effulgent relativity! There is no 'real' picture under there waiting to be revealed. What I've always said about life itself. We may scrape and spit and dab and rub, until the point when we declare that the truth stands plain before us, thanks to xylene and propanol and acetone. Look, no fly-shit! But it isn't so! It's just my word against everybody else's!' (Barnes, 1991, p. 120)

Oliver's conclusion – 'it's just my word against everybody else's!' – amounts to a deeply subjectivist form of relativism. It would fit well with the extreme postmodernists' belief that there is no difference between social scientific claims about reality and those of fiction. In this world view, all that matters is the perspective of the story-teller, of the speaker of his or her 'word'. This position seems to have received credibility from Gillian's comment that there is no real picture under there waiting to be revealed; Oliver revels in this because it is what he has always said about life itself. But Gillian's comment is ambiguous. Does she mean that there never was a real picture, that when the painting was first completed 'all those centuries ago' it did not possess, to use Bhaskar's term, an intransitive reality of its own? She surely is not saying this. Rather, she is saying that, although there was originally a specific (compositional, textural, toning and shading of colour) reality to the painting, there is now no way of knowing exactly what that was. The problem is not one of original intransitivity but of knowledge of what that intransitivity was. Paintings have to be restored because the original painting is no longer there exactly as it was. Gillian's point is that there are limits – I would say scientific, historical and artistic – to the knowledge we can have about what the chap would have seen before him all those centuries ago. It is this ignorance that dictates that 'it's an artistic rather than a scientific decision when to stop'.

If our ignorance were total, the relativist subjective autonomy of the restorer would then be total. In actual fact, a perspective on something is very rarely so totally and utterly uprooted from knowledge about that something. Certainly, it seems that in Gillian's case we are not talking about a *carte blanche* perspectivism but, rather, a knowledge that is limited at the margins. She, at least, believes that four different restorers would all get the picture roughly back to the same level. I very definitely do not want to downplay the lack of knowledge at the margins here, but I do want to distinguish between, on the one hand, the totally subjective relativism which the horrible Oliver wilfully extracts from Gillian's testimony and, on the other, a more restricted form of relativism, in which perspective and interpretation are in dialogue with traces of evidence, however imperfect and incomplete, relating to the intransitive reality that is the focus of their attention. The imperfection and incompleteness of evidence may increase the margins available for the construction of competing plausible interpretations of an intransitive reality, which is the focus of attention, but the evidence that is available – together with the regulative (ontologically informed) sense of an intransitive reality to which the evidence refers – will typically rule out many other interpretations as being implausible.

Extreme postmodernists, while not exactly or explicitly denying that one can ever obtain evidence about an intransitive reality – which would be very difficult to do – instead have a tendency to only discuss such evidence when its meaning, and hence its relationship to the reality it pertains to, is so outrageously indeterminate as to allow any number of interpretations. Typically, in these instances, our appreciation of the context in which a statement or an action was produced is playfully revealed to be wildly ambiguous. Evidence appears to be open to an interminable and exhausting number of interpretations – all with the same status – and the important thing becomes one's ability to seduce others with the power of one's own pragmatically preferred interpretation. A much cited example used to bolster the strategy I refer to is taken from Jacques Derrida's *Spurs: Nietzsche's Styles* (1979). Among the papers found at Nietzsche's death was one found with the words, in inverted commas, 'I have forgotten my umbrella'. As no sentence is intelligible without a context, Derrida uses this fragment of information to show that there is no end to the range of possible contexts, and thus meanings, that one could give to these words. As John Mepham has noted, Derrida uses this tactic as a general metaphor for the openness of all texts:

> Nietzsche's written remark, Derrida argues, is open to many possible interpretations. It may be a citation, a memorandum, an example he intended to use in an argument, a joke, or it may have been a demented verbal flourish devoid of meaning altogether. It may not even be Nietzsche's at all. Or perhaps it is a metaphor ('I am out, unprotected, in the storm…'). Perhaps it should be read as an expression of a disguised unconscious castration anxiety to be interpreted within a Freudian framework (note the use of umbrellas in D. M. Thomas' *The White Hotel*). We do not know. It may never be possible to disambiguate the sentence. We may never know what the context of the utterance was. The meaning of the remark will therefore remain forever undecidable. It is a text (Mepham, 1991, pp. 147–8).

Probably the most one can say about the text here is that if Nietzsche did intend it as a joke, he must have been an absolute hoot at parties. In any event, when faced with an example as bare in information and cues as this, one would hardly want to challenge the demonstration of radical undecidability. So much about the context of the sentence is unknown, and this includes our ignorance about the situation and state of mind, the perspective, of the writer – even if it were Nietzsche – when he wrote it. However, there are cases similar in structure to the Nietzsche example but in relation to which we happen to know much more about the context and perspective of the speaker, doer, writer, than in this case. As with restoring a work of art, the more we know about these things, then, *ceteris paribus*, the less unanchored will be the realm of evidence. The latter will still be more or less indeterminate, but it will not be as totally and completely open to any possible interpretation. Some, or many, interpretations will be ruled out as irrelevant or implausible, others will seem relevant and plausible – albeit still indeterminate. Once one has more than minimal information about the situation in which a practice took place, and/or about the perspective of the actor(s) involved, the reconstruction of context may then become an axis around which an argument allied to evidence, rather than unrestricted playfulness, can begin to rally.

Let us draw on another example discussed by Mepham. Although the spoken word 'Fire!' could mean a whole series of different things, information about the context in which it is spoken would soon help us to narrow down the possibilities and to work out whether we should interpret it as, for example, an order to pull a trigger and kill somebody, a warning that a building is going up in flames, part of an explanation of the basic categories of material being in classical Greek philosophy or a foreigner's request for a match (Mepham, 1991, p. 147). The crucial thing is the amount of relevant information one has about the situation towards which one's question is directed.

Guidelines for a Serious Scepticism

Having said this, however, it is still the case that the more restricted form of (realist and contextual) relativism that I propose is still a long way from the complacent truth claims of sociological modernists. And it is important to maintain the momentum on this sceptical side of the past-modern realist equation. Thus, if scepticism – doubt in relation to knowledge – is to be invested with as much authority as claims to know, and if scepticism is to be persuaded to work constructively in tandem with claims to know, we need to pay as much attention to the provision of guidelines for scepticism as we do to those for positive (albeit provisional) knowledge. We also need to show where the two sets of guidelines meet and how they relate to each other. On one level, the guidelines for scepticism should quite simply be the reverse side of the coin of the player guidelines for positive knowledge. In itself, reflexivity towards the elements in the player model would not only facilitate an understanding of one's presuppositions, field of vision, logic of selection and status of evidence – including its degree of contextualisation – but could also facilitate a healthy scepticism towards each of these.

This said, however, we can also introduce some more specific analytical guidelines, which can help us to identify and become reflexively aware of *different types of potential limitations* of our knowledge which rest specifically on questions of *evidence*. The analytical types are based upon the application of the spirit of postmodern scepticism to a past-modern realist project based upon the rich, complex ontology outlined in Chapter 2. The ontology provides the ruthlessly honest benchmark against which the imperious pretensions to exhaustive knowledge of old-fashioned, or modernist, realism can be laid bare. With the reminder, no doubt by now unnecessary, that all explanations and solutions are underdetermined by evidence alone, and that evidence therefore only makes sense from within a distinct perspective, I think it is useful to distinguish between the following *different types of sceptical questioning*, which we can take up in relation to evidential claims, and which I will discuss in turn. One can focus upon:

1 the *relevance or irrelevance* of evidence to a question, hypothesis, or claim to knowledge;
2 the *dubiousness or trustworthiness* of the (relevant) evidence that is available;
3a the *gaps* in the evidence about relevant sequence(s) of contiguous practices in time–space;
3b the *gaps* in the evidence about aspects of sequences of time–space contiguity that are relevant (or possibly relevant) to the formation of an agent's hermeneutic frame of meaning;
4 the *ambiguity and indeterminacy* of the evidence that is available and which there is no reason to believe is dubious or untrustworthy.

The Relevance or Irrelevance of Evidence to a Question, Hypothesis or Claim to Knowledge
The meaning of this is fairly self-explanatory, but as a methodological guideline it is not as straightforward to follow as it might at first seem.

The main reason for this is that one of the primary rhetorical devices of nonreflexive literary and sociological realism is the introduction of so many details – for example, all the paraphernalia and learning of whichever profession the heroine is engaged in – which give colour and surrounding and authority, but which are irrelevant to the development of novelistic plot or sociological answer to a specific hypothesis or question. In analysing literary narratives, Roland Barthes made a similar, although not identical, distinction in terms of nuclei and catalysers (Barthes, 1977; cf Lodge, 1986, p. 19). In the player model of analysis the *nuclei* might contain evidence of the actors' frames of meaning and the sequence of actions directly relevant to answering a question or substantiating a hypothesis: to the substantiation of a very specific and delineated claim that things were like this, that a causal sequence did proceed like that. We can distinguish the strictly relevant nuclei from *catalysers*, which are the many details, the padders, that fill up the space around and about the nuclei and coalesce to produce an authoritative 'reality effect' through sheer weight of reference to some reality, rather than through reference to the specific social reality that is relevant to the circumscribed question or hypothesis of the sociologist. In sociological analysis, as in literature, there is certainly a place for catalysers in, for example, producing a sense of atmosphere and place, but a reflexive awareness of their exact function is necessary in order not to allow them to stand in surreptitiously for the nuclei.

The Dubiousness or Trustworthiness of Evidence

Much of the evidence that we manage to acquire in the course of trying to answer a question comes in the form of traces or fragments. We look for traces of what really happened in the past, and for fragmentary hints of the realities that are happening now, fragments that we can piece together into discernible pictures. But how are we to trust the evidence we receive? This is not to ask about how we are to understand its true meaning; we shall come to this later. It is the more prosaic question about how we know that the evidence itself – quite apart from its adequacy or inadequacy to the puzzle at hand – is not a forgery. How do we know that the evidence has not been fabricated or doctored in some way? This could happen – could have happened – in its incipience, if, for example, disingenuous answers have been given to probing questions, or when the 'finding' of evidence is the result more of wishful thinking than of anything in the world available to be found. Or it could happen at a later date, as evidence is tampered with, damaged, lost or otherwise altered in part or whole, form or content.

Social agents can have many reasons not only for nondisclosure, but also for the active bending of the truth, for promoting a false impression for instrumental purposes. One aspect of this circumspection and improvisation can often be power, the power relationships between the agents who provide knowledge and evidence, and those who are ready to listen. Those who listen are often also the ones who will write and, like Vonnegut's narrator (see Chapter 3), they do not generally require a gun in order to maintain a fair degree of control over their subjects. This is an area to which qualitative interviewers have become particularly sensitive in recent years, and it has been highlighted most acutely in the discussions of anthropologists and feminist methodologists, whose awareness of power relationships in colonial and gender relationships respectively has made this a pressing issue central to both ethical and epistemological concerns.

In *Writing Culture: The Poetics and Politics of Anthropology*, edited by James Clifford and George E. Marcus, one of several key books influenced by literary criticism and postmodernism that have had a revolutionary effect on debates within anthropology, one of the contributors, Renato Rosaldo, focuses closely on the way in which the power-saturated conditions of the production of evidence can be evaded, smoothed over and submerged as the evidence and its conditions of production come to be represented in documentary or textual form. In particular, Rosaldo notes how Emmanuel Le Roy Ladurie's *Montaillou*, a reconstructed 'ethnographic' account of a fourteenth-century French village, presents, in italicized citations, 'the purportedly free direct speech of the peasants, verbally presented as if one were eavesdropping in the village itself' (Rosaldo, 1986, p. 79). Drawing on this convention of novelistic realism, the speakers are characterised as articulate and insightful about the conditions under which they live. Rosaldo remarks that the rich, vivid descriptions, quite unlike those in other historical works concerned with medieval villagers, make compelling 'ethnographic' reading. However, he goes on to contrast this representation with the fact that the source of the peasant's words is an Inquisition Register. This is, of course, acknowledged by Le Roy Ladurie, but only to be submerged and downplayed by the forms of textual presentation. As Rosaldo writes, the conventions of a naïve transparent realism that are employed in the text immediately arouse the scepticism of ethnographers who have become accustomed to questioning – to use the title of one of his subsections – 'the use and abuse of ethnographic authority':

> From the outset the historian's innocent tone gives reason to pause. How can his data ('the direct testimony of the peasants themselves') have

remained untainted by the context of domination ('the Inquisition Register')? After all, the inquisitor extracted the testimonies as confessions; he did not overhear them as conversations in everyday life. What could motivate the historian to separate the data from the instrument through which they were collected? (Rosaldo, 1986, p. 79)

This question of the status of available evidence, presented or footnoted, has proved to be a consistent source of fascination and exploration for postmodern novelists. Their play illuminates the fragility of our certainties and undermines the false solidity of much that is presented as knowledge of reality. In a parody of the spurious precision of journalistic and governmental 'truth', *Midnight's Children* tells of radio broadcasts during the Indo-Pakistani War: 'what destruction, what mayhem! In the first five days of the war Voice of Pakistan announced the destruction of more aircraft than India had ever possessed; in eight days, All India Radio massacred the Pakistan Army down to, and considerably beyond, the last man' (Rushdie, 1982, p. 339 cited in Alexander, 1990, p. 138). Through the use of irony, parody and the stylistic foregrounding of conventions, postmodern novelists manage to contest and undermine too sanguine a belief in the probability that evidence is authentic.

Giving Visibility to the Gaps in Our Evidence: 'Are We Allowed To Guess?'

We have already noted that the ontological complexity of contemporary social theory includes a keen appreciation of the time–space location of social practices and causal sequences. If we are really going to take seriously the idea of complexity and contextualisation, we need to acknowledge the multiplicity of moments in space that both act as the vehicle for, and help to constitute, any given set of social practices. There is a whole lot going on out there, in spaces, in moments, some of which we know about and some of which we do not. If we take on board the filtering process that is enacted by, for example, the questioner and the question, we can say that some of the moments and spaces are relevant to our question, and some are not. This narrows down the field, but we will almost certainly still be left with a whole lot of moments, a whole lot of spaces, in which, and through which, social practices and causal sequences were enacted. We will know about some of these, and we will be ignorant of most. There will be gaps, huge gaps, in what we know about what we need to know. We need to be much more reflexive, frank and unpretending about how much we do know, about for how long, how far and with how much vision we have tracked our prey (or retraced its footprints). In this respect, we need a revolution in our thinking. The gaps, the absences, the silences in what we know and what we tell, must be winched up high so that they are just as visible as, if not more visible than, the typically more meagre moments of sequences, and parts of moments, to which we manage to give shape and colour.

It seems to me that the reflections of postmodernist literary critics such as Linda Hutcheon have much to offer a sophisticated realism, particularly with their determination to explore the boundaries of knowledgeability, to question all sorts of complacencies that we have in regard to the evidential basis of what passes for knowledge. Hutcheon argues that postmodern literature is intrigued and obsessed by the distinction between the real events – with, we might say, their own existential independence (see Chapter 1) – and the way in which historians give these events meaning in the present – for us, now – by inferring from fragmentary and circumstantial traces of evidence about those past, absent, events. She makes us think carefully about how the epistemological barriers to an ideal evidential base may tempt us, before we know it, into crossing the grey boundary between reality and fiction:

> Must a historical account acknowledge where it does not know for sure or is it allowed to guess? (Hutcheon, 1989, p. 72).

Ajay Khandelwal, in a graduate essay on realism, hermeneutics and postmodern scepticism (1993), brings out well some of the implications of gaps in our apprehension of real sequences through his choice of, and discussion of, a passage from Michael Ondaatje's *The English Patient* (1993). The nurse, in the passage, carries on reading after the patient has fallen asleep, and recommences the story on the next occasion without rereading the sections that she has read alone. In order to recover the plot, the patient must rely on his knowledge of the overall story, the parts of it that he does know and from which he can reconstruct a general map. His map may be more or less accurate depending upon the extent to which he can find and piece together reliable clues as to the contours and features of the missing sections:

> She would sit and read, the book under the waver of light… The book lay on her lap… [she had] two bottles of wine, and each night after she had lain with the Englishman and he was asleep, she would ceremoniously pour herself a small beaker and carry it back to the night table just outside the three-quarter closed door and sip away further into whatever book she was reading… So the books for the Englishman, as he listened intently or not, had gaps of plot like sections of a road washed out by storms, missing incidents as if locusts

had consumed a section of tapestry, as if plaster loosened by the bombing had fallen away from a mural at night... She was not concerned about the Englishman as far as the gaps in plot were concerned. She gave no summary of missing chapters. She simply brought out the book and said 'page ninety-six' or 'page one hundred and eleven'. That was the only locator (Ondaatje, 1993, pp. 6–8 cited in Khandelwal, 1993).

The contours and features of the missing sections of a sociological analysis – the gaps –are cavernous holes that contain all sorts of mysterious possibilities for the potential falsification of whatever general map, whatever answer to one's question, one manages to draft. Gaps are the other side of contextualisation; the more contextualised an account, the fewer the gaps, the more gaps – in sequences of moments and in relevant aspects of moments – the more an account will best be characterised as 'floating'. In relation to Figure 3.3, illustrating levels and types of contextualisation, three dimensions of time–space contiguity were emphasised: biographical time–space paths, current day-to-day time–space paths and systemic interconnections across time and space. Methodologically, one can look at any one of such sequences of contiguous practices in time–space either from a theorist's pattern point of view or from a point of view that includes relevant actors' conduct analysis. The existence of, and the nature of, silences, absences, gaps in any one particular account of real processes and events can be measured against the appropriate dimension of time–space contiguity. Their existence, as we shall now see, should also be judged according to whether the *claims* to knowledge are made according to a theorist pattern or an agent's conduct perspective.

Gaps in Contiguity Are Relevant to both Theorist's Pattern Analysis and Agent's Conduct Analysis

At first sight, a tracing of sequences and gaps in the three areas of time–space contiguity might seem to be primarily applicable to the theorist pattern aspect of accounts. However, this is not so. As noted already, all three areas contain sites that may have, or may have had, a relevant formative effect on the constitution of an actor's frame of meaning. Thus, if we do not know about the site, we will not know whether what we have missed is significant or insignificant. The unknown site will always be a potential source of falsification. In looking at the state of mind and understandings of agents in relation to their biographical experiences, their current everyday tasks or their agent's context analysis of system interconnections, we are dealing with something more complicated than practices apprehended according to a theorist's pattern analysis.

In terms of agent's conduct analysis, we are often working on a number of levels: on an immanent level, a specific experience, located in a particular time and place; on another level, the way that experience can help us to understand the frame of meaning of an actor in relation to another state of affairs, social practice or decision – maybe the same day or perhaps years later – that we are currently trying to understand or account for. A significant event in someone's past, and the way in which they reacted to it, talked about it, expressed opinions about it, were passionate or carefree about it, can often be relevant in constructing an agent's perspective in relation to a present event. Sometimes the relevance can extend so far as to illuminate directly the present content of the frame of meaning of the agent, past practices constituting the structural raw materials (in this case, of memory) that present agency draws on in the constitution of present action.

In terms of the player model of research (see Figure 3.2), the category of 'theory' is, by its very nature, closely related to gaps in analysis. Theoretical categories are constructed in order to facilitate analysis. They typically do this either by their encapsulation of a stock of grounded knowledge gleaned from previous player studies of similar phenomena, or simply by abstract reflection. In either case, the proper role for theoretical categories within a player study is the heuristic one of pointing to appropriate – possibly fruitful – sites of empirical research. The theoretical categories – of gender, class, the state, the interpretative TV audience, patriarchal relations in the workplace, business strategy, modernity and genocide, system articulation and so on – may be taken up and used as a means of guiding the exploration of social relations in the particular time and place of a new specific case study. These categories will take on a more substantive, fleshed out form as the empirical research proceeds. At the other extreme, theoretical categories may be introduced only as markers, which are then not followed through and developed in relation to the specific case study. In this case, they will not be able to tell us anything about the case study: they will signify a possibility left unexplored or, in other words, an empty space, a gap in the analysis of a specific set of social relations in a particular time and place. The result will, *ceteris paribus*, be a gap in the sociologist's knowledgeability about those social relations.

The Test of Translation

The distance between a theoretical category and its evidential support within the player gridlines of a Contextualised ACA (that is the top left-hand corner of Figure 3.3) – which, as the most detailed kind of analysis, is a useful point of comparison – can be measured according to what I will refer to simply as the *test of translation*, and which I will outline in a moment. The test of translation is a way of using the Utopian benchmark of exhaustive contextualisation in order to expose any surreptitious reductionism whereby theoretical categories are presented as equivalent substitutes for a contextualised analysis. The test of translation draws attention to what a theoretical category leaves unexplored. It insists that what we know – or do not know – about the relationship between the theoretical categories and the particular agents performing (or not performing) practices in particular contexts, is spelt out clearly. Thus, for example, when we are told that 'the strategy of the ruling class was... ', or that 'patriarchal forces were determined to... ', we are bound to ask who exactly are the agents constituting the ruling class or patriarchal forces?

And, once the agents have been identified more concretely, one can ask whether the intentions, feelings, desires and objectives attributed to them are the imputations of sociologists or whether they are based on a hermeneutic analysis that has made an attempt to understand the way in which the identified actors themselves view the world, and their actions in that world. In order not to be falsified as characterisations of a particular actor's conduct analysis, the more abstract theoretical categories would be required to pass the test of translation into, at least: (1) empirically definable agents; with (2) detailed, empirically rich, accounts of their intentions, motives, desires, feelings, objectives or whatever is relevant. As agent's conduct analysis is interested in the social practices of these agents, in addition to their hermeneutic views of the world *per se*, the test of a researcher's ability to translate her abstract account into contextualised categories would also involve the ability to specify (3) the time at which an event took place, and/or the duration of the practices referred to, and (4) the spatial site or sites in which, and through which, the key events or practices took place. Most of these tests are so rudimentary that the difficulties that they would undoubtedly pose to so many confident claims to knowledge is a telling testament to our careless and reductionist ways with theory. The less we reify, the less we reduce complexity, the more we will be enabled to notice and to acknowledge the gaps in our analyses. The more we acknowledge the gaps, the easier it will be to combine an acceptance of the limited and provisional nature of our knowledge with an appetite for, and an appreciation of what would be involved in, the extension of that knowledge.

Ambiguity and Indeterminacy of Evidence that is Available and which There Is no Reason To Believe is Dubious or Untrustworthy

Ambiguity and indeterminacy of the kind illustrated earlier in the chapter – which was suggested to be of greater or lesser degree depending upon the level of (relevant) contextualisation – should be approached in the light of the other three types of scepticism outlined above. Within the context of the guidelines already outlined in Chapters 3 and 4, this framework of reflexivity allows a greater degree of precision in assessing the amount, the status and the limitations of the knowledge one has about a slice of social reality. An important corollary of this is that one is much better placed to judge where an argument requires an *extension* of evidence, whether this be in order to cross-question a dubious piece of evidence, to fill in a significant gap or to increase the amount of knowledge one already has in relation to an event or process in order to reduce ambiguity or indeterminacy.

The crucial balance to achieve is the one between knowledge and doubt, between the ultimate inclination of a sophisticated realism and the ultimate inclination of postmodern scepticism. We saw how this balance could work out in a case of the restoration of a work of art – enough mutual confidence in mutually accepted traces of knowledge to get the painting roughly back to the same level, but not enough so that different restorers would agree exactly when to stop. There could be nowhere near even this level of confidence – misguided or not – about Nietzsche's umbrella. In any case, another way of thinking about the balance is in terms of practical adequacy versus epistemic certainty (see Chapter 1). While it is important to remember that we can never attain total epistemic certainty, and that scepticism and the refusal of closure are potentially fruitful reminders of this, it is equally important to understand that we still have to act in the world. While greater circumspection, humility and tentativeness should be applied just as much to knowledge used for practical endeavours, we will, in these cases, have to opt for what we feel is the most adequate interpretation and assessment of the limited evidence available to us. We will judge on the basis of practical adequacy as opposed to epistemic certainty.

In fact, the organisation of many human enterprises is premised upon an attempt to reduce the scope for misunderstanding and misjudgement in practical social interactions. Training programmes and rationalised bureaucratic systems are devised with the purpose of inculcating shared and/or compatible understandings that can facilitate the successful accomplishment of practical tasks. These cannot produce a guarantee of practical success, let alone a royal road to epistemic truth, but they do, in practice, allow us to accomplish many social tasks and, in doing so, reveal the performative contradiction in the claim of the defeatist postmodernists to eschew any notion of a reality that is out there. Air traffic controllers and pilots, as we have noted, have to be able to recover each other's intentions if they are not to cause a disaster. This is the significance, for example, of Quentin Skinner's forgivable irascibility with interpreters of Derrida who refuse to admit of anything except radical indeterminacy:

> My precepts, in short, are only claims about how best to proceed; they are not claims about how to guarantee success… I protest only at the assumption that it follows from this that the kinds of intentions I have been discussing are, as Derrida claims, in all cases 'in principle inaccessible'. If this were true, the effect would not only be to cut off the type of hermeneutics in which I am interested; it would also be to render meaningless a whole range of practices extending from the conducting of orchestras to the assessment of criminal responsibility. Such scepticism strikes me as unhelpfully hyperbolical, especially when we reflect that even animals are sometimes capable of recovering the intentions with which people act. Dogs often disclose by their responses that they are able to distinguish between an accidental and a deliberate kick. Derrida ought surely to be able to rise to the same interpretative heights (Skinner, 1988b, p. 281).[1]

Skinner's main point is indispensable. How could we survive in a world in which we could not and did not understand each other and (at least part of) our contexts at least some of the time? This would seem to be a necessary condition of much social interaction (cf Benton, 1984, p. 194). We can accept this while still acknowledging that not all interpreters of Derrida attribute to him the same lack of appreciation of the need sometimes to emphasise decidability over indeterminacy (cf Norris, 1991, pp. 143–6). We can also note that the assessment of, for example, criminal responsibility does not always run smoothly along the tracks of epistemic truth (or truthfulness), as attested to by, among others, the recent cases of the Guildford Four and the Birmingham Six in the UK. We can also accept that practical adequacy is not the same as epistemic certainty, and that some sorts of communication are harder to achieve than others. It is one thing to follow the direction of a conductor – skilled as this accomplishment is – but, as

Barthes points out in *A Lover's Discourse* (1978), we operate at another level of unfathomability when we attempt, for example, to be sure that somebody loves us just as we would have them love us: 'whether he seeks to prove his love, or to discover if the other loves him, the amorous subject has no system of sure signs at his disposal' (Barthes, 1978, cited in Mepham, 1991, p. 149). We may never know the reality because, like Nietzsche's umbrella, love is that kind of text! Nevertheless, the epistemic uncertainty of love does not necessarily stop us 'going on', 'getting on' (relatively, after a fashion, doing our best) happily in everyday life.

Note

1 Skinner cites Derrida's *Spurs: Nietzsche's Styles*, 1979, p. 125 as his source here. He directs the reader to p. 133 for a generalisation of the claim.

Chapter 7

Past-modern Sociology and Textual Critique

There are things that a sociologist knows, thinks she knows, thinks she doesn't know, and doesn't know. And there are nuances within each of these variations on a theme. For example, the sociologist can 'think she knows' with more or less certainty, and can be bolstered in her almost conviction by more or less evidence, and that evidence can be considered to be more or less conclusive or indeterminate, more or less likely to be authentic, more or less complete or partial. The degree of certainty about knowledge, or the degree of provisionality and uncertainty, is something that takes shape both in the process of the research or analysis itself and in the writing (or speaking or whatever) of the text – a book, an article, a film – which presents the case study to an audience (often the actual processes are tightly intertwined, so that the researcher-author herself is not sure where one ends and the other begins). As audiences, we usually only have the text to go on, we do not have privileged access to the research process itself; we only have what has been revealed about it to us in the text. As texts are not transparent windows into the reality of the sociological analysis, as they have at least a relative autonomy with idiosyncrasies, conventions and rhetorics of their own, it is important that we learn to distinguish the knowledge claims *implied* by the rhetorical tropes and narrative structure of the text from the knowledge claims as systematically assessed according to the linguistic conventions and models of sociological research.

Sjuzet and Fabula: the Story Told and the Reality Implied

In order to begin to facilitate our ability to distinguish analytically between the knowledge claims authorised by the research and those implied in the textual presentation of it, I want to introduce and adapt the notions of *sjuzet* and *fabula* coined by the Russian Formalists for the purposes of analysing the form and composition of literary texts. The fabula, when applied to fiction, refers to the events as they would have actually happened in real time and space, while the sjuzet refers to the story as it is represented in the text (Genette, 1980; Rimmon-Kennan, 1983, pp. 43–85; Lodge, 1986, pp. 20–2, 38–40, 56–7; 1990, pp. 123–8).

There are all sorts of textual device that may be employed to produce an illusory effect of knowledgeability. The greater the sense of effortless fluency, the greater our reluctance to question the plausibility. The influential French narrativist Gerard Genette, whose work has included an extended and detailed analysis of Marcel Proust's *Remembrance of Things Past*, has distinguished two principal ways in which the reality, the fabula, is modified, re-formed or restructured, and inflected by the sjuzet. These are: point of view (equivalent to 'perspective' in the terms we have been using) and time (Lodge, 1986, p. 20; cf Chatman, 1978, pp. 63–79). Genette distinguishes three ways in which the temporal sequence of the real story can be filtered and reformulated by the sjuzet: order (for example flashbacks), duration and frequency; all three have promising critical potential for the analysis of sociological texts, although I will refer only to the latter two in the present study. I will say more about the terms as we meet them. I will also discuss further ways in which a real story can be modified by the textual sjuzet such as, for example, the way in which the use of metonymy (see below) serves to compress both time and space in order to make links between different episodes and aspects of the real.

In relation to fiction the fabula is inferred or reconstructed from the sjuzet, and a similar process, I want to argue, can be undertaken in relation to a sociological or historical sjuzet. The fabula in these latter cases, reconstructed from the textual sjuzet, is the account of reality that is implied by the story as it is told in the text – the '*implied fabula*' (in effect, the implied analysis). The recovery of the implied fabula from the sjuzet is often not an obvious and straightforward affair, and it is here that we need to draw upon all those tools that have been developed for the analysis of narrative and rhetorical strategies within the text. We need these tools because most stories, especially those told by social scientists, do not bring to the fore their textual strategies in the manner of the postmodern novelists discussed in Chapter 3. Consequently, we ourselves have to employ the services of textual analysis to enable us to tease the bare torso of the implied fabula out from under the theatrical costume of the sjuzet. The rhetorical tropes and narrative techniques need to be foregrounded – if not by the author, then by us – in order to make explicit the ways in which the sjuzet manages to effect the impressions, the implications, that it conspires to convey.

In other words, we need to be more aware of the effect that the sjuzet is having on us; we need to make it explicit and less subliminal. The implied fabula is, in effect, the analysis – the story of the real from within a certain perspective and with a certain account of relations of contiguity – we are being provided with by the textual account (once we have recovered it from the sjuzet). This, therefore, can be subjected, in turn, to the same critical criteria as we have suggested for all social analyses. Thus, the implied fabula can be critically assessed in order to test the knowledge claims contained within it. A cross-questioning reader will want to know whether the implied claims about knowledge of reality are well grounded. Critical analysis can be in terms of gaps and elisions in contiguity in the places where knowledge was implied; of an absence of agent's conduct analysis where such knowledge was implied; of a vaguely contextualised agent's conduct analysis where a highly contextualised one was implied; of a highly disjointed and staccato theorist pattern analysis of system interconnections across time and space where an agent's conduct analysis of highly contiguous system interconnections was implied; and so on.

Stages in a Cross-questioning Analysis of a Sociological Text

Adapting the fabula/sjuzet distinction in this way is particularly useful for my present purposes, because with its emphasis on point of view or perspective, on the one hand, and time and space, on the other, it parallels my emphasis on the (double) hermeneutic and time–space dimensions of ontological complexity. It allows one to focus on the textual representation of contextualised social processes in such a way that it draws attention to the mechanisms by which we writers pretend to know more than we do about all those moments, and all those thoughts and practices, that are going on in the world out there and the world in here. There are clearly two basic steps involved in the move from text to a cross-questioning assessment of the knowledge of the fabula contained within that text (Figure 7.1): first, the difficult critical literary task of recovering the implied fabula from the sjuzet, and, second, a critical sociological analysis of the implied fabula/ analysis on the basis of the player and/or dreamer models. The rich,

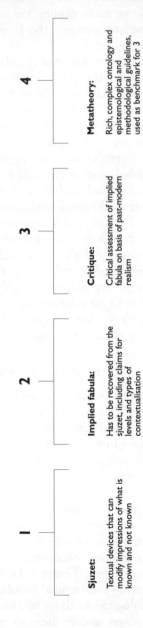

Sjuzet:

Textual devices that can modify impressions of what is known and not known

Implied fabula:

Has to be recovered from the sjuzet, including claims for levels and types of contextualisation

Critique:

Critical assessment of implied fabula on basis of past-modern realism

Metatheory:

Rich, complex ontology and epistemological and methodological guidelines, used as benchmark for 3

Figure 7.1 Stages in a Cross-questioning analysis of a sociological text

complex ontology of Chapter 2, together with the epistemological and methodological guidelines of subsequent chapters, can all the time act as benchmarks against which the methodological constructions of the implied fabula can be measured. In terms of Figure 7.1, the lessons of Chapter 6, 'A Positive Scepticism Towards Claims About Empirical Evidence' would be relevant at stage 3's critical analysis and reconstruction of stage 2. That is, having recovered the chronological reality of the story, as far as possible, from the way it was told (stage 2), stage 3 can then go on to assess how much of the evidence provided by the story is relevant to the question posed, sufficiently trustworthy to be acceptable, and sufficiently extensive to reduce ambiguity and indeterminacy to a worthwhile point. In other words, how much of what is implied to be appropriate and sufficiently valid knowledge of the real story can be accepted as such? And to what extent do the claims made or implied for the author's knowledge about the real represent delusions of grandeur rather than a realistic appraisal of the status of the knowledge? The present chapter is more directly focused upon stage 2's recovery of the implied fabula from stage 1, the sjuzet, although it obviously has implications for the other stage of critical analysis.

The Recovery of the Implied Reality from the Story as it Is Told (the Recovery of Stage 2 from Stage 1)

There are a number of ways in which the textual diegesis of the author can work to imply an authority for her research in ways that are not immediately transparent; and in traditional realist texts these techniques certainly do not have attention drawn to themselves as literary devices to establish epistemic authority. The converse is true, in the sense that the more invisible the techniques are, the more seamless the joins in the literary artefact, then the more the attention of the trusting reader is channelled into an unquestioning acceptance of the real world that is being so confidently represented. I will focus, in turn, upon four analytically distinguishable (but, in reality, overlapping) clusters of such textual devices, which for purposes of shorthand I will characterise as: (1) establishing my 'I'; (2) framing their words; (3) insinuating knowledge of where and when; and (4) painting diversionary distractions.

Each one of the clusters brings into focus a different aspect of the role of the author/sociologist in the production of the text. Each of them involves *the use of narrative diegesis*, which in social science genres usually means the voice of the researcher or theorist, *to control the story as it is told and, also, what it seeks to imply.* In relation to each of these techniques, past-modern sociology invites the cross-questioning reader to appreciate the ways in which the devices work, and also explicitly to reconstruct or decode, into the language of sociological analysis, the claims about the real world that are implied by way of allusion, connotation, insinuation, framing and authority. A reflexive sociological rendering of the implied fabula would enable a critical player analysis to evaluate the implied knowledge claims, not least in order to exercise a healthy postmodern scepticism towards the evidential basis of these claims.

Establishing my 'I': Ways in which the 'I' of the Diegetic Knower is Constituted as Authoritative

The American cultural anthropologist Clifford Geertz has written of the ethnographer's decidedly literary negotiation of the passage from what one has been through 'out there' to what one says 'back here' in the text. Geertz writes with respect to ethnographers working in the field, practising what he punningly calls the 'I-witnessing' approach. However, once one accepts the pivotal role of the sensibilities and perspective of the questioner in social research, then what Geertz says – with appropriate adaptation – has implications for all types of social scientist who attempt to negotiate any sort of passage from their research to their texts; to establish an authority for themselves as knowers of the first order.[1] Discussing the work of Bronislaw Malinowski, Geertz brilliantly encapsulates and categorises some of the surreptitious and skilful literary devices that are deployed by the most convincing realist chroniclers. Geertz writes of the distinctive problem, associated with an emphasis on the role of the questioner, of rendering your account credible through rendering your person so:

> To be a convincing 'I-witness', one must, so it seems, first become a convincing 'I'... Malinowski's main way of going about this formidable task was to project in his ethnographical writings two radically antithetical images of what he variously refers to (though, like the morning star, the evening star, and Venus, they all denote the same resplendent object) as 'the competent and experienced ethnographer', 'the modern anthropological explorer', the fully professional 'specialized fieldworker', and the 'chronicler and spokesman of... a few thousand 'savages', practically naked'. On the one side, there is the Absolute Cosmopolite, a figure of such enlarged capacities for adaptability and fellow feeling, for insinuating himself into practically any situation, as to be able to see as savages see, think as savages think, speak as savages speak and on occasion even feel as

they feel and believe as they believe. On the other, there is the Complete Investigator, a figure so rigorously objective, dispassionate, thorough, exact, and disciplined, so dedicated to wintry truth as to make Laplace look self-indulgent. High Romance and High Science, seizing immediacy with the zeal of a poet and abstracting from it with the zeal of an anatomist, uneasily yoked (Geertz, 1989, p. 79).

The textually inscribed pretensions of the narrator/researcher may or may not be true. The textually presented 'I' may or may not correspond to the reality of the 'I' who did the research. Literariness by itself does not necessarily imply untruth and dissembling. The point for me here is that it might, and that the more accomplished the performance, the more its intrinsic allure will serve to distract the unwary from questioning the authority that is insinuated.

Framing their Words: Ways in which the Diegetic Voice Infiltrates, Frames and Gives Commentary on the Perspectives and Mimesis of Other Actors, and Generally Attempts To Direct and Control the Reader's Understanding.

Hermeneutically informed accounts of social relations will usually include a dimension of mimesis – the words of actors – in their accounts. At the level of theorist's pattern analysis, the interpretation of mimesis will be focused upon the supposed public meanings of the actor's words as interpreted by the theorist, while at the level of agent's conduct analysis, the theorist's interpretation will be centred upon the motivations and linguistically embodied beliefs drawn upon by the actors in formulating their intended meanings. In this latter case, the theorist has the difficult task of reconstructing the internal process by which the agent chooses to say one thing rather than another, more precisely, of reconstructing the process by which an agent chooses to intend to mean one thing rather than some other thing (and of determining the extent to which the agent did in fact 'choose' to intend). This internal process is the very site of the duality of structure and agency, of what is perceived to be out there and what is to be done with it from in here.

This difficult interpretative task of reconstruction has to be accomplished on the basis of at least two major types of raw material: what agents do and what they say. The cross-questioning reader of an account purporting to be informed by agent's conduct analysis will want to assess the quality of a reconstruction, and will want to see some evidence of the raw material and of the chain of interpretative reasoning that has incorporated it (cf Skinner, 1988b, pp. 277–9). Of course, the adequacy of any particular reconstruction will depend on the claims being made for it, but, all other things being equal, levels of adequacy would tend to depend upon the density and breadth of the networks of opinions, attitudes, comments, speeches, angry outbursts, passionate declarations, gentle solicitations, firm remonstrations, 'don't forget' lists and so on, which are constructed into a frame of meaning – a frame of meaning relevant to the particular aspect of social relations which is the focus of the question. This reconstructed frame of meaning will take account of the actor's analysis of the practical context of action: of the immediate spatial site; of the hermeneutic constitution of the particular audience; of the importance of this site within the agent's hierarchy of priorities; of the relevance of events on this site for other sets of social relations that are important to her (what would the likely fall-out be from an utterance or action in one arena on relations in another – that is, what are the 'systemic' linkages?) (cf Stones, 1990). The reconstruction will also draw from words and deeds along the other two dimensions of contiguity – the biographical and the day-to-day.

Densities, Breadths and Types of Speech Presentation, and their Sociological Significance

Of the two sorts of raw material that form the basis for a reconstruction – what agents say and what they do – I want to concentrate primarily here on what agents say, and to do so in relation to how this is presented textually, that is, to look at the way in which the textual treatment of speech can be scrutinised in order to make the cross-questioning reader more or less comfortable with, and convinced by, a particular version of agent's conduct analysis. At one extreme, the speech of social actors can be shown directly, in quotation marks (*direct speech*), and, at the other extreme, it can be summarised diegetically by the author (*narrator's report of speech action*). There are various gradations in between these two poles such as: *free direct speech*, in which speech (or thought) is reported without any quotation marks or any other verbal framing cues from the author – this form is sometimes used in verbatim sociolological interviews; *indirect speech*, in which it is reported that someone said something but the confirmation of word for word faithfulness indicated by quotation marks is absent; and *free indirect speech*, used extensively in novels, in which there is an intermingling or fusing of actor's speech and author's diegesis so that one is not sure where one begins and the other ends (cf Leech and Short, 1981; Rimmon-Kenan, 1989, pp. 109–16; Simpson, 1993, pp. 21–30).

For the purposes of disentangling the evidence actually provided for an analysis from an implied fabula, the use of direct speech is clearly the most unambiguous type of speech presentation, and a browsing through random sociological texts would suggest that – in those instances in which concern of some kind is shown for the actual words of actors – the greater preference for the use of direct speech or free direct speech is something that seems to distinguish sociological writing in general from novels in general. There are many exceptions and caveats, however, and there seems to be a remarkable diversity in the density and breadth of direct speech/free direct speech (and other forms of speech representation) material that sociologists deign to be necessary in order to construct an actor's hermeneutic frame of meaning and the agent's conduct analysis that arises from it.

Towards one extreme, we could cite Stacey's ethnographic study of postmodern kinship patterns in California's Silicon Valley, *Brave New Families*, as an example of a relatively high level of contextualisation in terms of textualised evidence of speech. At the other extreme, we can cite those historical and political sociologists who, as in examples we shall come across later, confidently draw on summary phrases to characterise actors as 'profoundly ambivalent', 'embittered', 'irresolute' or 'loyal', while feeling only the slightest obligation, or no obligation at all, to provide textualised evidence of the speech acts (or other practices) upon which the characterisations have been so authoritatively inferred. Indeed, one often cannot help suspecting that the paucity of textual presentation reflects the paucity of the author's knowledge.

The textual effect of the summary characterisations is, as is the case with the narrative use of summary in general, to efface the particularity and individuality of the characters and their actions. In the very moment of seeming to tell the reader so much about an actor, the author reduces them to a vacant general type. Instead of the inferential construction of an actor's hermeneutic frame of meaning on the basis of a network of speech, and other, practices in a range of more or less interdependent contexts, we are given, if we are lucky, two or three sentences of an actor's utterances, diegetically framed to make a smooth fit with the author's argument-inspired characterisation. Compared with the densely packed 'thick descriptive mimesis' of a work such as Stacey's, the wafer-thin characterisations of these historical sociologists seem presumptuous in the extreme. We should be highly sceptical of – dubious of – their claims to the greater knowledge, which they do not see fit to allow us to judge for ourselves. From the perspective of a reader who wishes to cross-question a textual account, summary characterisations are little more than empty signifiers.

The thinner the presentation of mimesis in an account, the more open it is to manipulation by the author. The thinness gives the author much more leeway as regards interpretation and characterisation because, as we saw with Nietzsche's umbrella, the more uprooted the evidence of a frame of meaning is from its specific contexts (including the strategic context of interdependencies) then, *ceteris paribus*, the more indeterminate is the meaning. In addition to noting the differences that exist between studies with respect to the density and breadth of their speech presentation, we should also be aware that there is a whole range of devices for the diegetic framing of the words of actors (cf Todorov, 1984, p. 73; J. Hawthorn, 1992, pp. 18, 19), which cover not only the different forms of speech presentation but also such rhetorical framing devices as irony, parody, enthusiasm or scorn, sympathy or dismissiveness towards an actor's words. Here, as in other aspects of textuality, 'the performance consists in manipulating a certain degree of impressionism' (Barthes, 1990, p. 22): the lighter the touch the greater the connotative effect. Often the connotative effect is produced by a combination of these framing devices and a particular form of speech presentation.

Consider, for example, the difference between the reader's responsibility for interpretation in the free direct speech of Gillian and Oliver in the *Talking it Over* extract (see Chapter 6) – 'free' in the sense that it has no reporting clause – and the more cued direct speech included in a novel, an ethnographic account or a qualitative interview-based project, in which reporting clauses can play a subtle part in the direction of the reader, clauses such as these from Barry Unsworth's novel *Stone Virgin* (1986): 'Lattimer said, in his cold, deliberate voice', or '"All art tends to abstraction", Litsov said finally and magisterially', or '"It is there I disagree," Raikes said quickly and warmly' (Unsworth, 1986, p. 93). Consider also clauses such as these from Carolyn Steedman's social history-cum-autobiography-cum-cultural criticism, *Landscape for a Good Woman*: '"Your mother drank gin once," my father told me years later, with nostalgic regret', or 'Now I can feel the deliberate vagueness in her accounts of those years: "When did you meet daddy?" – "Oh, at a dance, at home." There were no photographs'; or, 'Now, thirty years later, I feel a great regret for the father of my first four years, who took me out and who probably loved me, irresponsibly ("It's alright for him; he doesn't have to look after you"), and I wish I could tell him now, even though he really was a sod, that I'm sorry for the years of rejection and dislike' (Steedman, 1986, pp. 30–6).

A Case Study in Words from the Silicon Valley: Judith Stacey Presents Pamela Gama

The scope for authorial commentary extends, of course, much further than the reporting clause of a speech act, important as this can be. *Brave New Families* (Stacey, 1990) is particularly useful at this point, not least because Stacey is unusually self-reflexive about her role in the ethnographic and textual processes. The episode I want to discuss is an interview that the author conducted with Pamela Gama during which it gradually dawns on Stacey that she is not hearing the story that she expected to hear. In a previous exploratory interview with Pam as program director for Social Opportunities and Services (SOS), the social service agency in Santa Clara County, Stacey had noted the expression 'of a variety of feminist and other progressive political sentiments, characterised by keen sensitivity to the plight of the regions' laid-off workers and low-income women' (Stacey, 1990, p. 42).

In this and other encounters, Stacey had also begun to discern a pattern in the recounted biographical experiences of a number of the women now working for SOS. Three of the women, Pam, Lorraine and Doreen, had in 1970 all been participants in Santa Clara County's first re-entry program for women at East Valley, a local community college. According to Pam, of the 25 women who had entered the program, all as 'happily married' housewives, only 2 or 3 were still in those same marriages (Stacey, 1990, p. 43). Stacey summarises the 'East Valley story' as it seemed to emerge from the accounts of Pam, Lorraine and Doreen as:

a history of paradoxical status and income mobility generated by the widespread national shifts in contemporary women's family and work patterns. East Valley had served these brides of the 1950s as a trapdoor out of the security and constraints of domesticity. Heady with new ideas, skills, self-esteem, and goals, each had begun a journey up the ladder of educational and occupational status, a journey that paradoxically hurtled each woman and her children precipitously down the economic pyramid. Although each was to increase her earning power over time, none would recover the level of material attainment she had enjoyed as an engineer's wife and homemaker before attending East Valley or that her former husband's new wife enjoyed. Downward economic mobility appeared to be one of the ironic consequences of increased educational and career achievement among many housewives. Women like Pam, Lorraine and Doreen, whose social class had once been determined by the men to whom they were related, now were determining their class positions by themselves, and the results were ambiguous and contradictory. Feminism, particularly the strand popular in the early 1970s that criticized female dependence and encouraged career ambitions, had proven to be incompatible with millions of marriages forged on 1950s premises. This appeared to be the hidden spring that had released the unsuspected trap (Stacey, 1990, pp. 45–6).

Stacey's interpretation of, and textual commentary upon, what she has heard from the three women draws upon her own perspective and generalised stocks of knowledge about aspects of the historical conjuncture. From these exploratory forays, we see that she begins to formulate hypotheses about unintended consequences, the causal interaction of various social and economic causal mechanisms, and the relative significance of one of these mechanisms in tipping the balance sufficiently in one direction rather than another – 1970s feminism seemed, to switch back to her metaphor, to be the hidden spring that had released the unsuspected trap. At this stage of the research process, Stacey felt that she had the beginnings of a player analysis that could go on to explore, in a more contextualised manner, the ways in which a range of different causal influences became interwoven in the lives of these women:

> The collective history of the East Valley circle I had stumbled upon seemed to condense most of the significant social, demographic, economic, and political transformations that had taken place in Santa Clara County over the past several decades. Most notable among these were the rise of the electronics industry, the escalation of female employment and divorce, the demise of the family wage system in the working class, and the rise and decline of grass-roots feminism. Recognizing this, I flirted with the notion that a case study of the original East Valley reentry cohort would be an ideal medium for exploring in greater depth the relationships between these changes as well as their contemporary implications. And that was what led me to my 'revelation' interview with Pam (Stacey, 1990, p. 46).

Spelling this out in terms of the test of translation, Stacey thus envisaged a contextualised ethnography that would allow the fleshing out of the abstract theoretical categories of 'social, demographic, economic, and political transformations' to the more specifically defined categories of 'the rise of the electronics industry, the escalation of female employment and divorce, the demise of the family wage system in the working class and the rise and decline of grass-roots feminism'. It would also allow, if she so wished, the further step of attempting to trace and analyse how these more specific categories translated, in turn, into: particular electronics companies with addresses and premises in locatable time and space; the precise employment tasks, terms and conditions of particular women in particular electronics companies; the relationship between this employment and adjustments in the women's relationships with their husband or partner, including the balance of earning power, the balance of domestic labour, the management of financial responsibility within the household, and the accompanying adjustments to the relationship in terms of the style, content and texture of talk and emotion, both in relation to each other, to any children and to others inside or outside the household; and the influence of feminism on the talk, the emotions, the perspectives and the conduct of the women (cf Hochschild, 1990, *passim*). The translation of theoretical categories or markers into an appreciation of the detailed texture of interactions – how influences are *articulated* – is a ground-level, experience-near affair. This is all the more so because the reality of contextualised articulations quite often contains a twist, a surprise, a veritable tale of the unexpected, which a dreamer would never dream of and a floater would be too far away to envision.

In Stacey's case, as we shall see, the lesson is pushed home with even greater force, because even though she was there on ground level, interacting directly with her subjects of research, her preconceptions (her side of the double hermeneutic) still led her to resist the surprise. Her resistance, moreover, was given a particular textual form, which reveals much about the way in which the diegetic commentary of the author can frame the words of the interviewees, the lay actors, in such a way that ambiguity and indeterminacy can be made to seem unambiguous and transparent. It also reveals much about the way in which the hermeneutic framework of the questioner can misleadingly dominate and subsume the hermeneutic framework of the lay actor. All this is easily revealed in Stacey's case because she allows her subject, Pam, to talk back, not just in the interviews and interactions during the ethnographic research process, but also after having been invited to read the final textual form of the narrative with all its selections and linkages, arguments, implications, balance of diegesis and mimesis, summary, commentary, reflexive asides and conclusions. Pam's response is included in an appendix (and partly in a prologue), and, as we shall see below, it challenges Stacey's interpretation of a significant dimension of her hermeneutic frame of meaning.

Indeed, Stacey's whole approach is extremely user-friendly as far as the cross-questioning reader is concerned. The aspects that facilitate cross-questioning derive to a great extent from a combination of: the explicitly dialogical strategy that Stacey takes, both in her initial analysis and in the invitation to her subjects to respond to the final text (and then to renew the final text with an account of their own response); her continual references within the text to aspects of her own identity as questioner and its relevance to her particular view on the relations she was researching – her feminism, her emotional response to various situations, the discomfort, and occasionally confusion, she experienced when confronted with views expressed by some subjects in the course of her research; and the additional sensitivity that these dialogic and self-conscious dimensions of the research and writing processes foster when it comes to a critic's textual analysis of the evidence and interpretation of speech acts. These dimensions, taken together, facilitate critical analysis and scepticism towards certain aspects of the implied fabula of *Brave New Families*, and they expedite the important first step in this process, of disentangling the implied fabula from the traditionally more seamless and rhetorically persuasive sjuzet.

We have seen how Stacey's initial encounters with the 'East Valley' women led her to form certain hypotheses and to develop a preliminary frame of expectations as to what she was looking for and what she would find. Subsequent to this, when she returned to interview Pam another time, she was all set to listen to her 'record her chronicle of the journey from fifties' domesticity through seventies' feminism' (Stacey, 1990, p. 47). When it happened, the interview turned out to be much more about the influence of religion than feminism. It centred upon the conversion to a form of evangelical Christianity of Pam's second husband, Al, and Pam's own subsequent conversion. Stacey conveys a clear sense of her shock at this revelation, being knocked off the track of her own preconceived itinerary. Listening to a tape-recording of the interview later, during transcription, she realised that she had 'ignored the existence of cues to an alternative narrative from the start' (Stacey, 1990, p. 47). I will cite at length Stacey's account of the episode at the centre of the revelation because it vividly captures the central dramatic chain of events and also illustrates the typically generous helpings of direct speech that Stacey intersperses with her own commentary. In the process, it also provides the raw material of direct speech from Pam that Stacey subsequently proceeds to interpret and textually frame in a manner, which, I want to argue, creates a sjuzet that implies a determinate and unambiguous meaning where an indeterminate, undecidable meaning would have been more appropriate:

> Late one summer night several months earlier, and six months after Pam and Al had separated, Al severely injured a young woman in an automobile accident. Al had had a few drinks before the accident and was driving

an inadequately insured vehicle registered in Pam's name. Several hours later, in the middle of the night, he arrived on Pam's doorstep, desperately shaken. All of their property, savings, retirement benefits, and future earnings were in jeopardy. 'An awesome thing had happened to this young woman, and it looked like an awesome thing was going to happen to both of us. And Al had just never been in a place like that before. I mean, he just basically controlled his environment and shut off anything he didn't care to be involved in. Of course, this was one thing he couldn't shut out.'

Terrified, remorseful, close to suicide, Al was driving to work several days later when 'a voice came to him and said – which feels like it was God speaking to him – and said, "Go see Katie", which is our middle child'. A secular nonbeliever, Al ignored the voice at first, but as it repeated itself insistently, he surrendered. He delivered himself to born-again Katie, who received and guided him 'through this big emotional thing where he accepted the Lord, and the whole bit, and asked for forgiveness for his sins… And just suddenly this total depression he'd been in, this one where life just wasn't even worth living, suddenly he felt totally different… in fact still does to this moment, even though things are real unsettled.'

Quite suddenly, and without comment, Pam shifted from a third- to a first-person account in this revelation narrative. By so subtle a maneuver did Pam disrupt my preconceptions and redirect the future course of my research as she informed me that just as Al suddenly accepted Jesus into his life, she had accepted both Al and Jesus back into hers. 'So we started going to just everything that Katie said, started looking for a church, began going to church. Global Ministries of Love [Katie's Christian community] has a lot of evening activities we went to. I hadn't had the experience Al had, but it felt okay to me because it was right in line with what I had been feeling all along.'

Pam reminded me of her earlier church involvements, then continued the tale of their marital redemption. She and Al started reading the Bible together, praying together, rededicating their relationship to each other and 'the Lord'. 'Because I really knew, clearly,' Pam explained, 'that there was something totally different about Al. And I knew on some very basic level that if we ever had a chance for our marriage to work out, it was right then' (Stacey, 1990, p. 54).

Stacey's response to this is to interpret Al's conversion as a genuine, almost textbook, example of sin, crisis, repentance and salvation, but to see Pam's conversion in a completely different light – a light, it seems to me, guided more by the force of Judith Stacey's 'secular feminist sensibilities' than by any cues offered by Pam – seeing it as a shrewd, instrumental and strategic manoeuvre by Pam to save her marriage rather than as a sincere and wholehearted embracing of the faith. Stacey does not comment upon Pam's own declaration that 'it was right in line with what I had been feeling all along', nor does she take up Pam's cue to probe further into her earlier church involvements. The authorial diegesis neglects any discussion of the theological, biographical or general existential bases for the conversion because it is preoccupied with the implications of the conversion for patriarchal marriage. Perspective and textual presentation are clearly focused upon a particular quest, immune to hints of alternative avenues of possible interpretation. In terms of Genette's discussion of the temporal relationship between the sjuzet and the (implied) fabula, Stacey's repeated reiterations of the same point is a clear case of the rhetoric of *frequency* in which the same event referred to again and again begins to take up an aesthetic and symbolic resonance within the text that far exceeds the power of the original event; in this case, by means of sheer insistence, the resonance of implied authority for Stacey's interpretation far exceeds the power of licence conferred by Pam's original words:

> Whereas the talk of Al's conversion followed almost a textbook script of sin, crisis, repentance, and salvation, Pam's own rebirth struck me as unusually self-conscious, methodical and strategic (Stacey, 1990, p. 55).
>
> Her responses suggested a selective, instrumental, and highly creative approach to Christian marriage (p. 56).
>
> The views of wifely subordination Pam depicted struck me as remarkably strategic (p. 57).
>
> She was no passive victim or dupe, no believer in the inferiority of women, and her turn to fundamentalist marriage was acutely self-conscious, willful and articulate (p. 57).
>
> From Pam's description, Christian marriage was demanding more profound changes in Al's prior ways of relating than in hers. Perhaps that was why, despite her egalitarian convictions, the doctrine of submission did not strike her as a bad deal (p. 59).

The adequacy of Stacey's interpretation is called into question quite explicitly by Pam in her reaction to the text of *Brave New Families*. In Stacey's words: 'what [Pam] found most unsettling was the instrumental account I had given of her reborn religious faith' (Stacey, 1990, p. xiii). And in Pam's own words, she felt that Stacey had labelled her and pushed her into a group in which she did not recognise herself: 'the group I felt I was in there is *Diary of a Mad Housewife* – you know that picture – "Tell me what you want me to be and I'll be it"? No values, nothing but a need to be accepted, with changes coming so fast, how could I keep up if I were in that group?' The fact that it is Stacey who chooses to include this reaction in the text – to give Pam 'the right to control its closing words' – is testimony not only to her integrity but also to the ingenuous nature of the powerful (and defensive) preconceptions that, against the reflexive grain, strove to convince her readers of determinacy when the explicit cues from Pam suggested otherwise.

Insinuating Knowledge of When and Where: Ways in which the Sjuzet's Treatment of Time–Space Contiguity Needs To Be Translated into the Form of the Implied Fabula

Summary and the Cloaking of Gaps

A textual account can cover a period of 50 years in 2 lines or 2 chapters, a period of 24 hours in 2 lines or a 600-page book. And the account can be more or less explicit about its coverage of events, more or less interested in drawing the reader's attention to its relative exhaustiveness or skimpiness. Relative skimpiness usually implies a form of authorial diegesis in which summary-telling rather than showing is dominant. The author *tells* us the way things were by way of a summary instead of showing us the details, colours and actions of the scenes. The duration of a summary account (for example how long it takes to read) will, naturally, be much shorter than the duration of the actual events themselves; this is less likely to be the case when an author *shows* the reader what happened – as in the recreation of the scene and conversation at a party – rather than tells it all in summary (cf Booth, 1991, pp. 3–20).

There is a cooked breakfast scene in Iris Murdoch's *The Book and the Brotherhood* (1987) in which we are virtually escorted from one character's plate to another – we see a boiled egg for Gulliver, fried eggs and bacon for Duncan, a piece of bacon and fried bread on Gerard's plate, eggs, bacon, sausage, fried bread and grilled tomatoes for Jenkin, and toast with home-made gooseberry jam for Lily. We are too late for Tamar, who had just toyed with her one piece of toast and rapidly vanished. Everyone has had coffee, except for Lily who has asked for tea. Our assumed interest in these and other details is indulged so punctiliously that we, no doubt, could have prepared, cooked and eaten a three-course meal, with wine and coffee, and a choice of mints, in the time of the telling (Murdoch, 1987, p. 228). Similarly, Nicholson Baker's *The Mezzanine* (1989) consists of an account of the lunch-hour of a single working day, as experienced by an office worker, in which 'time under the discursive microscope changed its nature. The [apparently] trivial and quotidian were dignified by the attention given them' (Baker, 1989; Mars-Jones, 1994, p. 3).

In the contrasting case of diegetic telling by way of summary, the particularity and distinctiveness of events, processes, characters and their actions are effaced by the 'conciseness and abstraction of the narrator's language' (Lodge, 1992, p. 122). Summary basically involves the compression of time and space in linking one topic or event with another. It is a particularly efficient way of concealing what is not known about; the narrative is accelerated so that we hurry past events, processes and details about which we are ignorant. Summary is also a good means of deflecting attention away from things that we do know about but that are troublesome and untidy for our argument. Summary is the natural textual partner of a TPA Floater analysis within the player model of research. While it is possible that the TPA Floater nature of an analysis, and the corresponding summary nature of its textual presentation, may be reflexively acknowledged for what they are – as I have been suggesting they should be – it is just as likely that there will be no acknowledgement of the many gaps, elisions, deflections and summary compressions.

Metonymy and the Cloaking of Gaps.   Summary is typically metonymic rather than metaphorical in structure, in the way in it connects one topic or event with another (cf Lodge, 1977). Metonymy makes links in a narrative not by means of metaphorical similarities, but by means of contiguity or association between part and whole, thing and attribute, cause and effect. Such narrative links can be spatial or temporal/historical, or a combination of both, thus the cinematic lingering of the camera upon a bread knife, followed by a more or less immediate subsequent scene of a body lying on the ground, blood trickling onto the kitchen tiles – we have not seen the killing but the metonymic connection of cause and effect has been established through spatial association or contiguity. Or a scene showing chiefs of staff arguing vigorously but unsuccessfully with their Minister of Defence for additional financing for personnel and armaments, interwoven – again, at greater or lesser narrative distance – with clips, sometime later, of the enemy tanks rolling onto home territory: the metonymic connection is clear, whereas the exhaustive causal sequence established in an open system with multiple social mechanisms will have been much more complex.

The initial contrast of metonymy with metaphor could suggest an account that is closer to the ground than the clouds, an account that has an interest in veracity or faithfulness to the real. It is as well to suspend any such assumption from the start, as there is no guarantee at all as to the actuality or depth of such a commitment. Moreover, as the principle figurative vehicle of summary in realist texts, metonymic language has the great advantage over literal language in the smoothness and flexibility it affords in the production of apparently seamless junctions between one event and another, one point in time and another. Metonymic linkages – whether figurative or literal in the language used[2] – are the primary means by which gaps and elisions in the analysis are concealed by the sjuzet.

Whenever a chain of real events (or aspects of real events) relevant to a question is not exhausted by a narrative account – which is most of the time – the narrative sjuzet will always be in a metonymic (or synecdochic)[3] relation to the implied fabula (cf Lodge, 1986, p. 22); certain events and details will be brought to the fore and others will be absent. Because of the limits of our knowledgeability – our inability to obtain exhaustive knowledge of social relations relevant to our question – and because of the exigencies of textual presentation (aesthetics, readability, space, publishing costs or author's patience), the use of metonymy in sociological accounts is, to a degree, inevitable. However, without adequate forms of reflexivity to acknowledge which areas of relevant knowledge are missing, or indeterminate, summary in general and metonymy in particular can serve the ends of intellectual despotism. Reflexivity in relation to both analysis and text can serve to highlight any inabilities of an account to pass an appropriate test of translation from implied causal connection to contextualised, literal and demonstrable causal connection, from implied linkage to contextualised contiguous linkages in identifiable times and places.

In a discussion of Charles Dickens' *Sketches by Boz* (1966), the American literary critic J. Hillis Miller shows how the novelist skilfully exploits the autonomy of the text to give himself the power to create an effect of realism freed from the constraints of having to represent what is actually real. In doing so, he gives us clear insights into those temptations available to sociological writers to write as if they know more than they do. The effect of realism is created in *Sketches by Boz* by means of a skilful use of metonymic chains of equivalence and substitution. Dickens always begins with a detailed, contextualised description of inanimate things, objects, and then moves from these to imagined characters, which he associates with them, and from there to tales or stories about them. The detailed contextualisation of the inanimate object, taken together with the confident suggestion of contiguous association, enables Dickens to create an effect of realism and intimate knowledge, which is, in fact, highly fictional in character. The extended knowledge, beyond the objects, is supposition, imagination, dressed up as realistic journalism.

Hillis Miller argues that metonymy provides a structuring dynamic for the *Sketches by Boz* in that 'a movement from things to people to stories is the habitual structural principle of the *Sketches*, the law which validates this movement is the assumption of a necessary similarity between a man, his environment, and the life he is forced to lead within that environment. As a man's surroundings are, so will his life be' (Hillis Miller, 1992, p. 297). Just as a sociologist may allow her argument-led preoccupations to dominate the links in her narrative, ignoring cues to the contrary thrown up in the sociological analysis, so Dickens allows – gives free rein to – his preconceptions of perspective to validate the links he forges between what is seen and known about, to what is not seen, not really known about. A metonymically implied spatial association or contiguity – thing next to person next to story – is linked with an implied knowledge of temporal contiguity – the character's life and the tales therein. The symbolic equivalence set up between different elements in the story smoothes the process of substitution of one element by another; a deft movement from the pallor of an object to the pallor of a life, or from the closely described hopelessness of one life to the hopelessness of another life by means of equivalence and substitution.

Hillis Miller shows us one technique by which this is effected in the *Sketches by Boz* when Dickens presents a scene in which individuals at different stages of their lives are placed side by side in order to encapsulate in the same tableau 'a progression which is achieved by a single individual only through a long period of his life. The presence in a single instant of more than one stage of such a progression strongly persuades the reader of the inevitability of the sequence' (Hillis Miller, 1992, p. 300). Hillis Miller cites one such scene in which Boz glimpses two young sisters, the elder defiant and the younger weeping bitterly, being taken from the Bow Street police station to the prisoners' van that will take them to jail:

> These two girls had been thrown upon London streets, their vices and debauchery, by a sordid and rapacious mother. What the younger girl was then, the elder sister had been once; and what the elder then was, the younger must soon become. A melancholy prospect, but how surely to be realised; a tragic drama, but how often acted!... The progress of these girls in crime will be as rapid as the flight of pestilence (Dickens, 1966, p. 274).

There is an all-knowingness about the *Sketches by Boz,* which is enacted by means of metonymic linkages. Imagination and invention are disguised by the smoothness of the literary transition from what is known about to what is not. It is the impression of all-knowingness so created that also allows the conceit of the attribution of inevitability to seem more than a loose hypothesis – a dreamer's tentative generalisation. The significant gaps are, in effect, covered over and effaced. In nonfiction, the writer would have to have far more gall actually to make up – or trippingly imagine – large swathes of reality in the detail that Dickens delivers (although near equivalents certainly exist).

Metonymy, Theoretical Critique and the Cloaking of Gaps.   An equivalent trick here, one we touched upon in Chapter 6 when discussing gaps in empirical evidence, lies in the use of theoretical categories to do the job of implying much knowledge where not a lot exists. The insinuation by the sjuzet of a 'wrapped up' causal explanation is typically effected by theoretical categories in one of two ways, that is, by introducing theoretical categories either to *compress* the many details of social practices that take place within a wider, longer, chunk of time and space, or to *efface* time and space altogether. In the first case, the case of compression, this happens by means of the metonymic (strictly speaking 'synecdochal') substitution of theoretical categories for the many details that would otherwise be necessary to tell the whole story. Theoretical categories are introduced into the midst of narratives that are telling about a particular sequence of events in time and space. Adapting the examples used in the section on gaps in empirical evidence, these could include: 'the strategy of the German ruling class was… ', 'patriarchal forces fighting the nineteenth-century Factory Acts were determined to… ', 'the aim of US-owned multinational business was to…', 'these measures were anathema to all fair-minded people who were acquainted with the facts', and so on. As the last two examples suggest, as the example from Dickens demonstrates and as we shall see again in subsequent chapters, the categories – signifiers – used can be more prosaic than academic theoretical categories. Whatever the level, whether the signifiers are reified theoretical categories or more grounded everyday words describing everyday things, they can still work in the same way within the narrative, smoothly and matter of factly affecting the compression of many details of practice and consciousness within time and space by means of a few summary phrases.

In the second case, that of the complete effacement of time and space, theoretical categories are used in an even more abstract manner to (supposedly) refer to contextualised instances that are never discussed except in relation to an abstract 'virtual' reality, which is timeless and spaceless. The contextualised instances are only virtually so. The sjuzet implies that the contextualised instances would be found to be X or Y if – *if* – they were investigated. Thus, the state in capitalist society will act in the interests of capital; the state in patriarchal society will act in the interests of patriarchal society; and self-identity in modernity is traversed by the experiences of trust, risk, doubt and reflexivity. Put as baldly as this, each of these statements completely effaces the rich potential diversity of many variations and exceptions to their abstracted pronouncement (hence the significance of the distinction between a dreamer or a despotic account – the former acknowledges its tentative, hypothetical and ungrounded nature). As in the case of compression, the categories substitute themselves metonymically for the many parts they subsume within their ambit.

However, whereas in the case of compression, the categories are introduced into a narrative that is already about a particular time and place, effacement involves a narrative that takes place in relation to a virtual, abstract, reality. It has no need for any particular times or any particular places because it is already about many times and many places – notwithstanding the contingencies of open systems and of agency. It is vital to continue to recognise the metonymic functions of such categories even when the language used is metaphorical; this is because it is typically a major part of the explicit purpose of these accounts to discuss relationships of contiguity – to insinuate knowledge of relationships of contiguity – albeit social relationships and interdependencies that exist in virtual as opposed to actual time and space.

Painting Diversionary Distractions: Ways in which the Details, the Padding, the Catalysers and their Connotations Coalesce To Insinuate an Intimate Acquaintance and Knowledge of all Aspects of the Story as it Really Happened

The roles of catalysers and detail was discussed above in relation to their strict relevance or nonrelevance to the question, hypothesis or claims of a player analysis. The importance of catalysers and details in the present context lies in the contribution they make to what Barthes calls the 'reality effect' (Barthes, 1992, pp. 135–41). Thus, to use and adapt one of Barthes' examples in which Flaubert, describing the room occupied by Madame Aubain, Felicité's mistress, tells us that 'on an old piano, under a barometer, there was a pyramid of boxes and cartons', we can say that he is providing us with data or descriptive detail of such innocence structurally that it contributes by default to the seamless quality of the sjuzet, to the way in which the sjuzet can effortlessly imply a fabula – or authoritative knowledge of a fabula – without seeming to have an interest in implying anything at all. The recovery of the implied fabula from the sjuzet is thus made more difficult.

The most effective accounts in traditional realism seem to be able to downplay their perspective and their literariness just at the point at which these attributes are being exercised most fully. One of the most effective ways of doing this is to direct the attention of the reader to the details and/or connotative chains of the real world, to immerse the reader in the richness, glamour and overwhelming diversity of what is out there. In his critique of *Montaillou,* referred to earlier, Rosaldo (1986) quotes the following passage as an example of the way in which Le Roy Ladurie carries to extremes novelistic realism's strategy of naming names, providing titles, citing specific places and referring to exact dates entirely for their own sake, to buttress the sense of the real (see my account of Radway in Chapter 5). The reader is supposed to take as read that the inquisitor produced an impeccably detailed and reliable account available for the historian's confident use over six centuries later. To this end, the inquisitor Fournier is portrayed as ambitious, industrious, talented and a tireless seeker of information:

> A few details will suggest how our dossier was built up. The inquisition court at Pamiers worked for 370 days between 1318 and 1325. These 370 days included 578 interrogations. Of these, 418 were examinations of the accused and 160 examinations of witnesses. In all these hundreds of sessions dealt with ninety-eight cases. The court set a record for hard work in 1320, with 106 days; it worked ninety-three days in 1321, fifty-five in 1323, forty-three in 1322, forty-two in 1324, and twenty-two in 1325 (Le Roy Ladurie, 1978, p. xiv, quoted in Rosaldo, 1986, p. 80).

Rosaldo comments that the imposing numbers heaped one upon the other in a manner familiar to sports fans, attempt to 'persuade the reader that they constitute an exact measure of the inquisition's degree of thoroughness... [the] piling up of statistics rhetorically makes it appear that Fournier's investigation was exhaustive and definitive' (Rosaldo, 1986, p. 80).

Barthes' book-length – phrase by phrase, sentence by sentence – structural analysis of Balzac's novella *Sarrasine* is a goldmine of examples and commentary upon the reality and connotative effects of seemingly innocuous detail. At the very beginning of the analysis in *S/Z*, Barthes discusses the following lines (lexias 2 to 7) from Sarrasine:

> I was deep in one of those daydreams which overtake even the shallowest of men, in the midst of the most tumultuous parties. Midnight had just sounded from the clock of the Elysée-Bourbon. Seated in a window recess and hidden behind the sinuous folds of a silk curtain, I could contemplate at my leisure the garden of the mansion where I was spending the evening.

Barthes notes that a metonymy leads from the Elysée-Bourbon to the signifier 'Wealth', since the Faubourg Saint-Honoré is a wealthy neighbourhood. In turn, the specific meaning of 'Wealth' connoted (implied) by the signifier of the Faubourg Saint-Honoré is the wealth of the *nouveaux riches,* as this neighbourhood refers, by synecdoche (that is, by being a part of something bigger, to which it alludes), to the Paris of the Bourbon Restoration, 'a mythic place of sudden fortunes whose origins are suspect; where gold is produced without an origin, diabolically' (Barthes, 1990, p. 21). Already, within a few sentences, Barthes argues, Balzac has conjured up the thematic signifier (the 'Seme') of wealth and has attached it in a chain of meanings to the signifiers of party, the Faubourg Saint-Honoré and a mansion.

Now, there is nothing whatsoever wrong with Balzac's subtle invocation of wealth, in itself. It is certainly not an inaccurate representation, and connotative equivalences, with all their magical charm, are legitimate in all forms of discourse (although, of course, less appropriate in some than in others!). However, when we are reading sociological texts, texts that purport to be taking a shot at intransitive reality, we should be consciously alert to the use of connotation and its power in order to know when an author – intentionally or not – is relying upon its charm and its magic to distract attention away from what is not known about, what is compressed and what is effaced. Barthes lectures, in his own lyrical and evocative style, on the surreptitious manner in which apparently innocent data coalesce to produce, in my terms, an implicit fabula, which is all the more effective for not literally speaking its name:

> The *Party,* the *Faubourg,* the *Mansion* are anodyne data, seemingly lost in the *natural* flow of the discourse; in fact, they are touches designed to bring out the image of Wealth, in the tapestry of the daydream... one cites the signified (wealth) to make it come forth, while avoiding it in the

discourse. This fleeting citation, this surreptitious and discontinuous way of stating themes, this alternating of flux and outburst, create together the *allure* of the connotation; the semes appear to float freely, to form a galaxy of trifling data in which we read no order of importance: the narrative technique is impressionistic: it breaks up the signifier into particles of verbal matter which make sense only by coalescing... the greater the syntagmatic distance between two data, the more skilful the narrative; the performance consists in manipulating a certain degree of impressionism: the touch must be light, as though it weren't worth remembering, and yet, appearing again later in another guise, it must already be a memory... (Barthes, 1990, pp. 22–3, original emphasis).

Notes

1 See the interesting discussion of the authorial narrative voices in the works of Garfinkel and Goffman respectively in Ira Cohen and Mary Rogers' article 'Autononomy and Credibility: Voice as Method' (1994).

2 Importantly for my argument here, Lodge notes that a narrative can be metonymically constructed even where it contains few metonymic tropes; that is, it can still be metonymical in structure, 'connecting topics on the basis of contiguity not similarity' (Lodge, 1977, p. 99). See footnote 2, below, for examples of metonymic and synecdochal tropes (figurative uses of language).

3 In his *The Modes of Modern Writing*, Lodge (1977) notes the close association between metonymy and synecdoche, and defines the latter as 'the substitution of part for whole, genus for species, or vice-versa'. He writes: 'The hackneyed lines, "The hand that rocks the cradle/Is the hand that rules the world" include both tropes – the synecdoche "hand" meaning "person" (by inference "mother") and the metonymy "cradle" meaning "child".' Lodge notes that in Jakobson's scheme, metonymy includes synecdoche (Lodge, 1977, p. 75).

Chapter 8

Exemplary Critiques of Sociological Modernism I: Comparative Citizenship and State Autonomy

In these final chapters, I want to concentrate upon sociological modernism, and to bring the spirit and the tools of a past-modern sociology to bear on the critique of specific examples of the most stubborn characteristics of modernist sociology. The authors of the examples chosen can be seen as representatives – more or less – of contemporary social theory's move away from ontological reductionism. All have gone out of their way to identify themselves with – again, more or less – a richer, more complex ontology. Thus, my critique, while partly focused on the need to push an ontological antireductionism even further, is directed first and foremost towards their failure to develop epistemological, methodological and textual approaches that can do justice to the richer, more complex, ontology that they, in part, recognise. I criticise them for their lack of epistemological and method-ological reflexivity, their consequent misunderstanding of the status of their own evidential base and their textual complacency, with its highly premature foreclosure on the pursuit of alternatives.

The examples chosen involve aspects of comparative citizenship, state autonomy, and patriarchal systems, and are all cases in which the modernist impulse is directed towards the big historical sweep and/or the large spatial canvas. Full-blown modernist forms of writing typically consume the complexity and diversity of the real. They manifest a desire, whether conscious or unconscious, to demonstrate total and exhaustive knowledge. The desire is tempered only by a relatively minimal sense of the difficulties of, and the obstacles in the way of, acquiring knowledge. Where past-modernist realists would luxuriate ostentatiously in a steep sweeping bow before the life-affirming goddess of doubt, modernists would, at most, give way to the slightly perceptible nod, the begrudged and hurriedly embarassed crimping of the knees. The three authors I will discuss here, while touched by contemporary social theory at the level of ontology, I judge to be typical of sociological modernists in their textual presentation and in the insistent confidence of their implied analyses. My criticisms may appear to be unkind – which is not to say unfair – and I can only stress that I have as my target the conventions that underpin and fortify these analyses. My aim is not to belittle or slight the scholarship and creativity involved in the production of these works, but it is most definitely to question – and to question deeply – the choice of those conventions. I have no illusions about the susceptibility of some of my own work to the same sorts of criticisms; the conventions, after all, have been hegemonic.

Comparative Citizenship from a Hot-air Balloon

Michael Mann's influential article on 'Ruling Class Strategies and Citizenship' (Mann, 1987, pp. 339–54) is an archetypal example of modernist historical sociology. The claims for knowledge are strikingly extensive and confidently insistent. However, one feels that the all-consuming breadth of the knowledge implied relies more on the literary sjuzet for its credibility than on an appropriately parallel all-consuming sociological analysis. On my reading, the article is, in fact, best characterised as a Floater TPA, which is highly indeterminate and ambiguous, and this form of analysis gives the author a great deal of leeway to construct a narrative with the minimal interference of empirical evidence.

Mann's analysis is ambitious in scope, covering numerous countries, and arguing that there were at least five viable ideal-type strategies for the institutionalisation of class conflict in the emergence of modern industrial societies. He argues this against T. H. Marshall's theory of citizenship, which he regards as Anglocentric and evolutionist, in not being able to see beyond the particular form that the institutionalisation of class conflict and the development of citizenship took in Britain. Mann sets himself the task of explaining the origin, development and durability of five types of 'ruling class strategies': liberal, reformist, authoritarian monarchist, Fascist and authoritarian socialist. He gives more than one national example for each of these categories, with, for example, Germany, Austria, Russia and Japan fitting into a category of countries that made similar transitions from absolutism to authoritarian monarchy (Mann, 1987, pp. 344–9). In a moment, I will focus on Mann's account of Russia for illustrative purposes, but in all of these cases, he is concerned to show that the ruling class strategy of authoritarian monarchy was a potentially durable one, and that the demise of these national strategies was contingent upon the external impact of war and geopolitics rather than upon a somehow inferior internal efficiency. He sets up Germany as the most successful of these countries and, with the other three countries, he brings out the ways in which they matched or fell short of the German ideal. In any event, his conclusion is that it is:

> plausible to conceive of the divide-and-rule, selective repression strategies, wielded by arbitrary authoritarian monarchies, surviving successfully today in Germany and Japan, and possibly also in Russia and constituent parts of Austria-Hungary... authoritarian monarchy... could probably have survived into advanced, post-industrial society, providing a distinctive, corporately organised, arbitrary combination of partial civil, political and social citizenship. This was not envisaged by Marshall, or indeed by any modern sociologist (Mann, 1987, p. 349).

The accounts of each country, however, that are given as evidence for the substantiation of this bold counterfactual conclusion, are broad and sweeping theorist pattern analyses and do not provide much for the sceptical or cross-questioning reader to go on. In addition to being a theorist pattern analysis, it is also what I have called a floater account, to be contrasted with more contextualised theorist pattern analyses (see Figure 3.3). This metaphor, as stated earlier, seeks to capture the way in which a certain type of study – and much comparative historical sociology is of this type – acquires a broader and longer perspective by means of floating over the surface of events as if in a hot-air balloon, from which one's view is extensive but lacking in detail. In the relevant section of Mann's account, the periods of time covered range from eight years in the Russian case to more than fifty in the German. There is no sense of the different regime dynamics that might exist in subperiods within these longer timescales, whose probable strategic importance is stressed by, for example, Jessop *et al.* (1988, pp. 20, 64–5) in relation to the stages of Thatcherism, and Poulantzas (1974) in relation to Italian and German fascism.[1] The local and the contextual fades very much from view in Mann's account, with the time–space positioning of events, processes, forces, divisions, places and people left very vague indeed. For the means of illustration and analysis, I will quote in full Mann's discussion of the Russian case:

> Less successful was Russia, whose regime generally favoured more repression and exclusion, yet vacillated before modern liberal and authoritarian

influences from the West. Two periods of regime concilliation (1906–7 and 1912–14) enabled the emergence of bourgeois parties of compromise and labour unions run by reformists. But each time the subsequent return to repression cut the ground from under liberals and reformists. They could promise their followers little. Many became embittered and moved leftward. Socialist revolutionaries took over the labour and peasant movements and even some of the bourgeois factions (see e.g. on the workers' movement, Bonnell 1983, and Swain, 1983). Divisions and vacillations at court prevented successful emulation of the German model. The ancien regime still possessed the loyalty of the nobility and propertied classes in general, but its modernization programme began to disintegrate from within (as Haimson, 1964, and 1965, classically argued). The regime lacked a corporate core of either liberal or conservative modernizers. Stolypin, the architect of the agrarian reforms designed to recruit the rich and middling peasant support, was the potential conservative saviour of the regime, yet his influence at court was always precarious. The divided regime became buffeted by the personal irresoluteness of Nicholas and the reactionary folly of Alexandra. When monarchy begins to depend on the personal qualities of its monarchs, it is an endangered species. Russia represented the opposite pole to Japan within the spectrum of authoritarian monarchy – no corporate regime strategy, much depending on the monarch himself. On the other hand, economic and military modernization was proving remarkably successful in pre-war Russia. Could the regime find a comparably coherent political strategy? In 1914 the answer was not yet clear. Though regime weaknesses had begun to create what later proved to be its revolutionary grave-diggers, their influence was still negligible in 1914 (Mann, 1987, pp. 346–7).

In this passage, the compression of time in the narrative is enacted by means of loose and indeterminate action sequences, in which the actors are figurative and abstract entities such as: 'Two periods of regime conciliation (1906–7 and 1912–14)' which 'enabled' a 'subsequent return to repression', which 'cut the ground from under…'; and 'Divisions and vacillation at court', which 'prevented…'. The degree of imprecision and ambiguity contained within these sequences can be grasped by attempting to think of the additional work that would have to be done in order for the account to pass the simple test of translation into a more contextualised and hermeneutic account. Needless to say, the account is dominated by authorial diegesis to the extent that mimesis is totally absent. The diegesis, moreover, is not brought to the fore as it would be in a postmodern literary text – in past-modern realism, highlighting the relationship between the autonomous elements of the research process and their relationship to the narrative text – it is presented with the omnipotent disposition of a nineteenth-century novel towards an effect of transparency, with the words on the page simply and unproblematically mirroring the world as it exists out there.

Indeed, the actual indeterminacy of Mann's account is shrouded and masked by a series of additional narrative devices, all familiar in nineteenth-century novels, which are conventionally deployed in this type of sociological study. References to proper nouns and dates give a sense of objective realism and authority, while personalised descriptive nouns and adjectives ('many became embittered', 'the personal irresoluteness of Nicholas', 'the reactionary folly of Alexandra') insinuate that the author is 'in the know' on a more cultural or hermeneutic level. A firm knowledge of the strategic context is implied in a string of phrases of authoritative certainty ('the ancien regime still possessed the loyalty of…', Stolypin's 'influence at court was always precarious', 'their influence at court was still negligible in 1914'), which fit perfectly the French literary critic Philippe Hamon's account of naïve realist discourse as managing to reject any reference to itself as a constructed discourse by means of being matter-of-fact and assertive – 'no verbs, turns of phrase, or adverbs such as: perhaps, probably, somewhat, a sort of, to seem, so to speak, one might say that, a certain, one would think, etc.' (Hamon, 1992, p. 175) By avoiding all 'distancing' of this type, naïve realist discourse presents itself as authoritative and transparent and militates against the raising of doubts. Reflexivity towards the research process as a whole, and methodology in particular, and towards the textuality of argument and evidence, is repressed in favour of the authority of 'seriousness', which Barthes regarded as the major characteristic of the readerly (*lisible*) text designed to induce passivity and trusting acceptance in the reader (Barthes, 1990; Hamon, 1990, p. 175).

The problem with Mann's account is not that it is a theorist's pattern analysis, nor that it is a floater analysis; one of my aims in outlining a realism beyond modernism is to find a legitimate means of looking at the large scale and the long term, and a Floater TPA can be a legitimate form of analysis. The problem is that, in order for it to be legitimate, it must be reflexively self-conscious as to its own character, and thus to its intrinsic limitations. The lack of reflexivity is important in Mann's account, and the many other accounts like his, because one cannot be sure how much or how little is being claimed. An ideal Floater TPA would be aware of its knowledge claims as partial, tentative, conjectural and fallible. It would be textually explicit as to what these claims were, and as specific as possible about their context. It should be aware of its possible function as a heuristic device, in which its arguments and (tentative) conclusions are treated as a provisional basis on which more contextualised and/or hermeneutically oriented hypotheses can be formed. It should be full of all the caveats, qualifications and other signposts of undecidability, which Mann avoids. The more of these there are, the easier it is for other sociologists, other researchers, to locate the gaps, the ambiguities and the uncertainties of knowledge in relation to a particular question. They facilitate the task of extending existing, highly tentative player knowledge gleaned at the Floater TPA level into islands of more contextualised and hermeneutically informed player knowledge.

Ironically, most of the space in the passage discussing Russia quoted above is intended to show the forces militating *against* the author's counterfactual claim that the Tsarist authoritarian monarchy could have survived through to the present day. It is only at the end of the passage that the purportedly superior 'arguments for' are brought in. The integrity inherent in this 'for' and 'against' procedure does not diminish any of my arguments about the type of analysis used in the article as a whole; the type of analysis is constant whether the arguments being made are pro or contra. To be sure, I certainly do not want to pass over or diminish the sort of conventional academic honesty contained in such procedures, nor, to repeat, do I want particularly to personalise my criticism of the type of argument that *Ruling Class Strategies and Citizenship* represents. The criticism of Mann's article is intended primarily as a criticism of a set of widely accepted conventions that constrain the extent to which the virtue of honesty about knowledge can be exploited.

For example, the usefulness of the arguments that Mann presents against his own thesis – the arguments that explore the weaknesses of the Tsarist regime – is severely abated by the absence of any acknowledgement of their limited contextuality. At one level, we would not need all the reflexive tools we have used to discuss Mann's article in order to see that his concluding question and answer in the section quoted above are extremely indeterminate: 'Could the regime find a comparably coherent political strategy? In 1914 the answer was not yet clear'. Mann could quite reasonably claim that the whole point about the section on Russia was to show that the survival of its authoritarian monarchy *was not out of the question* ('possibly' surviving today – I must acknowledge the one 'possibly'), not that it was definitely on the cards. However, a sceptic might surmise that the only reason this high level of indeterminacy is convincing might be because of the account's low level of contextuality. The introduction of a greater level of specificity could well have the effect of increasing our sense of the intractability of the obstacles to reform (which are mentioned but downplayed by Mann). At least one commentator on the Tsarist autocracy has concluded that the obstacles were indeed intractable:

> Neither the tardiness in the granting of political reform, nor the excesses of an extravagant and foolish nationalism, nor the personal limitations of the imperial couple began with the war or were primarily responses to the existence of the war. None of the consequences of these deficiencies were in process of any significant correction as the war approached. The spectacle of the final years of tsardom prior to 1914 is that of an impressive program of social, economic, and cultural modernization of a great country being conducted, somewhat incongruously, under the general authority of a governmental system that was itself in the advanced stages of disintegration (Kennan, 1972, p. 18).

Now, of course, the onus would also be on Kennan to translate these claims into a more contextualised and hermeneutic account in order to substantiate them and so falsify Mann's more open-ended picture of a possible political reform of Tsarist autocracy. The point is, however, that the indeterminate relationship between Mann's Floater TPA account and the rich complexity of real contextualised events means that his argument about what was possible is hardly constrained by empirical evidence. Given the low degree of contextualisation, and a high accompanying level of indeterminacy, Mann's narrative construction of his argument, culminating as it does with his claim that in 1914 the survival of the regime was still a real possibility, is arbitrary. Indeed, the account itself is superfluous because the names, dates, action sequences and everything else he says could have been included in exactly the same way, only this time to be followed by the conclusion that it was highly unlikely, in the face of all these obstacles, that the regime would have found a *political* strategy comparable in coherence to modernisation programmes in other areas. Certainly, there is no reason to believe that Kennan would be unhappy with anything in Mann's account except the conclusion.

On these grounds, it is fair to say that, in terms of the criteria that we discussed in Chapters 6 and 7, with regard to relevant and nonrelevant textual detail, Mann's account is so indeterminate as to be irrelevant to his question and argument, which demand a much higher level of contextualisation for their substantiation. Accordingly, to use and adapt Barthes' terms again, the whole of Mann's account on Russia functions solely in terms of the creation of a 'reality effect' whereby the 'effect' of having been convinced is derived from irrelevant descriptive details, fillers or padding (catalyses), superfluous to the argument itself but combining cumulatively to give readers an impression of the state of the real, which gives a false authority to the conclusion (Lodge, 1981; Barthes, 1992, pp. 135–41; Furst, 1992, p. 133).

Researching State Autonomy: the Slightly Perceptible Nod Meets the Steep Sweeping Bow

In *The Politics of Postmodernism,* Hutcheon points her finger at the shadowy world of 'paratextual conventions', especially that 'central mode of textually certifying historical events', the footnote. The footnote, says Hutcheon, is the main textual form by which 'believ-ability' is procured: 'Although publishers hate footnotes (they are expensive and they disrupt the reader's attention), such paratexts have always been central to historiographic practice, to the writing of the doubled narrative of the past in the present' (Hutcheon, 1989, p. 84). Thus, a thorough cross-questioning reader might find herself not only applying her metatheoretical rules of research to the study in hand, but also tracing back footnote sources to check on, for example, the degree of contextualisation or agent's conduct analysis within that source. More footnotes essential to the argument may, in turn, be found here, and so on. There is much room available for a writer to blur and fudge the boundaries of what is known and not known. And if the footnote is, indeed, a major form of legitimacy, the greater is the onus on sociol-ogists to be as reflexive and scrupulous about their use of footnotes as they should be in relation to the content of their main text.

Footnotes not only send one back to other sources. They can also directly provide additional, sometimes essential, argumentative and narrative backing for a text's central theses. Such footnotes may themselves rely upon their own footnotes, referring the reader to other sources. Both these last two points are pertinent to the example I will discuss in this section, which is taken from Geoffrey Ingham's *Capitalism Divided?: The City and Industry in British Social Develop-ment* (1984). Incidentally, Ingham's book is discussed by Giddens in *The Constitution of Society* (1984) as one of four works chosen as exemplary empirical illustrations of the spirit of structuration theory.

In the main body of the text in Chapter 9, 'Postwar Mercantile Revival and Industrial Decline', Ingham pursues his book's overall theme – the debilitating industry–City (financial sector) divide in Britain, and the City's dominance within that divide – in relation to the political support that the incoming Labour government of 1964 gave to the industrial sector ('productive capital and labour'). What were the ramifications of this political support for the industry–City split and for the City's erstwhile dominance?

The setting up of the Department of Economic Affairs (DEA), with the party's deputy leader George Brown as Minister, meant that for 'the only period in peacetime, productive capital had its own separate representative agency in the state, and a senior cabinet Minister in a government which was in accord with many of its views' (Ingham, 1984, p. 214). The DEA was to implement and manage the National Plan, which was publicly committed to 25 per cent growth for the economy over a period of five years, together with the maintenance of full employment. This was the medium- to long-term aim. On the other hand, the Treasury was still to retain control of the short-term management of the balance of payments and of sterling's exchange rate.

Ingham argues that this division of responsibility represented a fatal equivocation by Harold Wilson's Labour government and simply continued 'the historical fissure which had developed within British capital over a period of two centuries' (Ingham, 1984, p. 214). Despite the increasing political organisation of industry – the CBI was to be formed in 1965 – and the Labour government's overt public support, industry's bid for hegemony was destined to fail.

There are two main levels within Ingham's assessment of the situation at this stage. First, 'The City's unregulated global operations and sterling's role placed real constraints on the range of domestic policy options by means of the ever present threat of the collapse of the currency' (Ingham, 1984, p. 215), and, second, as a consequence of this situation, the Bank of England and the Treasury continued to be afforded a large measure of political independence in the management of the economy. The persistence of a certain set of institutional relationships and practices between the City, the Bank of England and the Treasury was the real underpinning of commercial and wholesale banking capital's continued hegemony. All three spheres possessed a relative autonomy from the other and each had their own particular *raison d'être* for sustaining the current pattern of their interrelationships. Against this background, Ingham argues that, despite 'Labour's explicit ideology of managed industrialism, the government seemed unable to perceive that profound changes in sterling's role and the City domination of the economy were required if the industrial strategy was to succeed' (38) (Ingham, 1984, p. 216).

The number 38 after this section of Ingham's argument directs us to a long footnote, which is designed to certify the account we have just been given. Ostensibly, it would seem that it is designed to procure the believability of the claim that the government was 'unable to perceive' that profound changes to sterling's role and the City's domination of the economy were necessary if the industrial strategy was to succeed. We will see, however, that this is not, in fact, the argument that Ingham makes in the footnote. I will cite the footnote at length because I also want to show that, despite the relatively contextualised nature of the focus, and despite the confident assertiveness of the style in which the argument is made, the certification we receive from it is actually extremely indeterminate. Any believability that is procured is purchased through ambiguity and the rhetoric of the text rather than through a systematic and ruthless tracking of the prey.

To highlight the way in which different textual strategies – just as much as institutions of the state and the economy – can have their own powerful relative autonomy, I will follow Ingham's footnote with an alternative version of my own, which will highlight some of the rhetorical strategies used. I will attempt to show that the argument proceeds by insinuating knowledge that appears to be strong and credible only because the evidence it is based on is not spoken out loud. In other words, the respect that the knowledge demands relies on the rhetoric of the text. Where there is little evidence given of a contextualised ACA then, instead, we have a no-nonsense adjective of incontrovertible force ('utmost', 'profound', 'willing') attached to the imputed verb of the action; and instead of 'probably's and 'seemingly's, there are clear and definite statements of 'did's, 'did not's and 'why's. With these points in mind, I will recover aspects of the implied fabula from the sjuzet in a very explicit and self-reflexive manner. In the process, I will reveal the indeterminacy and ambiguity of the evidence provided for the fabula implied from the perspective of the ontological and epistemological benchmarks of a past-modernist realism. This will be in marked contrast to the confidence and certainty with which Ingham plies his thesis, notwithstanding the slightest of nods to the contrary. A corollary of the indeterminacy and ambiguity of evidence is also the clear possibility of alternative accounts based upon the same evidence. A given pool of evidence can be construed in a range of different ways if the degree of contextualisation of that evidence is sufficiently indeterminate.

Geoffrey Ingham's Original Footnote

> On first inspection, Wilson's stance appears to lend support to the view that the City's existence constituted compelling power which the government opposed but was unable to resist. The hostility between the City and the government was openly and publicly expressed. Wilson, himself,

identified the 'currency speculators' and the 'gnomes of Zurich' as the perpetrators of the sterling crises. The City responded with the assertion that the government's policies were a genuine threat to international confidence in sterling and argued that unless public expenditure was reduced and the proposals for more stringent controls were dropped then sterling (and ultimately the economy) would collapse. In his speech at the annual Mansion House dinner in November 1964, Lord Cromer (Governor of the Bank of England) effectively gave notice that unless the government abandoned its plans for curbs on capital movements and introduced deflationary measures to ease the balance of payments deficits, he would be unable to organise the support of international bank capital to defend the pound's exchange rate. After further skirmishes, Wilson told the Governor that unless the financial support was organised then he would float the pound, dissolve Parliament and call a General Election on the issue of a 'banker's ramp'. The Governor acquiesced (see Michael Stewart, *The Jekyll and Hyde Years: Politics and Economic Policy Since 1964* (London: Dent, 1977, pp. 31–6). However, Wilson's overall position was one of profound ambivalence based on the simutaneous attachment to the contradictory strategies of both forms of British capital. His attacks on the City were focused on what he saw as the reprehensible and, in some cases, unpatriotic motives of individuals, and not the former's right to existence. Apart from some proposed controls, Wilson completely accepted sterling's international role and in so doing endorsed the existing structure of London's commercial markets; their integration with the world economy and, above all, the City's hegemony. In arguing against devaluation – as he did with the utmost resolution in opposition to members of his cabinet, Wilson stated that: 'there are many people overseas, including governments, market boards, central banks and others, who left their money in the form of sterling balances, on the assumption that the value of sterling would be maintained. To have let them down would not only have been a betrayal of trust, it would have shaken their faith about holding any further money in the form of sterling': cited in Longstreth [1979], 'The City, Industry and the State'. Such statements do not indicate a resistance to (and reluctant admission of defeat by) superior forces but, rather, a willing compliance with the hegemony which had dominated British policy making for over a century: Strange, *Sterling and British Policy* [1971], pp. 303–4. Further, the view that Wilson's stubborn refusal to consider devaluation as a means of making his industrial strategy viable was a result, however indirect, of City influence gains some support from the fact that by the time the pound was devalued in 1967 a significant change had already occurred in the City's practices and its views of sterling. According to Strange, the idea that the reserve and international transactions functions of a currency were separable began to emerge during the 1960s. As the *Banker* expressed it in 1967: 'A decline in the reserve role of sterling need not be too damaging to its use as a world trading currency. Britain remains a great trading country, and it will continue to be convenient to transact a great deal of world commerce in sterling. Similarly, the attraction of the City of London as a financial centre will survive the devaluation of sterling. Its remarkable success in Euro-currency business in recent years is evidence, if it still be needed, of its enterprise and adaptability, the pound will still be used as a leading world currency for trade and finance': quoted in Longstreth 'The City, Industry and the State', pp. 175–6. In other words, there are some grounds for believing that Wilson's submission to his cabinet colleagues' pressure for devaluation coincided with the withdrawal of opposition to such a move by the more enlightened and perceptive sections of the City. Furthermore, there was a growing realisation that uncertainty surrounding sterling impeded the smooth functioning of some of the City's operations. Although speculative activity on the foreign exchanges and short term money markets could produce large profits (and losses) it was the stability of sterling that was required to ensure the rational calculability which would permit the maximisation of exchange transactions. This division in the City emerged in the early nineteenth century, as I indicated earlier: see Stewart, *The Jekyll and Hyde Years*, 'Labour and the City's Hangups', pp. 31–6. (Ingham, 1984, pp. 285–6).

Alternative Footnote

I will take up my alternative footnote – as narrated by a hypothetical past-modern Geoffrey Ingham – as if from just after the Michael Stewart reference in the original as just quoted. Thus:

Wilson's position is difficult to fathom. Perhaps he was *profoundly ambivalent, attached simultaneously to the contradictory strategies of both forms of British capital.* Or, perhaps, he was genuinely committed to the strategy of industrial modernisation but was hampered in his pursuit of it, as I suggested in the main body of the text, because the ever present threat of the collapse of sterling placed real constraints upon the Government's policy. I have not really been able to unearth enough evidence to decide either way. I have said that Wilson was 'profoundly ambivalent', but I suppose that this was exceeding the realms of my authority.

Let me reconsider my evidence. On the one hand, I will stick to my claim that *Wilson's attacks on the City were focused on what he portrayed as the reprehensible and, in some cases, unpatriotic motives of individuals, and not on the former's right to existence.* But then, if you were worried about the collapse of sterling and its effects upon your industrial strategy, would you challenge the City's right to existence? This would not necessarily signify a lack of commitment to the industrial strategy.

If you were profoundly committed to an industrial strategy based, not least, upon an expansionary demand profile, you would most probably be highly wary of undermining the macro-economic conditions for this. Moreover, it is in fact possible that Wilson did attempt to curb the City's power as far as possible without causing the sort of panic run on sterling that would have fatally undermined his industrial strategy. Thus, while Wilson made no outright challenge to the City's right to existence he did, for example, introduce a series of controls upon sterling's freedom of exchange, controls that brought forth a heated response from City supporters.

This response could quite easily, I must admit, be interpreted as providing grist for the view that Wilson's attitude to the City and its values was totally instrumental and pragmatic. Still, I would like to maintain my assertion that when challenged at various intervals between 1964 and November 1967 by the prodevaluationists in his cabinet, Wilson stood by his position of defending sterling. One of the many things he said on one of these occasions, trying to convince his colleagues of his case, was: '*there are many people overseas, including governments, market boards, central banks, and others, who left their money in the form of sterling balances, on the assumption that the value of sterling would be maintained. To have let them down would not only have been a betrayal of trust, it would have shaken their faith about holding any further money in the form of sterling*': cited in Longstreth (1979), 'The City, Industry and the State'. However, it is difficult to be sure about the meaning of this one statement without providing much more of the context and background in which it was spoken.

In my previous rendering of this footnote, I wrote of *the 'utmost resolution' with which Wilson spoke*. Well, this is the way it seemed to me, although, to be frank, I haven't got too much of an idea about what lay behind that semblance of resolve. The level of my agent's conduct analysis of Wilson is at just about the lowest level of contextu-alisation possible – after all, I was writing a book covering over two hundred years of social development – so I suppose that in conveying something so solid about the strength of his motivation, I was drawing almost entirely upon the resources of textuality and literariness and hardly at all on those of analysis. In order to be able to say anything about Wilson's motivation or intentions in uttering that statement, we would, for example, have to know much more about Wilson's own analysis of context. We would have to know about his perception of the constraints posed by sterling's position: if the trust of central banks and governments in holding sterling balances had been shaken by an earlier devaluation, what would this have meant for the level to which sterling would have had to be lowered in order for it to be safe from further pressure? What would this have meant, in turn, for the growth strategy of 25 per cent in five years, based upon the steady expansion of demand? Would such an exchange rate level have put subsequent pressure on the US dollar, itself a weakening currency? What would this have meant for US and International Monetary Fund underwriting of sterling? And to what extent would all of these things have forced his government to take radical deflationary measures? With one sentence from the Prime Minister, the mimesis of direct speech though it is, we just do not know the answers to these questions. Where did this sentence fit into his general frame of meaning? To what extent did the specific audience (of the Cabinet) have an effect upon its authenticity, the degree of disclosure, the depth of discussion and the perception of the stage as 'front' or 'back'? To be blunt, I do not really have very strong grounds for believing that Wilson's talk of *not letting down the overseas holders of sterling was an expression of a normative commitment to, a willing compliance with, the values and principles of commercial and wholesale banking capital over and above the values and principles of industrial modernisation.* It is only by following through a much more complicated scenario of alternative possibilities available to Wilson that I could even begin to substantiate my, rather overenthusiastic, assertion that *Wilson's Cabinet statement did not indicate a resistance to (and reluctant admission of defeat by) superior forces but, rather, a willing compliance with the hegemony of the City.* In the event, I really don't seem to have acquired much evidence about Wilson's conduct or context analysis of his situation, certainly nowhere near enough to begin to confront the many conditionalities and caveats of counterfactual hypotheses.

The two additional pieces of implied evidence that I provide towards the end of my footnote – concerning the increase in Euro-currency business and the business advantages of stability on the foreign exchange markets – are really not very convincing; any persuasive effect they do have rests on a piling up of circumstantial evidence, not on a careful attempt to trace through causal chains – recognising gaps and indeterminacies – in order to narrow down alternative explanations. Indeed, the abscence of any real causal analysis is shrouded within the text by the simple strategy (albeit an intuitive one, I must add) of highlighting the spatiotemporal contiguity of these two concerns of the City with the decision to devalue – the explicit claim, it should be noted, is only the innocent temporal one that there are some grounds for believing that Wilson's decision 'coincided' with withdrawal of opposition by some elements within the City. Contiguous association is translated only implicitly into a (possible) causal relationship of the same hue. The sense of City influence on the devaluation decision derives from this very simple metonymic (spatiotemporal) chain of equivalence: the devaluation decision as part of the implied whole. My lightness of touch in backgrounding my nonanalysis of causal relations is facilitated, not least, by the (syntagmatic) distance between my previous confident assertions of Wilson's 'willing compliance' with the City – words now forgotten, sense remembered – from the remarks about 'coincidence': the whole makes sense simply by 'coalescing' (Barthes, 1990, pp. 22–3, see above).

Notes

1 This is not to say that both Jessop *et al.*'s account and that of Poulantzas could not be rendered in a more contextualised manner: they certainly could. The point is simply that their emphasis upon the different stages of a régime and its dynamics is the sort of framework that can open up the possibility of, and can provide a framework to give meaning to, greater contextualisation.

Chapter 9

Exemplary Critiques of Sociological Modernism II: The Flying Sorcery of Sylvia Walby's Patriarchal Systems

In this final chapter, I will discuss the attempt by Sylvia Walby, in the course of a number of linked publications, to establish a particular view of patriarchal systems. The critique will be informed by the guidelines of a past-modern realism in general but, more specifically, will be directed by the insistence (articulated in Chapters 2 and 4) that systems are ontologically the emergent properites of many local interactions and interconnections across time and space, and that, consequently, they cannot be treated any differently in terms of ontology than a single highly localised social event. In principle, systems can be analysed in the ACA Contextualiser frame of the player grid. In practice, this is hardly possible. The consequence is that epistemology and methodology are called upon to be creative, flexible and imaginative, to develop ways of thinking about the systems that traverse all our lives, but to develop them in ways that do not do violence to the rich, complex ontology that we have made central to the whole project of past-modern realism. To develop the capacity to think about systems in more adequate ways than hitherto is, to my mind, one of the most pressing tasks faced by sociologists. It is a task that has, thus far, frustrated some of the most well-equipped and agile minds (cf Joas, 1991, pp. 97–118; Habermas, 1991, pp. 250–64; McCarthy, 1991, pp. 119–39).

A major theme of this book has been that a sympathy, shared with postmodernism, towards the local and the contextual does not necessarily entail a rejection of thinking on the large scale, and I have suggested a number of ways in which a reflexively aware sociology can combine the strengths of both. In analysing Walby's work in some detail, I want to help push forward a little further this project of thinking anew, doing so by means of illustrating the inexorable problems, pitfalls and conceits of continuing to imagine that it is acceptable to think about systems in a largely unreconstructed modernist manner. Aware of the rather uncompromising tone of what follows, I must reiterate at this point that I regard Walby's work to be representative of an extremely widespread use of similar modernist conventions. One of the major reasons, besides its scope, that I have chosen Walby's work to criticise at length is that, notwithstanding the criticisms I will go on to make, I have learnt a lot from it. I have long appreciated her disaggregations of the sweepingly reductionist claims of previous theories of patriarchy, even though, by now, I do not think she goes far enough, stopping too far short of the demands of a rich and complex ontology. I have been an attentive reader of her work through the years and this – ironically, but also, in a way, inevitably – is why I know that work well enough to criticise it as I do. This is, for better or for worse, a not uncommon fate for those from whom we learn something that matters to us. It is, ultimately, I think (and hope), a satisfactory fate.

Walby's systems-thinking is very much in the tradition of the large sweep, both spatially and temporally, and is quintessentially modernist in its drive towards totalisation. In my terms, it is a clear example of the sort of sociological despotism that gives a good name to defeatist postmodernists. The despotism almost inevitably results from the failure to be reflexively systematic about the production and status of her knowledge claims. My critical analysis builds on the foundations of a critique of Walby's orientation to metatheory: to ontology and epistemology. I will argue that her attention to these dimensions is very slight and that her appreciation of their importance is damagingly underdeveloped. Although at the level of ontology, Walby has produced some valuable critiques of modernist reductionism, her accounts underplay both the richness and the research implications of the complex ontology of contemporary social theory. They lack a sense of the methodological guidelines appropriate to such a complex ontology. It is the latter that are an essential bridge enabling a realist ontology to give rise to systematic and consistent methodological consequences.

Each one of the relatively autonomous elements in the player model of research (see Chapter 3) is involved in the translation of a question or problem-to-be-solved (an *explanandum*) into a more or less satisfactory empirical resolution of that problem. It is important, as I have emphasised throughout, that in any research process, each element is compatible with each of the other elements: metatheory compatible with theoretical categories and claims; empirical evidence compatible with the reflexive frame and methodological bracketing, which themselves must be appropriate to the question and the related hypothesis; empirical evidence compatible with metatheory generally and ontology in particular – so that, for example, an ontology of a duality of structure and agency should not be combined with a presentation of empirical evidence to force through a structuralist explanation without reference to the hermeneutic contribution of agency; and so on.

Walby's metatheoretical weakness, I will try to show, has direct implications for her theoretical categories. The theoretical categories become overly simplified, flat and arbitrarily malleable as, in terms of the top row of the research models (see Figure 3.1), they are decoupled not only from the guiding presence of a complex ontology but also, too often, from the elements of questioner and question respectively. This implies, *a fortiori*, that they also tend to be decoupled from the guiding lights of the appropriate methodological brackets for a particular question. In short, there are no clear steps from theory to evidence, just *ad hoc*, unsystematic and relatively obscure affinities between a broad theoretical category and a piece of empirical evidence. Walby's overly confident and presumptious textual strategies are closely related to the above weaknesses. Lacking a reflexive awareness of the various dimensions of analysis, she inevitably lacks an ability to foster textual strategies that would respect the integrity and intricacies of a more sophisticated analysis.

I will present examples to illustrate my belief that most of Walby's analyses, and the evidence for them, are in fact best seen as constructed on the dreamer and TPA Floater models, with rare forays into the TPA Contextualiser frame (see Figure 3.3). However, in case after case, Walby believes she is doing more than she is: she believes that she knows more than she does, or, more precisely, she writes as if she knows more than she is telling us. She writes for trusting readers, not for sceptical readers who cross-question and reflexively monitor the evidence before them. A reflexive and sceptical reading of the evidence provided tells a different story to the one that is asserted. When Walby is dreaming, she believes that she is playing, and when she is floating she believes that she is contextualising. When she is carrying out a theorist's pattern analysis, she makes the sorts of claim only possible on the basis of an agent's conduct analysis.

A Patriarchal System of Six Structures

Walby's claim to distinctiveness is a theory of a patriarchal system that is made up of six main structures. The six structures are patriarchal relations in paid work, housework (the patriarchal mode of production), sexuality, culture, violence and the state (cf Walby, 1990, p. 16

and *passim*). These six structures are all involved in the maintenance of patriarchy, which Walby defines as 'a system of interrelated social structures through which men exploit women... The definition refers to a system of social relations rather than individuals, since it is presumed that it is at the level of a social system that gender relations may be explained, not that of individual men, nor that of discrete social institutions' (Walby, 1986, p. 51).

She argues that many of the existing grand theories of patriarchy have problems in dealing with historical and cultural variation because they are too reductionist. They tend to reduce the variety and complexity of the whole of patriarchal relations to one or two causes/bases, such as paid work/capitalism and housework, for example. Walby argues that this crude base-superstructure model, in which variety and complexity are seen as epiphenomena of whichever single base is chosen, is inadequate. Such models cannot understand variation and change. Walby triumphantly announces that 'this problem can be solved' (Walby, 1990, p. 16) by theorising causation in terms of six bases instead of one or two. She says that the six structures 'have causal effects upon each other, both reinforcing and blocking, but are relatively autonomous' (Walby, 1990, p. 20).

At the same time, it is important to note that examining causal relations within the system of patriarchy is not the same as examining causation within the system of gender inequality, as this would require an investigation of the intersection of patriarchy with capitalism and with racist structures (Walby, 1986, p. 69). Consequently, any 'specific empirical instance will embody the effects, not only of patriarchal structures, but also of capitalism and racism' (Walby, 1990, p. 20).

Walby's Dislike of too much Ontological Complexity: Six Structures *versus* Postmodernism

While Walby criticises overreductionist theories for not being specific and complex enough, she also criticises poststructuralist and postmodern approaches for being overly specific and too complex. In an article entitled *Post-Post-Modernism: Theorizing Social Complexity* (author's note – for 'Post-Post-Modernism' read 'Back to Modernism'), she specifically singles out the journal *m/f,* which, in an enterprise parallel to the one advocated by Joan Scott discussed in Chapter 1, takes as its project the breaking down of the unitary category of 'woman' because of its essentialism. Instead, *m/f* was marked by an emphasis on 'a number of cross-cutting discourses of femininities and masculinities which are historically and culturally variable' (Walby, 1992, p. 35). Walby gives an extended illustration of the sort of thing she means, which is worth quoting at length. For me it vindicates the *m/f* emphasis on contextuality and the significatory theory of language and meaning; it shows precisely that the notion of 'woman' can be, and is, constructed in variable, cross-cutting and highly specific ways, which are hardly accessible to the dreamers and TPA Floaters of this world. Walby summarises an article by Rosalind Coward, published in 1978 (Coward, 1978, pp. 7–24), which looks at the category of 'woman' in terms of its multiple representations in just one sphere of, to use Walby's terms, the culture structure available to British women, namely, contemporary women's magazines:

> There are many different ways in which 'femininity' is represented. In some, such as *Women's Own* and *Good Housekeeping*, femininity is seen in relation to family roles of cooking, cleaning and child-care. In others, such as *Cosmopolitan*, the focus is on the sexualization of the body of women in the context of successful careers and sexual and economic independence, and references to family roles are almost non-existent. In *Cosmopolitan* the glamour image is continued through the advertisements for related products such as make-up, soaps and body lotions. The film *Emmanuelle* offers yet another form of femininity, in which female sexuality is presented for the voyeuristic male gaze. Coward suggests that *Cosmopolitan* is a site of competing definitions of female sexuality, while that of *Emmanuelle* is foreclosed (Walby, 1992, p. 35).

Walby does not like this sort of analysis, and the project it is wedded to, because of the implication she believes it has that the categories of women and men have no use in social analysis:[1] 'The notion of 'women' and 'men' is dissolved into shifting, variable social constructs which lack coherence and stability over time' (Walby, 1992, pp. 34–5). This is a familiar theme for Walby. In *Theorizing Patriarchy*, she wrote that while postmodern critics

> have made some valuable points about the potential dangers in theorizing gender inequality at an abstract and general level... they go too far in denying the necessary impossibility and unproductive nature of such a project. While gender relations could potentially take an infinite number of forms, in actuality there are some widely repeated features. In addition the signifiers of 'woman' and 'man' have sufficient historical and cross-cultural continuity, despite some variations to warrant using such terms. It is a contingent question as to whether gender relations do have sufficient continuity of patterning to make generalizations about a century or two and a continent or so useful. While I agree that the answer to this cannot be

given at a theoretical level, I shall argue in this book that in practice it is possible; that there are sufficient common features and sufficient routinized interconnections that it does make sense to talk of patriarchy in the West in the last 150 years at least (Walby, 1990, p. 16).

Walby, it is clear, is not only arguing, *pace* postmodernism, that it is *possible* to theorise at an abstract and general level while simultaneously avoiding the potential dangers, but she is also quite confident that she has actually done this: 'in practice... there are sufficient common features and routinised interconnections that it does make sense to talk of patriarchy in the West in the last 150 years at least'. In my opinion, what she actually does is to acknowledge that postmodernists 'have made some valuable points' (largely unspecified), only then to ignore everything they have said. She leaves us in no doubt about the scale and the scope of the project that she feels is able to avoid those unspecified potential dangers of abstraction and generalisation, namely a century or two and a continent or so.

In addition, Walby feels that through their emphasis on language and representation, the postmodernists typically neglect the social context of power relations: 'in so far as power is discussed it is represented as highly dispersed, so dispersed as to preclude the possibility of noting the extent to which one social group is oppressed by another' (Walby, 1992, p. 35). Finally, postmodernists are also said to de-emphasise economic relations, making their analyses of gender overly free-floating (Walby, 1992, pp. 35–6).

So, in summary, Walby's position is that she does not like traditional grand theories of patriarchy because they are too reductionist: there is not enough complexity in their accounts. On the other hand, she does not like postmodern accounts because there is too much complexity and dispersion in these. Walby likes a little bit of complexity – six structures worth – but not too much. Moreover, in addition to their overenthusiasm for cultural and historical variability, she believes that postmodern accounts also emphasise representation and language at the expense of power and economics. It is not clear to what extent Walby feels that the second of these supposed weaknesses is a necessary product of the first, or just a contingent matter of emphasis. I certainly think that, to the extent that it is true, the relationship is contingent. In any case, I will concentrate upon the first of postmodernism's 'weaknesses'.

Beginning To Get the Picture: Piecing Together the Elements of Walby's Theory

The first thing to say in constructing a critique of Walby is that she is very explicit, albeit very brief, about her commitment to a realist ontology in which structures (hence her six structures) are emergent properties of social practices, which, following Giddens, contain a duality of both structure and action. She says that the theoretical project of *Theorizing Patriarchy* (1990) is realist, in the sense that it is engaged in an identification of the underlying structures of social life (Walby, 1990, p. 19). She acknowledges, like Bhaskar (whom she cites), that social systems are open. The system of patriarchy is thus, of course, seen as an open system (Walby, 1990, p. 19). Her formal commitment is thus expressly to the ontology used as the basis for this book, and which I have variously characterised as local, contextualised, complex and hermeneutic. On the basis of this ontology, it is clear to me why Walby does not like the reductionist theories that reduce the problem of patriarchy to only one or two of the six structures. There is clearly a disjunction between such reductionist ontological positions and the rich and contingent ontology of open systems we have been dealing with. On the other hand, it is not so clear why Walby should react so negatively to the rich and contingent ontology of the postmodernists/poststructuralists of *m/f,* or to the emphasis on shifting, variable social constructs that it allows. The objection does not flow logically from the ontology.[2]

If Walby's objection is not a necessary, logical one arising from a more reductive ontology, one might, first, reasonably surmise that it has something to do with her values and preferred objectives, with what she thinks is the purpose of theorising about gender or patriarchy. Her objection would then stem less from ontological differences and more from the purposes of the questioner and the questions or problems that she wishes to solve. We have seen in earlier chapters how contemporary social theorists and postmodernists have put increasing stress on the role of the questioner, her values, experience, objectives and textual devices. It is also fairly clear that this message has been listened to much more by researchers working at the local and contextual level than by those more concerned with the macro-scale. In texts that deal with the large scale, overt attention to the author, researcher, questioner and her values, purposes and/or experience tends to be reduced to the formalistic minimum. This is as true in Walby's case as it is in others.

However, there is a pointer to work with. One can see, without much difficulty, from what Walby writes that she is, at least, very concerned that forms of analysis should maintain the possibility of being able to note 'the extent to which one social group is oppressed by another' (Walby, 1992, p. 35). She never reflects upon why this is an important question to ask. It is not as obvious as it initially looks; there could be many reasons, each of them suggesting a different focus. In any case, the concepts of 'woman' and 'patriarchy' are important for her in this respect as they are used as the basis for macro-social theorising. They allow her to make those 'generalisations about a century or two and a continent or so' (Walby, 1992, p. 36). She believes that patriarchy, like racism and capitalism, remains a potent social force, and that all of these phenomena remain as 'virulent social divisions' (Walby, 1992, p. 33). These are all forms of social inequality that have a generality and a routineness about them, and the duty to grasp this should not be squandered by a retreat into the local and the contextual, into difference and fragmentation. In some ways Walby's project is, of course, laudable. How can we object to an attempt to root out common inequalities and expose deeply structured social divisions? The problem, as I see it, is that a much more effective way of pursuing these objectives would be to acknowledge the possibility of the fragmentation of reality, to take seriously the contingency, contextuality and potential variety of the social world as the basis on which to draw out any possible similarities between contexts, or affinities between mainly dissimilar contexts (see Chapter 2).

Walby starts with a whole series of assumptions about commonalities and similarities, in a way that necessarily downgrades difference, contextuality and hermeneutic specificities. From the very start, there is a bias in Walby's work towards her own abstract theoretical categories at the expense of the perspectives of lay actors. These categories are designed to silence and/or marginalise differences of context and meaning and to move commonalities to centre stage. In the process, we immediately lose the reflexive frame of hermeneutically informed contextuality for understanding the experience of lay actors, their hermeneutic perspectives, their agent's conduct and agent's context analyses. We lose the ability to focus in detail upon conjunctural constraints, opportunities and counterfactual possibilities, and the ethical issues related to all these elements. There is never any acknowledgement by Walby that these losses matter in any way whatsoever.

In ruling by fiat that her approach is superior to that of the postmodernists, Walby suggests that there is a necessary incompatibility between, on the one hand, the emphasis on contextuality and the deconstruction of macro-categories, and, on the other, her macro-theorising of similarities and systems. She suggests that hers is the only way to go. On the contrary, my argument in this book entails that the ontology we are supposed to share suggests that what she labels as the postmodernist approach – and whose broad ontological thrust, I have argued, is shared by a large segment of contemporary social theorists – must have a primacy with regard to the conditions of testability and falsifiability of research claims. Far from being able to dispense with the variety and detail of everyday life, Walby must be aware of its potential variability as a condition of the status of her own claims. All macro, large-scale research accounts should be able, in principle, to pass the test of extension to more contextualised descriptions, in the sense of being compatible with such 'thicker' descriptions. Respecting a realist ontology that stresses the integrity of the local, the contextual and the hermeneutic entails an understanding that it is at this level that events, processes and actions take place, whatever their wider conditions of existence. Any abstraction from this level needs to be keenly aware of itself as such. Equally, any methodological perspective on this level that brackets out the hermeneutic dimension needs to be sensitive to its partial take on the real, hermeneutically mediated, processes of causality. Furthermore, any methodological perspective that focuses on chronically reproduced institutional routines in abstraction from the complex and contingent processes by which they are produced in open systems should be continually aware of this missing causal dimension.

In constructing her system of patriarchy, which is constituted by six structures, Walby abstracts from the contextual frame; she is hooked on theorist's pattern analysis and generally has little time for the hermeneutic dimension, and she has much more interest in chronically reproduced institutional routines than in the contingent causal processes of structuration in open systems. Where she does look at the latter, she characteristically does so, as I will illustrate below, on the basis of a Floater TPA of the putative interaction of two or three different sets of routine institutional practices with a very low level of contiguity. Indeed, most of Walby's player analyses (or player illustrations for her dreamer theory) are pitched in the TPA Floater frame, with a very low degree of contiguity. However, she shows little awareness of the lightweight and highly indeterminate nature of the evidence she puts forward.

A Sophisticated Systems Analysis or Six Speculative Chapter Headings?

In discussing her system of patriarchy, Walby writes as if she is doing more than giving a list of six different broadly defined areas of gender oppression. We have already had a taste of the fact that her discussion of the six structures of the patriarchal system contains many references to their interconnectedness, to their causal effects upon each other (cf Walby, 1990, p. 177).

Indeed, she develops a distinction between *degrees* and *forms* of patriarchy, in which the first term refers to the intensity of oppression in one of the structures (for example the size of the wages gap between men and women)[3], while the second is explicitly geared to an analysis of the 'specific relations between the different patriarchal structures... In different times and places some of the structures are more important than others... Logically there could be many forms, since I have identified six structures within patriarchy and two other major systems with which it has been in articulation' (Walby, 1990, pp. 174, 177, see also Chapter 8, pp. 173–201). Walby argues that in recent Western history there have been two major forms of patriarchy; these are represented by her in Figure 9.1 (Walby, 1990, p. 24).

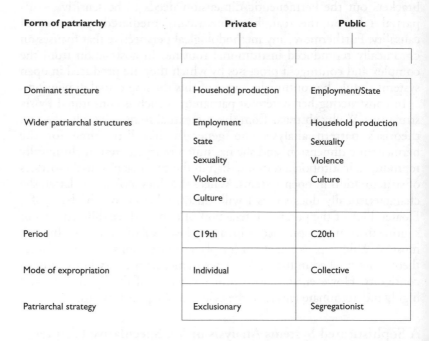

Form of patriarchy	Private	Public
Dominant structure	Household production	Employment/State
Wider patriarchal structures	Employment	Household production
	State	Sexuality
	Sexuality	Violence
	Violence	Culture
	Culture	
Period	C19th	C20th
Mode of expropriation	Individual	Collective
Patriarchal strategy	Exclusionary	Segregationist

Figure 9.1 Walby's 'private and public patriarchy' *(Reproduced from Walby, 1990)*

Figure 9.1 indicates that there has been a move from a predominantly private form of patriarchy in the nineteenth century, to a predominantly public form in the twentieth century. There has been a move from the individual woman's privatised oppression within the home in the last century, to a more collectivised public form of oppression in this century, women no longer being excluded from the public sphere but segregated and subordinated within it. This shift has its corollary in each of the six structures, so that, for example, on the level of the *cultural* discourse of femininity, there has been a shift 'away from private domesticity towards more public aspects of sexual attractiveness to men, outside as well as inside the family' (Walby, 1990, p. 108). Walby concludes that 'In each type of patriarchy the six structures are present, but the relationship between them, and their relative significance, is different' (Walby, 1990, p. 178).

On my reading, there is a clear tension in Walby's work between her use of the six structures as catch-all carriers in which to fling broadly similar types of social phenomena, looking for broad trends, and her seemingly more ambitious use of them as the constituent components of a definitely interrelated system of patriarchy, which can take different specific forms depending upon the exact forms of interdependency and mutual causation. The catch-all function of each structure – especially when each structure is used, as in *Theorizing Patriarchy* (1990), to give a heading to a chapter containing a review of all relevant literature and a survey of empirical data – tends to bring out the diversity of the social phenomena that are captured under each heading. So, for example, under the heading of 'violence', we have such disparate acts as: rape and indecent assault; wife beating; state policing of industrial relations disputes and employment law; various other types of state legislation; gender bias in the judicial system, from police procedures to forms of processing by the courts; and child sexual abuse (Walby, 1990, pp. 52–3, 128–49). Interconnections are, at times, implied by Walby, and we can see intuitively that there are many. However, an uneasy sense of the range and diversity of the practices that Walby wants *to conceptualise as a system* also begins to form. A contextualised player analysis of any one of these categories of violent practices would have many events and processes to choose from, to trace connections between.

If we remember that the structure of 'violence' is only one of Walby's six structures, each of which has at least as many types of practices under its umbrella (think of state practices!), and that we aspire to make claims about the interconnections between all of these elements, the thought of the exercise soon becomes overwhelming. In order for

Walby successfully to have undertaken this task, indeed to have the necessary capacities to undertake this task, she would, it seems to me, have to acquire the same sorts of power as the people from the planet Tralfamadore in Kurt Vonnegut's *Slaughterhouse Five* (1991). The Tralfamadorians, who come in a flying saucer to kidnap Vonnegut's narrator, Billy Pilgrim, on his daughter's wedding night, have the capacity to view the world in four dimensions instead of our limited earthling three dimensions. They can, Billy tells us, see all moments, past, present and future. These moments all exist at the same time to their four dimensional sight, they always have existed and always will exist. The Tralfamadorians 'can look at all the different moments just the way we can look at a stretch of the Rocky Mountains, for instance. They can see how permanent all the moments are, and they can look at any moment that interests them' (Vonnegut, 1989, pp. 19, 53). If Sylvia Walby is from the planet Tralfamadore, I will eat my words – I will eat the planet Tralfamadore.

It does not seem to me that Walby has succeeded in dispensing with the fragmentation and complexity of social processes emphasised by postmodernists, and I clearly would not expect her to succeed. Rather, she has found some broadly defined categories, in terms of which she can enter numerous dispersed and complex social processes into a limited number of files. The only way in which these processes need be similar is in terms of their seeming to fit under one of the six umbrella terms according to conventional language use. The idea that Walby has demonstrated more than this, to the extent of exhibiting system interconnections and causal chains within and between her six umbrella categories, is one that should be looked upon with generous helpings of scepticism. Her own archetypically modernist use of language certainly implies that she has a great and intimate knowledge of how the system interconnections and causal linkages look when one traces them out (cf Walby, 1990, pp. 178–9 and *passim*). This is clearly stated, for example, in her confident attribution of 'dominant structure' to household production in the nineteenth century and to employment/state in the twentieth. The relative causal significance of the collection of practices contained under these headings is said to be greater than that of the varied collection of practices contained under the other headings.

There are two points that I want to make about this. The first is that if Walby had succeeded in tracing through all the relevant causal processes, she would necessarily have had to have done so by means of returning to the local, to the contextual and to the different, as well as to the similar. She would have had to contextualise in context, to pass each part of the test of translation into the language of the contextual level, to trace through, in Cohen's words, 'the ordering and the articulations between interactions in time and space' (Cohen, 1989, p. 89), and to do so within the ACA Contextualiser frame (see Figure 3.3).

The second point is that Walby does not do this (how could anybody do this on such a scale?): her analysis is not a concerted and contextualised player analysis of system interconnections on such an enormous, mind-numbing scale, despite her implications to the contrary. The suggested precision of her theoretical formulations is never actually operationalised. Walby's six structures are rather thinly characterised theoretical categories, which, in accordance with what I have said above, are utilised as malleable and manipulable actors. The lack, not least, of a developed and systematic relationship to the discipline of ontological complexity allows the six structures to take on virtually any shape they like without changing their label. These categories (and the same is true of 'capitalism' and 'racism' in Walby's hands) thus function within her texts as metonymic (synecdochic) devices, which maintain the semblance of authority only by completely effacing the particularities of large chunks of time and space by substituting particular signs purporting to represent the whole (for example patriarchal violence) to stand in for the many, many parts in many, many times and places.

Cutting through the Pretensions of the Text: Walby's Speculative Hypotheses and their Evidential Support

Walby's remarks about patriarchy as a system, and about the articulation of the patriarchal system with the systems of capitalism and racism, would for the most part – and against the grain of her textually implied pretensions – best be treated as dreamer hypotheses. The illustrative examples of, or the substantive investigations of, these hypotheses come in two major forms:

1 The first, and most common, uses illustrations that are focused in the methodological bracket of institutional analysis (generalised practices and conversion relations between sets of these, see Chapter 4) and are given what detail they have in the TPA Floater frame with a very low degree of contiguity. (Another name for what Walby provides us with here, with which we are more familiar, is 'empirical correlations', but I think it is worth spelling out where I think such correlations fit in terms of reflexive frame and mode of bracketing).

2 The second, rarer, and more contextualised, form of dreamer analysis uses illustrations that are focused in the methodological brackets of systems analysis and theorist's context analysis (see Figure 4.2, and Chapter 4) and are fleshed out in the TPA Contextualiser frame (see Figure 3.3), with a variable degree of contiguity.

Both forms of hypothesis should be characterised as dreamer forms because of the way in which the illustrations are generalised beyond the specific illustrative instance to a myriad of other instances, which are not investigated – are not known about – as a means of bolstering the grand claims about patriarchal and other systems.

Given the ontology of open systems, one would expect these generalisations to be tentative and partial, to be agnostic about the specific manifestation of the phenomena in the other times and places, and to be ignorant about any contextual countertendencies that there might be. Walby rarely expresses such provisos. On those occasions when she does note the effects of the open system, it is to show the intervening effects of the systems of capitalism or racism on the systems of patriarchy, or to show the effects of one of the six structures on one or two of the others. When she does this, she seems to be beginning to recognise the importance of contextualisation and contingency to empirical realities in a way that would mean that her more homogeneous universalistic expectations – a century or two and a continent or so – would be undermined. But she never takes the hint.

Dreaming of a Continent or So, Floating over a Patch or Two: Capitalism, Racism and Patriarchy in the Inner Cities

The first type of example is occasionally presented purely as a player floater analysis of a particular case of system interconnections in its own right without its generalisation to other instances. More often, however, it is used to generalise, to bolster the universal claims. A good example of the latter is Walby's discussion of William Julius Wilson's *The Truly Disadvantaged: The Inner City, the Underclass and Public Policy* (1987) in her Post-Post-Modernism article. The textuality of Walby's analysis of Wilson's discussion is a perfect example of the way in which diegetic framing can be employed to overwhelm and glamorise the unsuspecting reader into a disposition of trusting admiration. She showers Wilson with adjectival plaudits, heaping authority and legitimacy upon him until, when the time comes to trump him, she is clearly trumping a genius, an authoritative genius with the most marvellous of grasps. One can feel the postmodern critics reaching for their copies of Nietzsche and Foucault, and who can blame them?

Wilson's book is said to be a highly sophisticated analysis of the intersections between class and 'race', and between class and gender, 'which engages with both theoretical and empirical issues of these intersections in carefully nuanced ways' (Walby, 1992, p. 40). His argument is 'consistently buttressed by extensive reference to empirical studies. It is a most impressive piece of scholarship. His correlations are impeccably established. His theoretical account of the relationship between "race" and class is sophisticated and subtly nuanced' (Walby, 1992, p. 41). It is too bad about his analysis of gender, which is 'much more crudely dealt with' (Walby, 1992, p. 41).

Rather quizzically, Walby observes that 'despite the call for complex accounts of social change... most sociologists in practice analyse at best only two out of the three of gender, "race" and class, and often only one of these!' (Walby, 1992, p. 33). I would have thought that an emphasis on complexity would help one to understand why it is not possible to understand everything at once. Analyses can always be extended, as long as they are as reflexive as possible about the specifics of their question, their perspective and their evidence. A subtle approach to complexity would be interested in these specifics, in achieving a level of contextualisation that is consonant with the claims that are made. In subject areas where there is a systematic neglect of certain questions, such as the situation that confronted Gilligan in relation to gender in child developmental psychology, there will be an obvious case for an adjustment of the balance, but even here, we will not be looking for all the new studies to necessarily include gender, race and class!

Walby presents Wilson's analysis, and her own 'corrections', as antidotes to the fragmentary excesses of postmodernism. It is given as an example of a study that manages to capture the articulation of the systems of class, race and gender. Wilson's analysis of the disadvantaged position of black people in US society is said to articulate race with class, in that it insists that the structure of the economy, particularly unemployment, must be taken into account in any explanation. Thus, '"race" cannot be understood outside of a class analysis' (Walby, 1992, p. 40). Gender is also introduced, in that one of the most immediate causes of poverty is said to be the increase in the number of female-headed households: 'He describes the significant increase in the proportion of black families which are female-headed, and correlates this with the increasing poverty among the black underclass' (Walby, 1992, p. 40). Wilson is said to have demonstrated clearly that male joblessness among blacks in the inner cities leads to female-headed households. For Wilson, this is simply because the increase in male black joblessness leads to a decline in the pool of marriageable black men. Walby claims, in addition, that the refusal to pay benefits to families that have a man present acts as an incentive for the man to desert the family or for the woman to leave the man (Walby, 1992, p. 41).[4] As an account that is supposed to show the strengths of grand theorising and to reveal the weaknesses and limitations of fragmentation and the deconstruction of catch-all concepts, Walby's commentary looks curiously antiquated. What she gives is an empiricist account of correlations between, for example, low household income and female-headed households, and between male joblessness and female-headed households. The sting in the tail – Wilson is said, in effect, not to take enough notice of ethnic, cultural influences on gender relations, hence to be too universalistic in his claims – comes with a further empirical correlation, in which Walby shows that the correlation between male joblessness and female-headed households does not hold for Asian households in Britain (Walby, 1992, pp. 41–2). These correlations seem to be the illustrative basis of her grand claims that we can articulate class with gender and both with race or ethnicity.

Such empirical correlations are interesting but hardly pathbreaking. Surely we have known about empirical correlations – and their limitations – for a long time, and we certainly do not need an elaborate edifice of system-talk to make sense of them. Above all, if we are seriously wanting to look at the way in which different practices articulate with each other, there is absolutely no way in which correlations can substitute for contextual, local and deconstructed analyses of the relationship between different causal mechanisms. There is a place for correlations of empirical instances with little regard for the contiguity of practices in specific spatial and temporal sites, but it is not a place that can substantiate claims about the contiguity of system articulations. Equally, there is a place for empirical correlations with no regard for the agent's conduct analysis of lay actors, but it is not a place that can substantiate claims about the causal duality of structure and agency in the production of system interconnections.

Walby's fixation on her own theoretical framework means that she surveys other studies from the all-too-settled vantage point of her own categories, and judges accordingly. She chides the postmodernists for getting too specific, getting too close to the plurality of different contextualities, and she chides Wilson for neglecting the contextuality of Asian ethnicity in Britain as compared with Black ethnicity in the inner cities of the USA. Walby has begun to fragment and deconstruct the unitary category of ethnicity, but she will presumably put a limit on how many categories are acceptable. But where does one stop? Will it depend on how many significant causal differences there are in the world, or will it rather be up to Walby's decision as to how many categories are suitable, elegant and neat? If it is the first, who can tell how many categories one would end up with; each player analysis would have to keep an open mind about the result. Ulitimately, it is not the categories that are important but the multiple, specifically located, causal configurations, which may or may not be similar to other causal configurations in other places and other times.

In moments of metatheoretical reflection, Walby herself recognises the importance of spatial variations: 'The specific forms of gender inequality in different spatial locations may vary as a result of the detailed differences in patriarchal and capitalist structures' (Walby, 1990, p. 45). She notes, for example, that some of the new forms of capital restructuring have been notable for their new use of space; and that women's employment rates differ markedly between individual regions in Britain, this being linked to the regional location of particular industries – for example, cotton textiles in the North West (high demand for female labour) and mining in Wales (no women underground workers) (Walby, 1990, p. 45). Presumably one's way of perceiving the world and one's agent's conduct/context analysis would be affected by the particular industry one is involved in and the regional location of that industry – the phenomenological side of space – which could quite well be affected by one's status as settled or migrant worker, as single parent or dual parent, or by one's ethnic culture, which itself will inevitably be of a varied hybrid nature, palpably so if one is, say, of Mexican or Costa Rican, or Bangladeshi or Pakistani, or Turkish origin living in the USA or UK or Germany respectively. The various hybrids will themselves all be specific and more or less regionalised, with a variety of implications for gender. Presumably the specificity of state policies on welfare and housing, industrial support, the regions, religious education and many other things, not to mention the local levels of racial and sexual tolerance, racial and gender stereotyping or harassment, the local spaces of youth and non-youth subcultures, both positive and negative, the influence of television, film (*Emmanuelle*, for example), video, magazines (*Cosmopolitan* and *Women's Own*, for example) and consumerism in general will also impinge, in different ways depending on social positioning, upon the hybrid identities and agent's conduct analyses of particular women.

It is important to be able to investigate whether Wilson and Walby's correlations and hypotheses (for example male joblessness leads to female-headed households, and that refusal to pay benefits to families that have a man present acts as an incentive for the man to desert or for the woman to leave the man – Walby, 1992, p. 41) are ontologically causal and are not just spurious correlations. This sort of knowledge is essential if we are to understand something more strategic or experiential about the unfolding causal conditions, in order to think about how they might be changed for the better. It is also a prerequisite for beginning to think about the nature and extent of the knowledge, including the gaps, elisions, doubts and ambiguities. Even if we are reflexively comfortable with strictly empiricist knowledge produced from within the TPA Floater grid – and there are many cases in which the ambitions of our project will call for nothing more – it is still the case that as soon as one begins to base any more ambitious causal claims upon such knowledge, then, for purposes of validation and falsification, it would have to be compatible with – and, therefore, in principle, be able to be extended to include – a hermeneutic, agent's conduct dimension, located in a specific time and place, which illustrates that there is a causal connection in terms of structural context, on the one hand, and agency understanding and motivation to act, on the other. With this, we would have a contextualised and hermeneutically informed causal account, and not just a TPA Floater correlation. Such contextualised accounts could serve as a basis of comparisons between instances, and between studies of different places and of different times, which did more justice to the potential plurality and variability of hermeneutically mediated causal linkages.

In the case of US welfare payments, Walby emphasises the distinctiveness of these practices from those in Europe. This is a putative difference in significant causal mechanisms between Europe and the USA. Walby, as we have seen, also recognises the potential for spatial and ethnic differences. Why does she resist *a priori* seeing potentially significant causal differences taking the shape of discourses? Why does she see varying welfare/state practices as signficant in relation to particular phenomena but not significant enough to disturb her edifice of 'sufficient common features and routine interconnections over a century or two and a continent or so'? Why can she stress the differences in mechanisms that she does – rapping Wilson over the knuckles – but chide the deconstructionists for going too far? One does not have to lose the general heuristic category of (patriarchal?) state practices, with welfare payments figuring largely in relation to certain questions (together with a general sense of the powerful resources that such payments potentially constitute in a hierarchical system), in order to accept that they may not be, and have certainly not been shown to be, part of a spatially and temporally uniform system of interdependencies. Walby's categories are useful as heuristic starting points for more specific studies – and, in this sense, the more subcategories the better – but they have not been shown to be anything like an integrated system of interdependencies.

Down to Earth at Last, but Dreaming Interferes with Play: Patriarchy and the Nineteenth-Century Factory Acts

An example of the second, and much rarer, type of illustration that Walby uses to substantiate her grand dreamer systems hypothesis is her relatively much more detailed case study of the nineteenth-century Factory Acts, which appears in *Patriarchy at Work* (1986, Chapter 4). Relatively speaking, the much more focused and more contextualised nature of this case study throws some of Walby's grander claims into relief. This is particularly so when we also throw into relief various aspects of the more focused study itself such as: aspects of textual duration, when compared both to real time and to the structure of the argument; the significant gaps in the analysis; the sketchiness of frames of meaning that are pivotal to the argument; and so on. Walby argues that the Factory Acts should be characterised as patriarchal, as opposed to their usual characterisation as reformist, whether this reformism be due to the influence of bourgeois philanthropists or, as in Marxist accounts, to the struggles of the working class against capitalists over the length of the working day. For Walby, the Acts are more appropriately described as patriarchal owing to their regressive effects on women. This applies particularly to 'those Acts which limited women's paid work more than that of men (which excludes the Acts before 1842 which refer only to children and young persons, and excludes those parts of Acts which refer to women and men equally)' (Walby, 1986, p. 101).

So far so good. Walby makes some valid and valuable points about the missing gender dimension in other accounts of the Factory Acts. Her new question, from a feminist perspective, sheds a different light on the implications of the Acts. However, there is a caveat, which should be remembered when we go on to look at what I will refer to as the second stage of Walby's analysis of these Factory Acts. (Walby does not make this distinction: she writes as if the two arguments are one – see below). The caveat is that Walby is doing no more, and no less, than using a gender-sensitive perspective to ask an unfamiliar question, using the very broad theoretical categories of capitalism and patriarchy. She is saying that there are implications not only for capitalism but also for patriarchy in the Factory Acts. Thus far the analysis does not need anything else except:

1 the definition of patriarchy as a system of interrelated structures through which men oppress women; followed by
2 the labelling of legislation that limited women's paid work more than that of men as an instance of such oppression; leading to
3 the characterisation of the Factory Acts as patriarchal.

We do not need to know anything about the details of the Acts beyond the sex difference in limits on hours. We do not need to know anything about how the women and men of the time felt about the Factory Acts in order to know that they were patriarchal in terms of Walby's twentieth century definition and characterisation. We do not need to know how the Factory Acts came about, who pushed them through, who resisted them, what the balance of forces was for and against them, who voted for and against in the crucial parliamentary votes. We do not need to know any of this because it is not relevant to the way the perspective, the problem, the theoretical category and the relevant evidence are related to each other.

Walby's second argument about the Factory Acts is more complex. This is a claim about the forces that were involved in the actual passage of the Factory Acts. It is thus addressing a different question. I am not convinced that Walby is, in fact, aware that she is asking two different questions within her case study, and I suggest that this is another example of the problems that arise from too unreflexive an orientation to metatheory – in this specific case, to epistemological guidelines. Walby examines the role of several groupings, which she says had distinct interests in the matter: male workers; different sets of manufacturers; bourgeois philanthropists; factory inspectors; the women's rights lobby, mainly women operatives; and the landowners. Walby argues that:

> The passage of the Factory Acts should be seen primarily as the outcome of the pressure from the male operatives and the Tory landed interest. The interests of the manufacturers and the women were defeated on this issue. This is not an unsurprising outcome given the different strengths of the groups in the nineteenth century. The male working class was growing in size and organizational power, albeit unevenly. The division of the bourgeoisie into the landed and manufacturing fractions and further divisions within the manufacturing interests were crucial in allowing the modest success of the male working class over this issue… The strength of male workers' demands was crucial to the passage of the legislation and the form of the legislation cannot be understood without an analysis of the

patriarchal relations which shaped it. This aspect of the analysis is missing from accounts of the battles between Tories and Whigs and the role of the working class. Yet the shape of the Acts cannot be understood if it is seen as merely Tory versus Whig, or worker versus manufacturers. While all those forces were present, patriarchal forces were crucial to the shape of the legislation as it differentially affected men and women (Walby, 1986, pp. 127–8).

This is about as detailed as the analysis gets as to the actual articulation of, and the respective causal effects of, the forces involved. As we saw with Mann's analysis, there is a systematic use of metonymic compression of time–space, together with the metonymic effacement of the details of agency and process. Malleable theoretical categories provide a metonymical substitute for the contextualised analysis that is implied. None of this subdues the knowingness that is assumed, the authority that is arrogated. Quite the contrary: Walby makes the confident and very specific pronouncement that the Acts represented 'a political response from patriarchal interests striving to re-establish patriarchal control which was threatened by the emerging capitalist reorganization of the sexual division of labour' (Walby, 1986, p. 111). For Walby, from the perspective of her systems theory, it is important that the Factory Acts seem to provide an example of a clash between capitalist forces, which preferred women and children in the workforce as sources of cheap and less militant labour, and patriarchal forces, which felt threatened by the autonomy this gave to women and the competition it gave to themselves. That is, it reveals the relative autonomy between capitalism and patriarchy; they can clash and patriarchy can come out on top.

The important point for me here is that Walby's question is now about the balance of forces that produced both the Acts and their patriarchal content. She is picking up on some well-made points earlier in the book, where she took to task theories of the capitalist state for failing to take into account women's political struggles. This latter omission, she pointed out, was serious because an account of the balance of forces at play in, for example, the development of the welfare state, which did not take into account the role of the political struggles of women as women would be seriously in error as to the political forces operating in that situation (Walby, 1986, p. 57). The Factory Acts offer a similar case, and Walby says that her conclusions are based upon an analysis that is structured around, first, a one-by-one discussion of the different competing groups and, second, 'a consideration of the overall structural configuration' (Walby, 1986, p. 109). This format would allow her to examine the positions of the various groupings and their power to mobilise resources in the struggles around the Acts, culminating, as we have seen, in an answer to the question of who were the most influential players in the passage of the legislation, and enabling us to identify the source(s) of its patriarchal content.

At first glance, Walby's second argument appears to be a contextualised, hermeneutically informed analysis of the balance of forces and processes involved in the passage of the Factory Acts. In fact, it is no such thing. The actual passage of the Factory Acts is hardly discussed at all. Of the two groups who are supposed to have been crucial to their successful passage, the male operatives and the Tory landed interest, the former had no direct representation in parliament, while the views and deliberations of the latter are deemed to be of so little importance that they receive seven lines, and all of authorial diegesis, in a sum total of 15 pages devoted to the six groups (Walby, 1986, pp. 125–6). The analysis is almost entirely focused on societal issues as opposed to state issues (cf Nordlinger, 1981; Evans *et al.*, 1985; and more recently, Marsh and Rhodes, 1992; Smith, 1993), and there is no discussion of the institutional arrangements and procedures of the state in general and of parliament in particular. (Walby tells us that one should not neglect the detailed working of parliament and the political parties, and then proceeds to do just that – Walby, 1986, p. 128). There are huge gaps in the analysis of significant relations of contiguity within the state, of the temporal and spatial sites within which societal and state influences articulate together and produce outcomes. Thus, for example, we are not told about any alliances between state and societal interests that might have given Walby grounds for her belief that the male workers were influential at the state level. Indeed, while we are assured that the Tory landed interest was strongly represented in parliament – which it seems they would have to be if Walby's claim about the two primary forces is to be believed – we are then rather confusingly told that 'the Tory party did not uniformly and whole-heartedly support the factory legislation. Such moves were supported by Ashley and the Tory Radicals such as Ferrand, but **not by the majority of the Tories**' (Walby, 1986, p. 128, my emphasis). In terms of the supposed patriarchal motivation of the legislation, we are left with one or two examples of clearly patriarchal attitudes expressed by bourgeois humanitarians, one or two of whom are possibly Tory MPs. The patriarchal attitudes are not shown to be related in any way to political strategy or to an analysis of the strategic context perceived by these players in the movement to reduce working hours.

As it stands, Walby's analysis is highly indeterminate as to the forces that converged to produce the passage and the form of the Factory Acts. This is made all the clearer when one considers an argument put forward by Marvel, which Walby dismisses. Marvel sets himself the task of explaining why the 1833 Acts, limiting child and female labour, could possibly be passed by a Whig government in which the manufacturers' interests were clearly represented. Marvel's answer is that the Act was supported by those manufacturers who were more advanced in terms of technology, and who had less need for child and female labour, in order to disadvantage their competitors in the older mills (Marvel, 1977; Walby, 1986, p. 123). The implication is that the motivation was more to do with profit than with patriarchy, and that the discriminatory effects on women were an acknowledged but unintended consequence. Walby concedes that there may be an element of truth in this but then, rather mystically, says that this is only in relation to the timing of that particular act. She uses similar arguments about timing in relation to a whole series of other events – from the repeal of the corn laws in 1846, which encouraged retaliation by the landed interest, to the depressed trade conditions of 1847, which encouraged the belief that the unemployed could be absorbed if hours were shorter – whose details, she says, should not be taken to explain the passage of the legislation. Rather, 'such events, manoeuverings and trade conditions merely assist in the explanation of the timing of the specific acts' (Walby, 1986, p. 128).

These arguments are resonant of the worst excesses of the base-superstructure metaphor. It seems that when empirical evidence does not fit, or is deemed not to be relevant to her purposes, Walby rules it out of court as surface level phenomena that pale against the deeper structural forces that constitute her impregnable and evasive systems. One gets the feeling that the structures cast their influence in the final instance that never comes. Today's events, it seems, are always epiphenomena; the real structures are always happening elsewhere. One begins to realise why Walby has so little time for the local, the contextualised and the hermeneutic.

The reason, I would suggest, why Walby is not at all interested in the specific contiguities and hermeneutics of legislative alliances and manoeuvres – in other words, in their hermeneutic contextualisation – is that her extended case study is ultimately irrelevant to her main thesis, which is based on her first, self-contained argument. She never distinguishes the two arguments herself, but she quite palpably has much more interest in the first, in establishing that the Acts were patriarchal according to her categories, than in undertaking the much more complex task of really tracing through the impulses and influences on the patriarchal content. Rather than going in for this, she reiterates the conclusions from the first argument but this time dresses them up as contextual and hermeneutic analyses. The attendant lack of an adequate evidential base is disguised by a combination of, on the one hand, bold and frequent assertions of knowledge and, on the other hand, the metonymic application of concepts to compress significant chunks of relevant time–space. In short, knowledge is implied by means of textual rhetoric rather than exhibited. Thus, 'patriarchal forces were crucial to the shape of the legislation as it differentially affected men and women' (Walby, 1986, p. 128); the factory legislation represented 'a political response from patriarchal interests striving to re-establish patriarchal control' (Walby, 1986, p. 111); 'the passage of the Factory Act cannot be understood without a concept of patriarchy' (Walby, 1986, p. 108).

The first argument is self-contained and irrefutable as it sets its own terms, and what little evidence that is needed is completely uncontentious. It thus becomes very difficult to challenge Walby's repeated assertions that the Acts were the result of patriarchal forces. Indeed, one would not necessarily want to, in those broad terms. What one would want to challenge is the insidious suggestion that Walby knows what these patriarchal forces were and how they manifested themselves at different stages of the overall struggle and legislative process. If one gets close enough to begin to question whether or not Walby does in fact know what she insinuates she does, then she tells you that the different stages and manoeuvrings, the calculations and hermeneutic understandings of the actors involved, do not matter, that they are only epiphenomena. What matters, as always, is not the timing or the conjunctures but the big, self-contained theory – which, used like this, can tell us no more than we would have been able to figure out anyway. Walby is typical of sociological modernists, in that ultimately, despite the moderate antireductionism of her six structures, she is more of a despot than a dreamer or a player. Caught within the conventions of sociological modernism, she flattens the complexity of reality at every turn, while denying that she is flattening anything.

Notes

1 Walby cites a letter to *m/f* by Barrett and Coward which she says substantiates this point (Walby, 1990, p. 35, n. 24, p. 51; Barrett and Coward, 1982, pp. 87–9).

2 One *could* conceive, for example, a conflict over the relative status of agency and discourse, in which there was disagreement about whether an emphasis on discourse is necessarily bound to impair the notion of agency and agency choice. Personally, I do not believe this to be a necessary incompatibility. In any event, Walby gives no indication of having any problem in this respect.

3 It comes as no surprise to find that Walby's conception of 'intensity' is pitched at the TPA level, and not at the level of the experience of the lay actor.

4 In fact, the situation is more complex and context-dependent than is allowed for by Walby. Since the 1960s, about half of all states have offered benefits to families where there is an unemployed man, and since 1990, all states do this. While it is true that the tightness of eligibility rules means that the take up is often very low, there are still significant differences between states, especially between urban Northern states and rural Southern states (cf Morris, 1994, pp. 64–70).

Conclusion

By now, I hope to have made a powerful case against my twin enemies of defeatist postmodernism and sociological modernism. I hope that I have succeeded in making their deficiencies very clear to the reader. Equally, I hope to have made a convincing case for the virtues of a sophisticated realism beyond modernism: a past-modernist realism whose acknowledgement of a rich, complex ontology is accompanied and matched by the adoption of a finely grained set of reflexive guidelines. It seems to me that such a sophisticated realism can avoid the dangers to sociology that are inherent in the alternative positions I have attacked.

The great intellectual and political danger of defeatist postmodernism is that by seeking to highlight the many deficiencies of modernism, while also rejecting any other form of realism, it strips sociology of any critical edge whatsoever; all stories become as good as each other. Foremost among the advantages of a past-modernist realism is the critical edge it can provide. It is able to make judgements about the status of knowledge claims and to judge claims about real events, and about real causal processes and responsibilities. It is able to identify some arguments as well grounded, others as less well grounded, and yet others as ungrounded, unfounded and falsifiable. It can say that some stories are more fictional than others, that some stories are more real than others. It can say that some stories have a cheek claiming to know all there is to know, to know the real story, when all they have to go on is a few facts marshalled more by expediency and rhetorical instrumentalism than by a systematic and rigorous journey from a rich ontology to a focused, evidential base. The latter journey much better equips its voyagers to make precise claims but, armed with a more refined sensibility as to the limits of their knowledge-ability, these travellers will be much more reluctant to claim that they know all there is to know. Claims to know will be accompanied by a highly developed reflexivity in relation to the means by which they believe they know, together with an urbane scepticism towards even that knowledge that, for the time being, seems to be the best available. A realism beyond modernism can allow us the resources through which to train our own (and others') practical aspirations towards society in a way that both sustains a necessary handle on the real and also cultivates a sensibility towards knowing which is less omnipotent, arrogant and instrumental, and which is more sensitive to the rich complexity of the local, the contextual, the hermeneutic and the ethical.

The guidelines for sociological research presented here only just begin to scratch the surface of possibilities available to a past-modern sociology. Each one of the elements in the player and dreamer models of research could be further elaborated, both individually and in combination, to fruitful effect. The rich, complex ontology I have presented, for example, is itself only a partial, incomplete elaboration of a potentially much richer, more complex ontology. Dimensions of ontology that I have particularly neglected or left underdeveloped could be further elaborated upon in relation to their implications for all the various elements in the research process. These additional aspects of ontology could include the power dimension, the unconscious, the body, the symbolic dimensions of time and space, the varieties in types of structural constraint, and various aspects of discourse and signification. Critical analyses of existing substantive research based on these areas of ontology could draw out the levels and types of contextualisation that are typical for particular subjects of study, and could also suggest ways of extending such studies to cover other areas of ontology, noting where and when there are windows of compatibility with other studies. Compatibility can mean extending a study focusing on, for example, specific aspects of power, to other such studies looking at other dimensions of power, or it could mean extending a study focusing on power to look at its points of contact and articulation with studies focusing on other dimensions, such as hermeneutics. In either case, there is much work to be done.

The significatory dimension of ontology, to take another example, is one whose epistemological and methodological dimensions could be explored much further. Thus, for example, while Chapters 8 and 9 of the present study have concentrated upon a critique of the residual sociological modernism within the works of a particular type of contemporary social theorist, it would also be interesting to critique the epistemology and methodology of those researchers whose influences at the ontological level lie more with poststructuralism than with other dimensions of contemporary social theory (for example Foucault, 1976, 1977; Scott,

1988; Hall, 1992; Laclau, 1994). A constructive critical analysis of the work of one of these writers, or of any other pertinent body of work – such as the one carried out in relation to Giddens' work in Chapter 4 – could be used as the basis for drawing out weaknesses, complacencies, compatibilities and points for elaboration with respect to the various dimensions of a past-modern realism. How far away, for example, are their claims for knowledge from the benchmark of exhaustiveness (see Chapter 3), and to what extent do they explicitly acknowledge this, or, alternatively, to what extent does their rhetoric subsume an otherwise yawning chasm?

With respect to many of the different specific elements of the research models of Chapter 3, there is already a good deal of highly interesting and innovative material being produced that it would be useful to analyse critically according to the guidelines of a past-modern sociology, looking for points of compatibility and the possibility of mutually strengthening alliances. To take just a couple of related elements to illustrate the point, it would be of great value, for example, if someone were to look at the wider related literature in order to try and develop the role of *questioner* in relation to the research models of Chapter 3, and/or the dimension of biographical analysis within the hermeneutic dimension of contiguous relations (see Chapter 4). One could draw quite readily here on a burgeoning literature concerned with the role of biography and autobiography in sociology, anthropology and oral history, and bring it into a critical dialogue with the guidelines outlined here (cf Thompson, 1978; Samuel and Thompson, 1990; Okley and Callaway, 1992; Josselson and Lieblich, 1993; Stanley and Morgan, 1993).

None of this is easy, but – to change the metaphor from the bridge of the introduction – the stretch of land between high theory and empirical research, between the peaks of philosophical and sociological theory and the valleys of evidential fragments and traces, has for too long been hidden from view. It is a forbidding territory for many reasons, but it is a territory whose contours, tracks and horizons it is essential to explore. The same is true of the relation between research analyses and their textualities. Texts have a relative autonomy from the analyses that result from the process of sociological research, and it is essential that a sophisticated sociology with a claim to realism begins to venture much further into the relationships that are typically set up between the textual sjuzet and the story of real events and processes that that discourse implies. We have seen that the story that is implied by the writer in flow is often a long way from the story that is licensed by the sociological analysis. There is much more for the cross-questioning *reader* of sociology to search out and cultivate in the skills of translation, interpretation and critique – from the sjuzet to the implied fabula, and from there to a critical analysis of the status of the implied analysis. For the *writer* of sociology, on the other hand, the urge to reflexivity provided by past-modern realism is simultaneously, and intrinsically, an exhortation to experiment with styles and forms of writing that can bring to the fore, and give the publicity that is due to, both the relative autonomy of the text and the robust epistemological scepticism that the genres of sociological modernism have smoothed into oblivion.

Bibliography

Alexander, M. *Flights from Realism: Themes and Strategies in Postmodernist British and American Fiction.* London: Edward Arnold, 1990.

Allen, R. C. On reading soaps: a semiotic primer. In Kaplan, E. A. (ed.) *Regarding Television.* Los Angeles: American Film Institute, 1983.

Ang, I. *Watching Dallas: Soap Opera and the Melodramatic Imagination.* London: Routledge, 1985.

Austin, J. L. *How to Do Things with Words.* Cambridge, Mass.: Harvard University Press, 1975.

Ayer, A. J. *Hume.* Oxford: Oxford University Press, 1980.

Baker, N. *The Mezzanine.* Cambridge: Granta Books, 1989.

Barnes, B. Thomas Kuhn. In Skinner, Q. (ed.) *The Return of Grand Theory in the Human Sciences.* Cambridge: Cambridge University Press, 1985.

Barnes, J. *Talking it Over.* London: Picador, 1991.

Barret, M. and Coward, R. Letter. *m/f,* 7, 1982, pp. 87–9.

Barthes, R. Introduction to the structural analysis of narratives. In Heath, S. (ed.) *Image, Music, Text.* London: Fontana, 1977.

Barthes, R. *A Lover's Discourse: Fragments.* New York: Hill & Wang, 1978.

Barthes, R. *S/Z.* Oxford: Basil Blackwell, 1990.

Barthes, R. The reality effect in descriptions. In Furst, L. (ed.) *Realism.* London: Longman, 1992, pp. 135–41.

Bauman, Z. *Modernity and the Holocaust.* Cambridge: Polity Press, 1989a.

Bauman, Z. Hermeneutics and modern social theory. In Held, D. and Thompson, J. (eds) *Social Theory of Modern Societies: Anthony Giddens and his Critics.* Cambridge: Cambridge University Press, 1989b, pp. 34–55.

Bauman, Z. *Intimations of Postmodernity.* London: Routledge, 1992.

Bellow, S. *Herzog.* London: Penguin, 1965.

Benhabib, S. *Situating the Self: Gender, Community and Postmodernism in Contemporary Ethics.* Cambridge: Polity Press, 1992.

Benton, T. *The Rise and Fall of Structural Marxism: Althusser and his Influence.* London: Macmillan, 1984.

Benton, T. Realism and Social Science. In Edgley, R. and Osborne, R. (eds) *Radical Philosophy Reader*. London: Verso, 1985.

Berger, J. G. London: Hogarth Press, 1989.

Bettelheim, B. *The Informed Heart*. London: Penguin, 1986.

Bhaskar, R. *A Realist Theory of Science*. Hassocks: Harvester Press, 1978.

Bhaskar, R. *The Possibility of Naturalism: A Philosophical Critique of the Contemporary Human Sciences*. Brighton: Harvester Press, 1979.

Bleicher, J. *Contemporary Hermeneutics: Hermeneutics as Method, Philosophy and Critique*. London: Routledge & Kegan Paul, 1980.

Bonnell, V. E. *Roots of Rebellion: Workers' Politics and Organisations in St Petersburg and Moscow 1900–1914*. Berkeley: University of California Press, 1983.

Booth, W. C. *The Rhetoric of Fiction*. London: Penguin, 1991.

Borgman, A. *Crossing the Postmodern Divide*. Chicago: Chicago University Press, 1992.

Brooks, P. The melodramatic imagination: the example of Balzac and James. In Thorburn, D. and Hartman, G. (eds) *Romanticism: Vistas, Instances, Continuities*. Ithaca: Cornell University Press, 1973.

Browning, C. *The Final Solution and the German Foreign Office: A Study of Referat DIII of Abteilung Deutschland*. New York: Holmes & Meier, 1978.

Browning, C. The government experts. In Friedlander, H. and Milton, S. (eds) *The Holocaust: Ideology, Bureaucracy and Genocide*. New York: Kraus International Publications, 1980.

Browning, C. *The Fateful Months: Essays on the Emergence of the Final Solution*. New York: Holmes & Meier, 1985.

Browning, C. *Ordinary Men: Reserve Police Batallion 101 and the Final Solution in Poland*. New York: HarperCollins, 1992.

Browning, C. Beyond 'Intentionalism' and 'Functionalism': a reassessment of Nazi Jewish policy from 1939 to 1941. In Childers, T. and Caplan, J. (eds) *Reevaluating the Third Reich*. New York: Holmes & Meier, 1993, pp. 211–33.

Bryant, C. and Jary, D. *Giddens' Theory of Structuration: A Critical Appreciation*. London: Routledge, 1991.

Burrin, P. *Hitler and the Jews: The Genesis of the Holocaust*. London: Edward Arnold, 1994.

Calhoun, C. Culture, history, and the problem of specificity in social theory. In Seidman, S. and Wagner, D. G. (eds) *Postmodernism and Social Theory: The Debate Over General Theory*. Oxford: Basil Blackwell, 1992, pp. 244–88.

Carey, P. *Oscar and Lucinda*. London: Faber & Faber, 1989.

Chatman, S. *Story and Discourse: Narrative Structure in Fiction and Film*. Ithaca: Cornell University Press, 1980.

Chodorow, N. *The Reproduction of Mothering: Psychoanalysis and the Sociology of Gender*. Berkeley: University of California Press, 1978.

Clifford, J. and Marcus, G. *Writing Culture: the Poetics and Politics of Ethnography.* Berkeley: University of California Press, 1986.

Cohen, I. J. The status of structuration theory: a reply to MacLennan. *Theory, Culture and Society,* vol. 3, no. 1, 1986, pp. 123–34.

Cohen, I. J. *Structuration Theory: Anthony Giddens and the Constitution of Social Life.* London: Macmillan, 1989.

Cohen, I. J. and Rogers, M. F. Autonomy and credibility: voice as method. *Sociological Theory,* vol. 12, no. 3, 1994, pp. 304–18.

Collier, A. *Critical Realism: An Introduction to Roy Bhaskar's Philosophy.* London: Verso, 1994.

Cottingham, J. *Rationalism.* London: Paladin, 1984.

Coward, R. Sexual liberation and the family. *m/f,* vol. 1, 1978, pp. 7–24.

Craib, I. *Psychoanalysis and Social Theory: The Limits of Sociology.* London: Harvester Wheatsheaf, 1989.

Craib, I. *Anthony Giddens.* London: Routledge, 1992.

Craib, I. Review of *Structuration Theory* by I. J. Cohen and *Social Theory of Modern Societies* edited by D. Held and J. B. Thompson. *Theory, Culture and Society,* vol. 9, no. 2, 1992a, pp. 175–8.

Craib, I. *The Importance of Disappointment.* London: Routledge, 1994.

Cuff, E. C., Sharrock, W. W. and Francis, D. W. *Perspectives in Sociology,* London: Unwin Hyman, 1990.

Culler, J. *On Deconstruction: Theory and Criticism after Structuralism.* London: Routledge, 1983.

Derrida, J. *Speech and Phenomena, and Other Essays on Husserl's Theory of Signs.* Evanston, Illinois: Northwestern University Press, 1973.

Derrida, J. *Writing and Difference.* London: Routledge & Kegan Paul, 1978.

Derrida, J. *Spurs: Nietzsche's Styles.* Chicago and London: University of Chicago Press, 1979.

Dickens, C. Sketches by Boz. *The Oxford Illustrated Dickens.* London: Oxford University Press, 1966.

Douglas, A. Soft-porn culture. *New Republic,* 30 August, 1980, pp. 25–9.

Douglas, J. D. *The Social Meanings of Suicide.* Princeton: Princeton University Press, 1967.

Doyal, L. and Harris, R. *Empiricism, Explanation and Rationality: An Introduction to the Philosophy of the Social Sciences.* London: Routledge & Kegan Paul, 1986.

Durrell, L. *The Alexandria Quartet.* London: Faber & Faber, 1961, 1963.

Dworkin, R. *Taking Rights Seriously.* Cambridge, Mass.: Harvard University Press, 1978.

Elster, J. *Sour Grapes: Studies in the Subversion of Rationality.* Cambridge/Paris: Cambridge University Press/Editions De La Maison Des Sciences De L'Homme, 1985.

Evans, P., Rueschmeyer, D. and Skocpol, T. (eds) *Bringing the State Back In.* Cambridge: Cambridge University Press, 1985.

Faludi, S. *Backlash: The Undeclared War Against Women.* London: Chatto & Windus, 1992.

Faulkner, W. *The Sound and the Fury.* London: Picador, 1989.

Foucault, M. *The Birth of the Clinic: An Archaeology of Medical Perception.* London: Tavistock Publications, 1976.

Foucault, M. *Discipline and Punish: The Birth of the Prison.* London: Allen Lane, 1977.

Fowles, J. *The French Lieutenant's Woman.* London: Jonathan Cape, 1969.

Fowles, J. *The French Lieutenant's Woman.* London: Triad/Granada, 1977.

Flax, J. *Thinking Fragments: Psychoanalysis, Feminism, and Postmodernism in the Contemporary West.* Berkeley: University of California Press, 1990.

Fraser, N. and Nicholson, L. Social criticism without philosophy: an encounter between feminism and postmodernism. In Nicholson, L. (ed.) *Feminism/Postmodernism.* New York and London: Routledge/Chapman & Hall, 1990.

Furst, L. (ed.) *Realism.* London: Longman, 1992.

Gadamer, H.-G. *Truth and Method.* Berkeley: University of California, 1976.

Geertz, C. *Works and Lives: The Anthropologist as Author.* Cambridge: Polity Press, 1989.

Gellately, R. *The Gestapo and German Society: Enforcing Racial Policy 1933–1945.* Oxford: Oxford University Press, 1990.

Gennette, G. *Narrative Discourse.* Ithica: Cornell University Press, 1979.

Giddens, A. *New Rules of Sociological Method: A Positive Critique of Interpretative Sociologies.* London: Hutchinson, 1976.

Giddens, A. *Central Problems in Social Theory: Action, Structure and Contradiction in Social Analysis.* London: Macmillan, 1979.

Giddens, A. *A Contemporary Critique of Historical Materialism, Volume One.* London: Macmillan, 1981.

Giddens, A. *Profiles and Critiques in Social Theory.* London: Macmillan, 1982.

Giddens, A. *The Transformation of Intimacy: Sexuality, Love and Eroticism in Modern Societies.* Cambridge: Polity Press, 1992.

Giddens, A. *The Constitution of Society: Outline of the Theory of Structuration.* Cambridge: Polity Press, 1984.

Giddens, A. *The Nation State and Violence: Volume Two of a Contemporary Critique of Contemporary Materialism.* Cambridge: Polity Press, 1985.

Giddens, A. *Social Theory and Modern Sociology.* Cambridge: Polity Press, 1987.

Giddens, A. A reply to my critics. In Held, D. and Thompson, J. (eds) *Social Theory and Modern Societies: Anthony Giddens and his critics.* Cambridge: Cambridge University Press, 1989.

Giddens, A. *The Consequences of Modernity.* Cambridge: Polity Press, 1990.

Giddens, A. *Modernity and Self-Identity: Self and Society in the Late Modern Age.* Cambridge: Polity Press, 1991.

Giddens, A. *New Rules of Sociological Method,* 2nd edn. Cambridge: Polity Press, 1993.

Gilligan, C. *In a Different Voice: Psychological Theory and Women's Development.* Cambridge, Mass.: Harvard University Press, 1982.

Gilligan, C., Ward, J. V. and Taylor, J. M. *Mapping the Moral Domain: A Contribution of Women's Thinking to Psychological Theory and Education.* Cambridge, Mass.: Harvard University Press, 1988.

Gilligan, C., Lyons, N. P. and Hanmer, T. J. *Making Connections: The Relational Worlds of Adolescent Girls at Emma Willard School.* Cambridge, Mass.: Harvard University Press, 1990.

Goldthorpe, J., Lockwood, D., Bechhofer, F. and Platt, J. *The Affluent Worker in the Class Structure.* Cambridge: Cambridge University Press, 1969.

Gregson, N. On the (ir)relevance of structuration theory to empirical research. In Held, D. and Thompson, J. B. (eds) *Social Theory and Modern Societies: Anthony Giddens and His Critics.* Cambridge: Cambridge University Press, 1989, pp. 235–48.

Habermas, J. *The Theory of Communicative Action, Volume Two: Lifeworld and System: A Critique of Fuctionalist Reason.* Cambridge: Polity Press, 1989.

Habermas, J. *On the Logic of the Social Sciences.* Cambridge: Polity Press, 1990.

Habermas, J. *The Theory of Communicative Action, Volume One: Reason and the Rationalization of Society.* Cambridge: Polity Press, 1991.

Habermas, J. 'A Reply'. In Honneth, A. and Joas, H. (eds) *Communicative Action: Essays on Jürgen Habermas's* The Theory of Communicative Action. Cambridge, Mass.: MIT Press, 1991a, pp. 214–64.

Haimson, L. H. The problem of social stability in urban Russia 1905–1917, parts 1 and 2. *Slavic Review,* vols 23, 24, 1964, 1965.

Hall, C. Missionary stories: gender and ethnicity in England in the 1830s and 1840s. In Grossberg, L., Nelson, C. and Treichler, P. (eds) *Cultural Studies.* London: Routledge, 1992, pp. 240–76.

Hamon, P. The Major Features of Realist Discourse. In Furst, L. (ed.) *Realism.* London: Longman, 1992, pp. 166–85.

Hartsock, N. The feminist standpoint: developing the ground for a specifically feminist historical materialism. In Harding, S. (ed.) *Feminism and Methodology: Social Science Issues.* Bloomington/Milton Keynes: Indiana University Press/Open University, 1987.

Hawthorn, G. English Channel. *Times Higher Education Supplement,* no. 911, 1990, p. 21.

Hawthorn, G. *Plausible Worlds: Possibility and Understanding in History and the Social Sciences.* Cambridge: Cambridge University Press, 1991.

Hawthorn, J. *A Concise Glossary of Contemporary Literary Theory.* London: Edward Arnold, 1992.

Held, D. Power and legitimacy in contemporary Britain. In McLennan, G., Held, D. and Hall, S. (eds) *State and Society in Contemporary Britain*. Cambridge: Polity Press, 1984.

Held, D. and Thompson, J. B. (eds) *Social Theory of Modern Societies: Anthony Giddens and his Critics*. Cambridge: Cambridge University Press, 1989.

Heller, J. *Good as Gold*. New York: Simon & Schuster, 1980.

Hochschild, A. *The Second Shift: Working Parents and the Revolution at Home*. London: Piatkus, 1990.

Holub, R. C. *Jürgen Habermas: Critic in the Public Sphere*. London: Routledge, 1991.

Honneth, A. and Joas, H. (eds) *Communicative Action: Essays on Jürgen Habermas's* The Theory of Communicative Action. Cambridge, Mass.: MIT Press, 1991.

Hoy, D. Couzens (ed.) *Foucault: A Critical Reader*. Oxford: Basil Blackwell, 1986.

Hume, D. *Enquiry Concerning Human Understanding*. Oxford: Oxford University Press, 1975.

Hutcheon, L. *The Politics of Postmodernism*. London: Routledge, 1989.

Hutcheon, L. Discourse, power, ideology: humanism and post-modernism. In Smyth, E. J. (ed.) *Postmodernism and Contemporary Fiction*. London: Batsford, 1991, pp. 105–22.

Ingham, G. *Capitalism Divided? The City and Industry in British Social Development*. London: Macmillan, 1984.

Ingram, D. *Habermas and the Dialectic of Reason*. New Haven: Yale University Press, 1987.

Isaac, J. *Power and Marxist Theory: A Realist View*. Ithaca: Cornell University Press, 1987.

Ishiguro, K. *The Remains of the Day*. London: Faber & Faber, 1989.

James, H. *What Maisie Knew*. London: Penguin, 1985.

Jameson, F. *The Prison House of Language: A Critical Account of Structuralism and Russian Formalism*. Princeton: Princeton University Press, 1972.

Jary, D. 'Society as time-traveller': Giddens on historical change, historical materialism and the nation-state in world society. In Bryant, C. and Jary, D. (eds) *Giddens' Theory of Structuration: A Critical Appreciation*. London: Routledge, 1991, pp. 116–59.

Jessop, B., Bonnett, K., Bromley, S. and Ling, T. *Thatcherism: A Tale of Two Nations*. Cambridge: Polity Press, 1988.

Joas, H. The unhappy marriage of hermeneutics and functionalism. In Honneth, A. and Joas, H. (eds) *Communicative Action: Essays on Jürgen Habermas's* The Theory of Communicative Action. Cambridge, Mass.: MIT Press, 1991, pp. 97–118.

Josselson, R. and Lieblich, A. *The Narrative Study of Lives*. London: Sage, 1993.

Kalberg, S. *Max Weber's Comparative–Historical Sociology.* Cambridge: Polity Press, 1994.

Keane, J. More theses on the philosophy of history. In Tully, J. (ed.) *Meaning and Context: Quentin Skinner and His Critics.* Cambridge: Polity Press, 1988, pp. 204–17.

Kennan, G. F. The autocracy's many shortcomings brought its collapse. In Adams, A. E. (ed.) *The Russian Revolution and Bolshevik Victory: Causes and Processes.* Lexington, Mass.: D. C. Heath, 1972.

Kershaw, I. *The Nazi Dictatorship: Problems and Perspectives of Interpretation.* London: Edward Arnold, 1989.

Khandelwal, A. Graduate essay for 'Current Disputes in Sociology', University of Essex, 1993.

Kuhn, T. S. *The Structure of Scientific Revolutions.* Chicago: University of Chicago Press, 1970.

Kundera, M. *The Unbearable Lightness of Being.* London: Faber & Faber, 1985.

Laclau, E. (ed.) *The Making of Political Identities.* London: Verso, 1994.

Laclau, E. and Mouffe, C. *Hegemony and Socialist Strategy: Towards a Radical Democratic Politics.* London: Verso, 1985.

Leech, G. and Short, M. *Style in Fiction: A Linguistic Introduction to English Fictional Prose.* London: Longman, 1981.

Levi, P. *If This is a Man* and *The Truce.* London: Abacus, 1987.

Lodge, D. *The Modes of Modern Writing: Metaphor, Metonymy, and the Typology of Modern Literature.* London: Edward Arnold, 1977.

Lodge, D. *Working with Structuralism: Essays and Reviews on Nineteenth- and Twentieth-Century Literature.* London: Ark Paperbacks, 1986.

Lodge, D. *After Bakhtin: Essays on Fiction and Criticism.* London: Routledge, 1990.

Lodge, D. *The Art of Fiction: Illustrated from Classic and Modern Texts.* London: Penguin, 1992.

Longstreth, F. The city, industry and the state. In Crouch, C. (ed.) *State and Economy in Contemporary Capitalism.* London: Croom Helm, 1979.

Lowry, M. *Under the Volcano.* London: Penguin, 1962.

Lyons, P. *Literary and Theological Responses to the Holocaust.* PhD thesis, University of Bristol, 1988.

Lyotard, J-F. *The Postmodern Condition: A Report on Knowledge.* Minneapolis: Minneapolis University Press, 1984.

McCarthy, T. Complexity and democracy: or the seducements of systems theory. In Honneth, A. and Joas, H. (eds) *Communicative Action: Essays on Jürgen Habermas's* The Theory of Communicative Action. Cambridge, Mass.: MIT Press, 1991, pp. 119–39.

McEwan, I. *Black Dogs.* London: Jonathan Cape, 1992.

Mann, M. Ruling class strategies and citizenship. *Sociology,* vol. 21, no. 2, 1987, pp. 339–54.

Bibliography 243

Marcus, G. and Fischer, M. *Anthropology as Cultural Critique: An Experimental Moment in the Human Sciences.* Chicago: Chicago University Press, 1986.

Marrus, M. R. *The Holocaust in History.* London: Penguin, 1993.

Mars-Jones, A. Larceny: review of Nicholson Baker's *The Fermata. London Review of Books,* vol. 16, no. 6, 1994, pp. 3–5.

Marsh, D. and Rhodes, R. A. W. *Policy Networks in British Government.* Oxford: Clarendon Press, 1992.

Marvel, H. P. Factory legislation: a reinterpretation of early English experience. *Journal of Law and Economics,* October, 1977, pp. 379–402.

Mepham, J. Narratives of postmodernism. In Smyth, E. (ed.) *Postmodernism and Contemporary Fiction.* London: Batsford, 1991, pp. 138–55.

Miller, J. Hillis, The fiction of realism. In Furst, L. (ed.) *Realism.* London: Longman, 1992, pp. 287–318.

Mills, C. Wright. *The Sociological Imagination.* New York: Oxford University Press, 1959.

Modleski, T. *Loving With a Vengeance: Mass-produced Fantasies for Women.* London: Routledge, 1988.

Modleski, T. *Feminism Without Women: Culture and Criticism in a 'Postfeminist' Age.* London: Routledge, 1991.

Mommsen, H. Die Realisierung des Utopischen: Die 'Endlösung der Judenfrage'. In *Dritten Reich, Geschichte und Gesellschaft 9,* 1983.

Montgomery, M., Durant, A., Fabb, N. and Mills, S. *Ways of Reading: Advanced Reading Skills for Students of English Literature.* London: Routledge, 1992.

Morris, L. *Dangerous Classes: The Underclass and Social Citizenship.* London: Routledge, 1994.

Morrison, T. *Beloved.* London: Picador, 1987.

Mouzelis, N. P. *Back to Sociological Theory: The Construction of Social Orders.* London: Macmillan, 1991.

Murdoch, I. *The Book and the Brotherhood.* London: Penguin, 1987.

Nelson, G. Undergraduate essay for 'Political Sociology and Contemporary Social Theory', University of Essex, 1993.

Nicholson, L. On the postmodern barricades: feminism, politics and theory. In Seidman, S. and Wagner, D. G. (eds) *Postmodernism and Social Theory: The Debate Over General Theory.* Oxford: Basil Blackwell, 1992, pp. 82–100.

Nordlinger, F. A. *On the Autonomy of the Democratic State.* Cambridge, Mass.: Harvard University Press, 1981.

Norris, C. *Deconstruction: Theory and Practice,* 2nd edn. London: Routledge, 1991.

Okely, J. and Callaway, H. *Anthropology and Autobiography.* London: Routledge, 1992.

Ondaatje, M. *The English Patient.* London: Picador, 1993.

Outhwaite, W. *Understanding Social Life: The Method Called Verstehen*, 2nd edn. Lewes: Jean Stroud, 1986.

Outhwaite, W. *New Philosophies of the Social Sciences: Realism, Hermeneutics and Critical Theory.* London: Macmillan, 1987.

Popper, K. *The Logic of Scientific Discovery.* London: Hutchinson, 1968.

Poulantzas, N. *Fascism and Dictatorship.* London: New Left Books, 1974.

Radway, J. *Reading the Romance: Women, Patriarchy and Popular Literature.* London: Verso, 1987.

Rainwater, J. *Self-therapy.* London: Crucible, 1989.

Reiner, R. *Chief Constables: Bobbies, Bosses, or Bureaucrats?* Oxford: Oxford University Press, 1991.

Rimmon-Kenan, S. *Narrative Fiction: Contemporary Poetics.* London: Routledge, 1983.

Rorty, R. *Philosophy and the Mirror of Nature.* Oxford: Basil Blackwell, 1980.

Rorty, R. Method, social science and social hope. In Gibbons, M. (ed.) *Interpreting Politics.* Oxford: Basil Blackwell, 1987, pp. 241–59.

Rorty, R. *Contingency, Irony, and Solidarity.* Cambridge: Cambridge University Press, 1989.

Rosaldo, R. From the door of his tent: the fieldworker and the inquisitor. In Clifford, J. and Marcus, G. (eds) *Writing Culture: The Poetics and Politics of Ethnography.* Berkeley and Los Angeles: University of California Press, 1986.

Rosenau, P. *Postmodernism and the Social Sciences.* Princeton, New Jersey: Princeton University Press, 1992.

Rushdie, S. *Midnight's Children.* London: Pan, 1982.

Samuel, R. and Thompson, P. (eds) *The Myths we Live by.* London: Routledge, 1990.

Sarup, M. *An Introductory Guide to Post-structuralism and Postmodernism.* London: Harvester Wheatsheaf, 1988.

Saussure, F. de. *Course in General Linguistics.* London: Fontana, 1974.

Sayer, A. *Method in Social Science: A Realist Approach.* London: Hutchinson, 1984.

Scott, J. W. *Gender and the Politics of History.* New York: Columbia University Press, 1988.

Seidman, S. The end of sociological theory: the postmodern hope. *Sociological Theory*, vol. 9, no. 2, 1991a, pp. 131–46.

Seidman, S. Postmodern anxiety: the politics of epistemology. *Sociological Theory*, vol. 9, no. 2, 1991b, pp. 180–90.

Sereny, G. *Into That Darkness: From Mercy Killing to Mass Murder.* London: Andre Deutsch, 1974.

Simpson, P. *Language, Ideology and Point of View.* London: Routledge, 1993.

Skinner, Q. (ed.) *The Return of Grand Theory in the Human Sciences.* Cambridge: Cambridge University Press, 1985.

Skinner, Q. 'Social Meaning' and the explanation of social action. In Tully, J. (ed.) *Meaning and Context: Quentin Skinner and His Critics.* Cambridge: Polity Press, 1988a, pp. 79–96.

Skinner, Q. A Reply to my critics. In Tully, J. (ed.) *Meaning and Context: Quentin Skinner and His Critics.* Cambridge: Polity Press, 1988b, pp. 231–88.

Smith, M. J. *Pressure, Power and Policy: State Autonomy and Policy Networks in Britain and the United States.* London: Harvester Wheatsheaf, 1993.

Stacey, J. *Brave New Families: Stories of Domestic Upheaval in Late Twentieth Century America.* New York: Basic Books, 1990.

Stanley, L. and Morgan, D. (eds) Special issue: biography and autobiography in sociology. *Sociology,* vol. 27, no. 1, 1993.

Stanley, L. and Wise, S. Method, methodology and epistemology in feminist research processes. In Stanley, L. (ed.) *Feminist Praxis: Research, Theory and Epistemology in Feminist Sociology.* London: Routledge, 1990.

Steedman, C. *Landscape for a Good Woman: a Story of Two Lives.* London: Virago, 1986.

Stevenson, R. *Modernist Fiction: An Introduction.* London: Harvester Wheatsheaf, 1992.

Stones, R. Government–finance relations in Britain 1964–7: a tale of three cities. *Economy and Society,* vol. 19, no. 1, 1990, pp. 32–55.

Stones, R. Strategic context analysis: a new research strategy for structuration theory. *Sociology,* vol. 25, no. 3, 1991, pp. 673–95.

Strange, S. *Sterling and British Policy: A Political Study of an International Currency in Decline.* London: Oxford University Press, 1971.

Swain, G. *Russian Social Democracy and the Legal Labour Movement 1906–1914.* London: Macmillan, 1983.

Swanson, G. *Dallas,* part 1. *Framework,* no. 14, 1981.

Swift, G. *Waterland.* London: Heinemann, 1983.

Taylor, C. *Human Agency and Language: Philosophical Papers, 1.* Cambridge: Cambridge University Press, 1985.

Taylor, S. *The Sociology of Suicide.* London: Longman, 1988.

Thompson, P. *The Voice of the Past: Oral History.* Oxford: Oxford University Press, 1978.

Thrift, N. Bear and mouse or bear and tree? Anthony Giddens' reconstitution of social theory. *Sociology,* vol. 19, 1985.

Todorov, T. *Mikhail Bakhtin: the Dialogical Principle.* Minneapolis: University of Minnesota Press, 1984.

Tully, J. *Meaning and Context: Quentin Skinner and his Critics.* Cambridge: Polity Press, 1988.

Unsworth, B. *The Stone Virgin.* London: Penguin, 1986.

Vonnegut, K. *Slaughterhouse 5.* London: Vintage, 1991.

Vonnegut, K. *Breakfast of Champions.* London: Vintage, 1992.

Walby, S. *Patriarchy at Work: Patriarchal and Capitalist Relations in Employment.* Cambridge: Polity Press, 1986

Walby, S. *Theorizing Patriarchy.* Oxford: Blackwell, 1990.

Walby, S. Post-Post-Modernism? Theorizing social complexity. In Barrett, M. and Phillips, A. (eds) *Destabilizing Theory: Contemporary Feminist Debates.* Cambridge: Polity Press, 1992, pp. 31–52.

Wallerstein, J. and Blakeslee, S. *Second Chances.* London: Bantam, 1989.

Warnke, G. *Gadamer: Hermeneutics, Tradition and Reason.* Cambridge: Polity Press, 1987.

White, S. *The Recent Work of Jürgen Habermas: Reason, Justice & Modernity.* Cambridge: Cambridge University Press, 1988.

White, S. *Political Theory and Postmodernism.* Cambridge: Cambridge University Press, 1991.

Willis, P. Notes on method. In Hall, S., Hobson, D., Lowe, A. and Willis, P. (eds) *Culture, Media, Language.* London: Hutchinson, 1980.

Wilson, W. J. *The Truly Disadvantaged: The Inner City, the Underclass and Public Policy.* Chicago: University of Chicago Press, 1987.

Winch, P. *The Idea of a Social Science.* London: Routledge & Kegan Paul, 1958.

Wittgenstein, L. *Philosophical Investigations.* Oxford: Blackwell, 1973.

Index

Agency, 43–59, 61–62, 67,
 98–102, 104, 110–114 and
 passim
Agent's Conduct Analysis (ACA),
 xii, 70, 71, 75, 78, 92, 93–94,
 99–102, 105–108, 133–134,
 138–139, 161–163, 173–174,
 199, 201, 204, 207, 209, 219,
 223
 and use of acronym ACA to
  encompass both agent's
  conduct analysis and agent's
  context analysis, 99
Agent's Context Analysis (ACXA),
 98–99, 105–108, 223
 role of lay agent's perspective
  within, 98
 role of social theorist's
  perspective within, 98–99
Air traffic controllers, and the
 reality of mutual understanding,
 43–45, 50
Alexander, M., 69, 159
Allen, R. C., 150
Ang, I., 138–143, 145, 146,
 148–150
 Watching Dallas, 138, 139, 143
Anthropology, 64, 158, 172
Austin, J. L., 16, 17
Authoritarian Monarchies,
 193–195
Autobiography, 176, 234
Ayer, A. J., 15

Baker, N., 183
 Mezzanine, The, 183
Balzac, H., 190
 Sarrasine, 190
Barnes, B., 17
Barnes, J., 152, 153
 Talking it Over, 152, 176
Barthes R., 166, 176
 A Lover's Discourse, 166
 and narrative technique,
  188–191
 and S/Z, 188–191
 and the readerly (lisible) text,
  196
 and the reality effect, 157, 188,
  198–199
 on nuclei and catalysers, 157
Bauman, Z., 6, 24, 40
 and critique of Giddens,
  115–117
 and habitat, 61
 and pragmatically useful next
  moves, 62
 and a tension within his work,
  128–129
 as part dreamer, part floater,
  119–121
 emphasis on context and
  complexity, 61–62
 Intimations of Postmodernity, 61,
  128
 on *Modernity and the Holocaust*,
  119–129

on monotony, homogeneity and
equilibrium, 61
view of totality as kaleidoscopic
and transitory, 61
Bellow, S., 69
Herzog, 69
Benhabib, S., 136
Benton, T., 6, 39, 150
and a degree of mutual
understanding as a necessary
condition of survival, 165
Berger, J., 15, 19
Bhaskar, R., 5, 6, 33, 39, 40, 41,
46, 64, 153, 213
and existential reality, 31–32
and intransitive reality, 31–32
and intrinsic causal powers,
28–29
and stratification of reality,
29–30
on epistemic fallacy, 28
open systems and the
differentiation of reality,
30–31
Biography, 68, 75, 99–100, 123,
139, 140, 161, 174, 180, 182,
234
Black Underclass in the USA, 220
Bleicher, J., 39
Bonnell, V. E., 195
Booth, W.,
on showing and telling, 183
Borgmann, A., 95
Britain, 193, 199, 200, 202, 222,
223
Browning, C., 121, 122, 123,
124, 125, 126, 127, 150
Ordinary Men, 123
Burrin, P., 127

Calhoun, C.,
and epistemic gain versus
absolute truth, 22
Capitalism and Capitalists, 67, 95,
188, 199, 210, 214, 220, 225,
227

Capitalism Divided, 199
Carey, P., 55–58
Oscar and Lucinda, 55
Catalysers, 157, 198–199
Causality, 27–38, 47ff, 59, 67,
113–115, 157, 159, 178, 184,
206, 210, 215, 217, 218, 222,
223, 224, 227
Charlemagne, 114
Chatman, S., 168
Chief Constables, 101
Chodorow, N., 133, 144
Citizenship, 11, 192, 193–199
City of London, 11, 199–206
Clifford, J. and Marcus, G.,
Writing Culture, 158
Cohen, I. J., 89, 87, 90, 95–97,
103, 107, 109, 111, 219
and relations between
metaphysics and empirical
claims, 36–37
and systems analysis, 95–98
on the metaphysical core of a
theory, 111
Collier, A., 39
Communicative Ethics, 135–138
Complexity and Richness of Social
World, 5, 33, 40–63, 74, 76,
77, 82, 88, 105, 136, 156, 163,
169, 188, 192, 208, 232
in relation to dreamer theory,
79, 82
Contemporary Social Theory, 1,
4, 5, 6, 8, 11, 12, 40, 61, 64,
233
as an Ideal Type, 12
Context, the Contextual, 5, 7, 8,
61, 65, 112, 118, 135, 155,
213, 218, 219, 222, 233
as more than the geographical
local (*see also* questions and
their significance), 49
Contextualisers, Contextualisation,
6, 11, 49, 71, 72–76, 83,
89–90, 99–102, 102–103, 118,
129–135, 196–213, 207, 208,
219, 220

absence of in Giddens' historical
sociology, 102–105, 110–115
Contiguity, relations of, 6, 7,
75–78, 123, 151, 156,
161–162, 169, 174, 183–188,
205–206, 215, 219, 220, 222,
228, 234
Contingency, 5, 24, 31, 33, 35,
40, 45, 54, 55, 57, 59, 60, 61,
62, 89, 110–115, 124, 127,
129, 136–138, 194, 211, 212,
213, 214, 215, 220
Cosmopolitan, 211, 223
Cottingham, J., 28
Counter-factuals, 59, 113–115,
197, 205, 214,
Coward, R., 211, 231
Craib, I., 40, 92
and the disappearance of
openness in Giddens'
historical sociology, 113
critique of Giddens'
presentation of the self in late
modernity, 87
'unreason' in the production of
knowledge, 118
Cross-questioning Analysis of a
Sociological Text, Stages in,
169–171ff
Cross-questioning Readers of
Sociological Texts, 173, 174,
179
Cuff, E.C., Sharrock, W. W. and
Francis, D. W., 16
Culler, J., 18

Dallas, and the sociology of soap
operas, 138–143, 145, 146,
148–150
Defeatist Postmodernism, 2, 4, 5,
9, 11, 12, 13, 20, 21, 22, 26,
38, 60, 67, 90–92, 115–117,
118–119, 134, 151, 208, 232
as an Ideal Type, 12
Derrida, J., 16, 25, 49, 154, 165,
166

Spurs: Nietzsche's Styles, 154, 166
Despots and Despotism, in the
practice of sociology, 6, 12,
82–83, 104, 114, 185, 208,
230
Developmental Psychology,
129–135
Diary of a Mad Housewife, 182
Dickens, C., 14, 185–187
Sketches by Boz, 185, 186, 187
Diegesis, 85, 142, 171, 174–176,
179, 184, 195, 228
Differentiation of Reality, 30–31
Dilthey, 16
Direct Speech, 172, 173, 174, 180
Divorce, 177–178
and self-reflexivity, 80–81, 111
Dogs, and their interpretative
capacities, 165
Douglas, A., 147
Douglas, J., 72–74
Social Meanings of Suicide, The,
72
Dreamers and Dreamer Theory, 6,
7, 78–83, 102–105, 110, 112,
118, 119–121, 136–138, 140,
144, 149, 209, 219–220
and methodological bracketing,
90–102
and multiple research
destinations, 104–110
and Richard Rorty's
*Contingency, Irony and
Solidarity,* 136–138
Dukheim, E., 31
Durrell, L.,
Alexandria Quartet, The, 69
Dworkin, R., 150

Elias, N., 31, 41
Emmanuelle, 211, 223
Empiricism, 30
Epistemic Certainty, 22, 164–166
Epistemic Fallacy, 28
Epistemological Agnosticism, 62
Epistemological Caution, 64

Elliott, G., 14
Ethics, 8, 129–138
Ethnomethodology, 40
Europe, 11, 53, 114–115, 224
Evans, P., Rueschmeyer, D. and
    Skocpol, T., 228
Existential Reality, 31–32, 39
Extension, of the present state of
    knowledge, 7, 115, 134, 150,
    164, 197, 215, 233

Fabula, Implied Fabula, 167–172,
    175, 182, 183–188, 189, 190,
    201, 234
Factory Acts of the Nineteenth
    Century, 187, 225–230
Falsification, 9, 134, 161, 224,
    232
Faludi, S., 129, 133
Fascism, 194
Faulkner, W.,
    Sound and the Fury, The, 69
Feminism, 25–26, 64, 129, 136,
    147, 158, 177, 178, 180, 181,
    225
Feyerabend, P., 118
Fiction, in relation to the claims
    of social science, 2, 5, 14–15,
    19–22, 81, 85, 151, 156–157,
    168, 185–186, 232
First World War, 115
Flax, J., 24, 61
Floaters, 6, 11, 12, 75, 77, 83,
    102–104, 106, 109, 110, 114,
    119–125, 133–134, 138, 139,
    161, 179, 193, 196, 197, 209,
    211, 215, 219, 220, 224
    and summary, 184
Focalisation, 68
Foucault, M., 221, 233
Foundationalism, 3–4
Fowles, J., 15, 85
    French Lieutenant's Woman, The,
    15, 85
Fraser, N. and Nicholson, L., 129,
    132–134

Free Direct Speech, 174–176
Free Indirect Speech, 174
Furst, L., 199

G, 15
Gadamer, H-G., 16, 33, 39
Garbage Dump Romances, 146,
    147
Geertz, C., 172–173
Gellately, R.,
    Gestapo and German Society,
    The, 122
Gender, 5, 25–26, 68, 129–135,
    158, 162, 209–230
Genette, G., 182
    and temporal duration, 168
    and temporal frequency, 168
    and temporal order, 168
    and the modification of the
        fabula by the sjuzet, 168
Germany, 121–128, 193–194,
    223
Giddens, A., 5, 6, 7, 8, 11,
    32–36, 40–45, 47–48, 50, 51,
    63, 70, 72, 79–81, 82, 87,
    88–117, 134, 199, 213, 234
    and actors' wants and
        motivations, 44
    and methodological bracketing,
        92–95
    and stratification model of the
        agent, 43–45
    as defeatist postmodernist,
        90–92
    as realist beyond modernism,
        92–95
    Central Problems in Social
        Theory, 103
    Consequences of Modernity, The,
        103
    Constitution of Society, The, 41,
        89, 93, 103, 104, 199
    Contemporary Critique of
        Historical Materialism, A, 103
    context and hermeneutics in
        structuration theory, 41–45

knowledgeability of agents,
43–44
lack of interest in epistemology
and methodology, 89–90
Modernity and Self-Identity, 79,
104
*New Rules of Sociological
Method,* 103, 115, 116
reflexive Monitoring, 43
*Social Theory and Modern
Societies,* 90
Transformation of Intimacy, The,
104
writing assessed in relation to
four senses of contingency,
110–113
Gilligan, C., 129–135, 138, 139,
221
and Kohlberg, 130
and malestream bias in
developmental psychology,
130
and moral choices embedded in
relationships, 131–132, 135
and the strengths of her form of
argument, 132–135
and the use of studies as
orienting heuristics, 134
In a Different Voice, 129, 138
postmodern critiques of,
132–133
Goffman, E.
and Breaking Frame, 85
Goldthorpe, J., Lockwood, D.,
Bechofer, F. and Platt, J.,
*Affluent Worker in the Class
Structure, The,* 101
Good Housekeeping, 211
Goring,
and a 'total solution', 127
Grand Narratives, 7, 12, 22–24,
36, 95, 119, 133, 138
Gregson, N., 90, 117
Guildford Four, Birmingham Six
and the travails of epistemic
certainty, 165

Habermas, J., 6, 28, 33, 39, 40,
62, 136, 207
and analytical aspects of social
reality, 45–47
and communicative action,
45–47
and claims to normative
legitimacy, 46
and 'repair work', 49–52
and the hermeneutic focus of
actors, 49–52
and truth claims, 45–46
and truthfulness, 45
and validity claims, 46
Haimson, L. H., 195
Hall, C., 234
Hamon, P.,
and naïve realist discourse, 196
Hawthorn, G., 92, 114
Hawthorn, J., 176
Held, D., 90, 110
Heller, J.,
Good as Gold, 85
Hermeneutics (*see also* agent's
conduct/context analysis), 6, 7,
16, 19, 27, 33–36, 41–61, 65,
98–102, 112
and open systems, 35–36
and its relation to the
Constraining Context, 55–60
and the Skilful Accomplishment
of One's Own Subordination,
52–55
and the Skilful Defiance of a
Normative Framework,
55–58
Historical Sociology, 7, 77,
110–115, 193–199
Hitler, 126, 127
Hochschild, A., 179
Holocaust, 119–129, 150
Holub, R. C., 39
Hoy, D. Couzens, 18
Hume, D., 15
Hutcheon, L., 15, 85
and de-doxification, 87

and paratextual conventions,
199
on postmodern literature's
preoccupation with
historiographic metafiction,
160
Politics of Postmodernism, The,
87, 199

Ideal and Failed Romances,
146–148
Indeterminacy, 8,152–155, 156,
164–166, 167, 179, 185, 198,
195, 198
Ingham, G., 11
critique of, as sociological
modernist, 199–206
Institutional Analysis, 94–98,
105–108
International Monetary Fund, 205
Intransitive Reality, 31–32, 39,
153, 154, 160, 190
Isaac, J., 28, 34
Power and Marxist Theory, 34
Ishiguro, K., 52–53, 65
Remains of the Day, The, 52

James, H., 68,
What Maisie Knew, 68
Jameson, F., 14
Jary, D., 95
on Giddens' historical sociology,
113–115
Jessop,B., Bonnett, K., Bromley, S.
and Ling, T., 194, 206
Jews, 121–128
Joas, H., 207
Josselson, R. and Lieblich, A., 234

Kalberg, S., 39
Kennan, G., 198
Kershaw, I., 127
Khandelwal, A., 160–161
King Lear, 49

Knowledgeable Agents, 9, 43–52,
54, 57, 58–59, 68–70, 75,
80–81, 93–94, 98–100,
111–112, 160, 161–162, 232
Kuhn, T., 17
Kundera, M., 59–60, 113
*Unbearable Lightness of Being,
The,* 59

Labour Government in Britain,
1964–70, 199–206
Laclau, E., 234
Leech, G. and Short, M., 174
Levi, P., 123
If This Were a Man, 123
Literary Criticism, 14–15, 160
Literature, 5, 9, 10, 14–15, 40,
64, 83–87, 159–160
Lodge, D., 85, 157, 168, 191, 199
and diegesis, 85
and Russian Formalism, 85
and textual summary, 184
Modes of Modern Writing, The,
191
on metonymy and summary,
184–185
on the sjuzet's metonymic
relation to the fabula, 185,
191
Longstreth, F., 203, 204
Love, and indeterminacy, 166
Lowry, M., 69
Under the Volcano, 69
Lyotard, J-F., 12, 24

m/f, 210, 213, 231
Mad Max, 49
Mann, M., 11, 227
critique of, as sociological
modernist, 193–199
on ruling class strategies and
citizenship, 193–195
on Tsarist autocracy, 194–195
Marcus, G. and Fischer, M., 24
Marrus, M. R., 126, 127, 150

Marsh, D. and Rhodes, R. A. W.,
228
Marvel, H. P., 229
Marxism, 2, 34, 40, 74
McCarthy, T., 207
McEwan, I., 31
Mepham, J., 166
  on Nietzsche's umbrella and the
    undecidability of texts,
    154–155
Metaphor, 77, 184, 188, 191, 194
Methodological Focus, 7–8,
  66–67, 70–71, 74–78, 78–82,
  88–117, 208
Metonymy,
  and the cloaking of gaps,
    184–187
  contiguity and the critique of
    theories which claim too
    much, 187–188
  and summary, 184
  and synecdoche, 191
Miller, J. Hillis,
  on metonymic chains of
    equivalence and substitution,
    185–187
Mills, C. Wright, 118
  Sociological Imagination, The,
    118
Mimesis, 101, 142, 173–176,
  179, 195, 205
Modernism, 1, 2, 3, 4, 5, 6, 8, 9,
  11, 12, 22, 24, 26, 61, 62, 82,
  84, 92, 152, 192, 193, 208,
  230, 232, 235
Modernism as an Ideal Type, 12
Modernism, in literature, 9,
  68–69, 84
Modernism, in the arts, 9
Modernity, 61, 68, 79–81, 95,
  103, 104, 113, 119–129, 134,
  135, 162
Mommsen, H., 126
Morris, L., 231
Morrison, T., 58
  Beloved, 58
Mouzelis, N.,

on mega-actors, 114, 125–126
Murdoch, I., 183
  Book and the Brotherhood, The,
    183

Narrative, 5, 7, 10, 12, 15, 68, 74,
  83–87, 142, 145, 146, 148,
  157, 167–191
Nationalism, 115, 284
Nazi Germany, 171–178
Nelson, G., 58–59
Nicholson, L., 129, 132, 133, 134
Nordlinger, E. A., 228
Normative Commitment, 46–48,
  54, 110, 205
Normative Framework, 50, 55–58
Norris, C., 18, 165
Northern Ireland, 94
Nuclei, 157

Ondaatje, M., 160
  English Patient, The, 160
Ontology, 1, 5, 6, 7, 9, 11,
  40–63, 66–67, 76, 77, 89, 92,
  192, 232, 233
Open systems (*see also* the
  differentiation of reality),
  30–31, 40, 60, 103, 110–113,
  188, 213, 215, 220
Ottoman Turks, 114
Outhwaite, W., 6, 30, 37
  and methodological
    consequences, 37
  and realism as ontologically
    bold and epistemologicallly
    cautious, 64

Past-modern Realism, Past-
  modern Sociology 1, 4, 8, 10,
  11, 13, 23, 25, 37, 38, 71, 95,
  152, 170, 172, 195, 196, 207,
  232–235
Patriarchy, 11, 68, 143–148,
  207–231

Performative contradiction, 46, 165
Perspective(s), 2, 119, 128–129, 133, 144, 153, 154, 156, 161, 168–169, 182, 214, 215, 221, 225
  limitations of, 9, 64–65, 68–70, 156
  plurality of, 22–23
  greater latitude for, and reflexive monitoring of, 92–93, 105–110
Phenomenology, 40, 223
Philosophy, 5, 9, 15–19, 28 , 40, 64, 155
Players and Player Theory, 6, 10, 65–78, 82–83, 88, 156–157, 161–164, 172, 178, 184, 196–197, 208–209, 215, 217, 219–220, 223, 230, 233
  and Carol Gilligan's *In a Different Voice,* 129–135
  and Ien Ang's *Watching Dallas,* 138–143, 148–150
  and Janice Radway's *Reading the Romance,* 143–148, 148–150
  and methodological bracketing, 90–102
  and multiple research destinations, 104–110
Popper, K., 9, 28
Postmodern novelists, 9–10, 84–87, 159, 160
Postmodernism, 2, 4, 5, 6, 7, 8, 12, 13, 15, 20–27, 37, 38, 61–62, 90, 115, 129, 144, 152, 158, 199, 207, 210–212, 220, 221, 232
Poststructuralism, 5, 11, 15, 40, 210, 213
Poulantzas, N., 194, 206
Practical Adequacy (versus epistemic certainty), 22, 164–166
Processual Nature of Social Being, 48–49

Proust, M., 168
  Remembrance of Things Past, 168
Provisionality in relation to knowledge claims, 13, 20–22, 38, 76, 78–79, 82–83

Questioners, and their significance, 68–70, 160, 169, 171, 179, 213–214, 234
Questions, and their significance, 7, 66, 68–72, 78, 91–92, 107, 129, 156–157, 188–191, 192, 208, 213, 221
  comparing Ang's questions about soaps with Radway's about romances, 148–150
  in assessing the relevance of Mann's historical evidence, 197–199
  in relation to Gilligan and the postmodern critique of her work, 132–135
  in assessing the evidence in Walby's analysis of the Factory Acts, 225–230

Race and Ethnicity, 133–134, 139, 140, 220–223
Radway, J., 139, 143–149, 189
  Reading the Romance, 139, 143
Rainwater, J.,
  Self Therapy, 81
Realism, 1, 2, 3, 4, 5, 10, 13, 14, 15, 19, 20, 22, 23, 24, 25, 26, 27, 29–37, 40, 64, 95, 120, 151, 153, 154, 155, 160, 185, 196, 213, 232, 234
  and methodological consequences, 66–67
Reality Effect, 157, 188, 198–199
Reflexive Monitoring, 43, 93
Reflexivity, 4, 10, 11, 43, 48, 88–89, 96–97, 115–117, 159, 192, 196, 209

and guidelines for a past-
modern sociology, 64–87,
88–89, 92–102, 155–166,
167–190
Reiner, R., 101–102
Relativism and Indeterminacy,
152–155
Relativism, subjective and
restrictive forms of, 152–155
Religious Evangelism, 180–183
Representation, 2, 14, 20, 69, 87,
169, 211
Retroduction, 37
Rimmon-Kenan, S., 168, 174
Romance Novels and their
Readers, 68, 138, 143–150
Rorty, R., 92
and nature's own language, 18
and dreamer hypothesis,
136–138
and ethical sensibilities,
136–138
Rosaldo, R., 158–159, 189
Montaillou, 158, 190
Roseanau, P., 20
Routine Social Practices, 35, 45,
94–98, 102, 109–113, 224
Ruling Class Strategies, 193–199
Rushdie, S., 159
Midnight's Children, 159

Samuel, R. and Thompson, P.,
234
Santa Clara County, 177, 178
Sarup, M., 24
Saussure, F. de., 16, 18
Sayer, A., 6, 30
Scepticism and the status of
knowledge claims, 151,
155–166, 169–171ff
Schleiermacher, F., 16
Scott, J. W., 5, 25–26, 210, 233
*Gender and the Politics of
History,* 5, 25
Seidman, S., 24, 39
Sereny, G., 123

Into That Darkness, 123
Signifieds, 18
Signifiers, 18
Silicon Valley, USA, 139, 175,
177
Simpson, P., 174
Sjuzet, 167–191, 193, 201
Skinner, Q., 17, 166, 174
and conditions of mutual
understanding necessary for a
range of practices, 165
Slavery, 58, 59
Smith, M. J., 228
Smithton, USA, 143–148
Soap operas, the sociology of,
138–143 ,148–150, 196
Sophisticated Realism, 4, 10, 13,
26–36, 64, 95, 160, 164, 232
Space, 6, 27, 42–43, 91, 161,
168, 169, 183–188, 233
Stacey, J., 11, 139, 175, 177–183
Brave New Families, 11, 139,
175, 177, 180, 182
and reflexive ethnography, 177,
179
and reflexive textuality,
179–183
and the rhetoric of frequency,
182
Stanley, L. and Morgan, D., 234
Stanley, L. and Wise, S., 71
State Autonomy, 192, 199ff
Steedman, C.,
Landscape for a Good Woman,
176
Stewart, M.,
Jekyll and Hyde Years, The, 202,
203
Stones, R., 87, 96, 97, 174
and strategic context analysis
(*see also* agent's context
analysis), 98
Strange, S., 202
Sterling and British Policy, 202
Strategic Conduct Analysis (*see
also* agent's conduct analysis),
70, 92–94, 98–102

Strategic Context Analysis (*see also* agent's context analysis), 98
Stratification of Reality, 29–30
Structuration Theory, 5, 32–37, 40–45, 47–49, 63, 80, 88–117, 199, 213
Structure(s), 3, 33, 47–48, 67, 209, 216, 217, 218, 219, 230 233
Suicide, 181
agency and the dialectic of control, 94
the sociology of, 72–74
Summary and the Cloaking of Gaps, 183–184
Swain, G., 195
Swanson, G., 142
Swift, G.,
Waterland, 15
Synecdoche, 185, 187, 191
Systems, 30–31, 35–36, 42–43, 61–62, 94–98, 99–100, 106–108, 111, 113, 192, 198
and the holocaust, 119–129
and patriarchy, 207–231
Systems Analysis, 95–100, 105–108, 161–162, 215–219

Taylor, C., 22
Taylor, S., 73
Sociology of Suicide, The, 73
Test of Translation, 163, 178, 234
Textual Foregrounding, 9–11, 65, 83–87, 88, 159, 171–172
Textuality, 9–11, 83–87, 167–191, 196, 199, 205–206, 234
Theorist's Pattern Analysis (TPA), 70, 71, 75, 76, 78, 96–98, 106–115, 138, 161–162, 173, 184, 193, 194, 196, 197, 209, 211, 215, 219, 220, 224, 231
Theory and Theories,
and distinguishing from ontology, 67–68
and the compression of social processes, 187–188

and the effacing of time and space altogether, 187–188
example of dreamer model of theory construction, 79–81
example of player model of theory construction, 72–74
Theory of Communicative Action, The, 87
Therapy, and self-reflexivity, 81, 111
Thompson, J., 90
Thompson, P., 234
Todorov, T., 176
Tragic Structure of Feeling, 139–143, 146, 149
Transparent Realism, 4, 13, 20, 158
Triangulation, 77–78
Tsarist Russia, 194–198

Unacknowledged conditions of action, 43, 52, 57, 59, 99, 112
Undecidability, 8 (*see also* indeterminacy)
Unfolded Social Relations, 59, 111, 123–125
Unfolding Nature of Social Being, 59–60, 111, 113, 123–125, 138, 224
Unintended consequences of action, 43, 63, 80, 112
United Kingdom, 165, 223
United States of America, 46, 52, 68, 115, 139, 143, 185, 187, 205, 221, 222, 223, 224, 231
Unsworth, B.,
Stone Virgin, The, 176
Utopian Benchmark of Exhaustive Contextualisation, 7, 9, 76, 99, 163

Verstehen (*see also* hermeneutics), 16
Vietnam, 35–36, 128
Vonnegut, K., 85–86, 158, 218
Breakfast of Champions, 85
Slaughterhouse Five, 218

Walby, S., 11, 207–231
  critique of, as sociological
    modernist, 207–231
  on inner cities, the underclass,
    and the articulation of
    capitalism, racism and
    patriarchy, 220–225
  on patriarchy as a system of six
    structures, 209–210,
    213–219
  on postmodernism, 210–212
  on the nineteenth-century
    Factory Acts, 225–230
  Patriarchy at Work, 225

Theorizing Patriarchy, 211, 213,
    217
Wallerstein, S. and Blakeslee, S.,
    80–81
  Second Chances, 80
Warnke, G., 16
White, S., 136
Wilson, Harold, 201–206
Wilson, W. J., 220–225
  Truly Disadvantaged, The, 220
Winch, P., 16, 17, 33
Wittgenstein, L., 16, 17
Women's Own, 211, 223